Dona L. Seacat

SO-AYW-520

HOW TO WRITE A PLAY

LORI GUM

LITERACY VOLUNTEERS OF NEW YORK CITY

HOW TO WRITE A PLAY was made possible by a grant from the Hale Matthews Foundation.

ATTENTION READERS: We would like to hear what you think about our books. Please send your comments or suggestions to:

The Editors
Literacy Volunteers of New York City
121 Avenue of the Americas
New York, NY 10013

Copyright © 1991 by Literacy Volunteers of New York City Inc.

All rights reserved. This book may not be reproduced in whole or in part, in form or by any means, without permission.

Published by Literacy Volunteers of New York City Inc., 121 Avenue of the Americas, New York, NY 10013.

Printed in the United States of America.

97 96 95 94 93 92 91   10 9 8 7 6 5 4 3 2 1

First LVNYC Printing: March 1991

ISBN 0-929631-34-X

Cover designed by Paul Davis Studio; interior designed by Helene Berinsky.

Executive Director, LVNYC: Eli Zal
Publishing Director, LVNYC: Nancy McCord
Managing Editor: Sarah Kirshner
Publishing Coordinator: Yvette Martinez-Gonzalez

LVNYC is an affiliate of Literacy Volunteers of America.

ACKNOWLEDGMENTS

Literacy Volunteers of New York City gratefully acknowledges the generous support and encouragement of the Hale Matthews Foundation that made the publication of this book possible.

We deeply appreciate the contributions of the following suppliers: Cam Steel Die Rule Works Inc. (steel cutting die for display); Boise Cascade Canada Ltd. (text stock); Black Dot Graphics (text typesetting); Horizon Paper Company and Manchester Paper Company (cover stock); MCUSA (display header); Delta Corrugated Container (corrugated display); J.A.C. Lithographers (cover color separations); and Offset Paperback Mfrs., Inc., A Bertelsmann Company (cover and text printing and binding).

For their guidance, support and hard work, we are indebted to the LVNYC Board of Directors' Publishing Committee: James E. Galton, Marvel Entertainment Group; Virginia Barber, Virginia Barber Literary Agency, Inc.; Doris Bass, Bantam Doubleday Dell; Jeff Brown; Jerry Butler, William Morrow & Company, Inc.; George P. Davidson, Ballantine Books; Joy M. Gannon, St. Martin's Press; Walter Kiechel, *Fortune*; Geraldine E. Rhoads, Diamandis Communications Inc.; Virginia Rice, Reader's Digest; Martin Singerman, News America Publishing, Inc.; James L. Stanko, James Money Management, Inc. and F. Robert Stein, Pryor, Cashman, Sherman & Flynn.

Thanks also to Joy M. Gannon and Julia Weil of St. Martin's Press for producing this book; Andrea Connolly for her thoughtful copyediting and suggestions; Helen Morris for her dedication and helpful contributions at so many stages of the book; to Carol Fein for proofreading and to Martin Duberman for his expertise. Most of all, our thanks to Lori Gum for taking on this daunting project and mastering its challenges.

Our thanks to Paul Davis Studio and Myrna Davis, Paul Davis, Jeanine Esposito, Alex Ginns and Frank Begrowicz for their inspired design of the cover of this book. Thanks also to Helene Berinsky for her sensitive design of the interior of this book and to Ron Bel Bruno for his timely help.

And finally, special credit must be given to Marilyn Boutwell, Jean Fargo and Stephanie Butler of the LVNYC staff for their perceptive comments and suggestions.

To obtain a copy of *Selected from Contemporary American Plays,* please send your check to Publishing Program, Literacy Volunteers of New York City, 121 Avenue of Americas, New York, NY 10013. Books are $3.50 each. Please add $1.50 per order and .50 per book to cover postage and handling. NY and NJ residents, add appropriate sales tax.

CONTENTS

INTRODUCTION

You might be asking yourself, Why write a play? What makes a play special?

Plays are special because they bring the written word to life. When you watch a play, you *see* and *hear* the characters as they live their lives. You experience the story as it unfolds.

Even if you have never seen a play in a theater, you have probably seen movies or television comedies and dramas. (Writing these kinds of plays is called screenwriting.) People like plays because they mirror real life.

Your life and the lives of those around you can become the subject for a play. You only need to learn to shape these experiences into a dramatic event. You will use what you learn in this book and your own imagination to turn your experiences into drama.

You can write a play by yourself, but you may also enjoy writing one with other people. Because of the special form of a play, it can be a very satisfying project for a group to work on.

NOTE TO THE READER

In this book, you will learn, one step at a time, how to write a play.

Each chapter of this book explains a particular part of playwriting. Within each chapter are exercises to help develop your understanding and playwriting skills. Read each exercise all the way through once or more, then go back and do it step by step. The book uses as an example a scene about two characters named Julie and Tony. This scene is developed step by step to illustrate the exercises. You should take as much time as you want with each exercise. You don't have to do each one in one day.

Each exercise builds on the one before. You will use what you write in the exercises to build a scene. If you want to go further, you can use your scene as part of a play. When you complete an exercise, date it and save it in a three-ring notebook. You will need to be able to remove each exercise for review.

Divide your notebook into two sections. One section will be for your exercise pages. Keep the other section for note taking. Playwrights often make note of interesting conversations they have heard or situations they have seen. The world is rich with situations and events that can be used in writing plays.

You will need the companion volume, *Selected from Contemporary American Plays,* along with this book. Specific plays from that book are used as examples of the techniques of playwriting we will discuss. You might find it helpful to look at these examples before you start an exercise. They may give you ideas and help you with your own playwriting.

1

WHAT MAKES A PLAY A PLAY

A playwright looks for a situation in life that can be dramatized. In a novel, the author can describe and tell the reader many things. In a play, the people in the play, or the *characters*, must tell the story. They tell it through spoken words, or *dialogue*, and actions. It seems as if the story is happening as you watch it.

A playwright tries to entertain the people who see the play, or the *audience*. The playwright hopes the audience will recognize something about themselves and their lives when they see the play. Perhaps they will even learn something.

Plays are made up of *scenes*. Each scene takes place at a particular time in a particular place. And each scene has a beginning, middle and end.

Scenes are like chapters in a book. Several scenes are put together to form an *act*. A play may have one act or many acts. An act may take place over the course of one day or over many years. An act builds, scene by scene, from beginning to middle to end.

The written form of a play is the *script*. The script is used by all the people involved in putting on a play, or the *production team* (see the diagram on page 64). Its special form makes it easy for every member of the team to read it and know what he or she is responsible for doing.

In the back of the book on page 62 is a glossary of many of the words playwrights use. These words will be used often in this book. Take some time to look them over and to discuss them with others in order to become familiar with what they mean. Learning these words is a good introduction to the world of playwriting.

EXERCISE 1: Seeing and Reading a Play

To understand how a play is put together, it is helpful for you to see, hear and read how other playwrights have created their plays.

STEP 1. There are many plays being presented in every town and city across this country. High schools, colleges and community theaters are excellent places to see plays. Find out about a play being performed in your area and go see it.

STEP 2. When you sit in the audience, notice the information that you are made aware of and how you are made aware of it.

STEP 3. After the play is over, think about how you learned about each character's personality and what he or she wanted. What made you like or not like the characters? Did you think they seemed like real people?

Think about what moved or inspired you about the play, or what made you laugh. Was the story believable? Do you think the play would be better if something in it were changed? Discuss what you think with others who have seen the play.

STEP 4 (*optional*). If it is available, buy a copy of the script of the play you have seen. Or perhaps someone in the cast will lend it to you. Read the play and compare what the playwright wrote with what you saw on stage. Notice what information the playwright gives to the production team. Remember the performance and think about things that you saw that are not in the script.

STEP 5. Based on this experience of seeing a play, begin to think about how some event in your life could be turned into a play.

2

USING YOUR OWN WORLD

It is often said that the best advice any writer can follow is, "Write what you know." Many playwrights bring to the stage the stories of their families, friends and, most importantly, themselves. As writers we are inspired by the world around us and we attempt to write what *we* see and how *we* see it.

Your own life is full of drama, conflict and emotion. And who can better tell your story than you?

EXERCISE 2: Selecting an Event

This exercise will help you discover what your play will be about. By process of elimination, you will pick one event that you want to write about. This will be the basis for a scene. By the end of this book, you will have shaped this event into the dramatic scene around which you can build your play.

Select an experience from your own life because that is what you know and understand best. If you prefer not to use an event from your own life, be sure to pick an event about which you know many details.

STEP 1. Take some time to think about your life. Remember the events that seemed to change your life or about which you had strong feelings. Talking with others may help you come up with ideas.

In choosing an event, it is important to consider three things. First, does it have *conflict*? The playwright looks for a story that has conflict. Conflict results from differences between people. They may have different interests, ideas or expectations. Conflict can also be caused by people's actions or changing circumstances in someone's life. The play is about how this conflict is worked out, or *resolved*.

Conflict creates drama and emotion. Suppose you are unhappy with your job and want to quit, but your family wants the extra income. These two opposing "wants" cause conflict.

Second, is the event simple to describe? Try to

pick an event that only involves two people in one place. Later, if you choose to develop your scene into a play, you can add more people and places.

Third, can you tell the story with words and actions alone? Can you make the story happen before the eyes of the audience? Because you are writing a scene, it is best to pick a story that doesn't need a lot of background information to be understood. You must be able to tell the story as if it were actually happening. And the story must be able to be understood through the characters' words and actions.

STEP 2. At the top of a piece of paper, write EVENTS. List five ideas that come to your mind. Focus on situations that happened on one day or evening, not ones that took place over many days. The events might be amusing, frightening or even sad. Sometimes our most vivid memories are the most painful. It might be the morning you left home, the afternoon you met a special person in your life or the night that a dear friend died.

STEP 3. Look over your list carefully. Is there one event that stands out? One that affected you the most? Is there one you remember most clearly? Which one could be a scene to start your play? Pick the event that you think could make a dramatic scene. Circle or highlight your chosen event and save this sheet in your notebook.

We have chosen an event to develop to show you how to do the exercises in this book. It is about a turning point in a new relationship. You will follow this event in future exercises.

EXAMPLE

Read the selection "Fences" in *Selected from Contemporary American Plays.* What is the conflict between Troy and Cory? Notice that the scene has only two people in one place. Think about how August Wilson, the playwright, tells the story through words and actions alone.

EXERCISE 3: Outlining Your Scene

You will learn how to take your event and use it to create an outline for a scene. The outline will help you organize the information for your scene.

STEP 1. Reread the event you have chosen. Close your eyes and picture the moment in time when that event happened. Think about who was there, where it took place, when it took place and what happened.

Who, where, when and what are important questions to ask yourself whenever you write. They help you give a complete picture of what you're writing about.

STEP 2. Take a piece of paper and title it OUTLINE. Below this, write *Who*. Beside it, write down who the people in your event are. For example, for our date, we might write: 1. my new friend Joe, 2. myself.

STEP 3. Next write *Where* and beside it, write where the event took place. For example: Outside his apartment building in Brooklyn.

STEP 4. Now write *When* and beside it, put when the event took place. For example: An early spring evening in 1985.

STEP 5. Next write *What* and beside it, write down what took place during the event. You don't have to write everything about what took place. Just put down a few words that will help you remember the event later. For example: I wanted to spend more time with Joe but I had to get home to my kids. Joe asked me to bring them next time so we could have more time together.

If you have trouble describing your event like this, don't be afraid to go back to your list of events and choose another that you can picture and write about more easily. Writing is a process of making choices and decisions.

EXAMPLE

Choose a scene from *Selected from Contemporary American Plays*. Read it and identify the "who, what, where and when" of the scene. Reading the editors' introduction to the scene may help you answer these questions.

EXERCISE 4: Turning Your Real People into Characters

Most playwrights agree on one thing. The characters are the most important part of a play. Without them, the story cannot be told. It is through the words and actions of your characters that you breathe life into your scene.

Their words and actions come from you, the writer. You control the language they use, their personalities, their emotions and personal experiences. It will take thought and time to create characters that really walk and talk on stage.

STEP 1. Get out your outline from Exercise 3. Look at the *Who* section. You should have two people listed, yourself and another person.

STEP 2. Think about the other person. On a new piece of paper, titled CHARACTERS, make up a name for and describe this person. Include facts such as how tall he is, what he weighs, how old he is and what kind of clothes he wears. Your description will be read by someone who does not know this person, so be sure to describe him or her clearly.

To use our example, we will make up a name for Joe—we'll call him Tony. He is twenty-nine years old. He is tall and thin.

STEP 3. Now write a little bit about the person. Describe the person's personality and point of view. For example, is the person happy or lonely? Does he always look on the bright side of things? Or does she have a chip on her shoulder? Write six or seven sentences that really show what this person is like.

To use our example: Tony is very straightforward

and kind. He is sure of himself yet he seems self-conscious.

STEP 4. On the same piece or a new piece of paper, describe the other character: yourself. Do what you did with the first character in Steps 2 and 3 of this exercise, but this time, describe yourself. Write about how you look and what your personality is like. Do not use the word "I." Give yourself another name. Instead of saying, for example, "I am twenty-two," write "Julie is twenty-two." You are writing about yourself as if you were another person. For our example, we would write: Julie is twenty-two. She is shy and reserved. She is very pretty but doesn't seem to know it.

Through this exercise, you have started to turn real people into characters. By inventing names for these characters, you began to free yourself from the real event and people. A playwright uses his imagination to make a real event into a dramatic event. By taking a step back from the real event, you free your imagination to take control and change the event.

Reread the descriptions of your two characters. Think about them and how their past has brought them to the moment in your event. Think about how they became who they are.

Spend a few days thinking about these characters. Add any new thoughts you have to your descriptions. You will be spending a lot of time with them as you write your scene. It is important to get to know them very well.

In the next section, we're going to put the characters aside for a while to think about *where* the scene took place.

EXAMPLE

Read the character descriptions before the selection from "'Night, Mother" in *Selected from Contemporary American Plays*. Notice what Marsha Norman tells us about her characters, and think about how this description will help you understand them.

The Senses

Now that you have thought about your characters, it's a good time to turn to the *setting*: the place where your characters will walk and talk. To re-create the time and place where your event happened, use your senses.

We absorb the world around us through our five senses. Hearing, sight, touch, taste and smell combine to give us a picture of our environment.

Senses contribute to how we think, feel and act. Look around you. What are your senses absorbing now? How do your senses contribute to your experience? As a playwright, you can use your senses to bring your remembered event to life.

Think how hearing an old song or smelling a food can bring back a flood of memories. Your memory of that time is tied to the sensory experience you had at the time. Senses make the memory more real.

Sometimes playwrights exaggerate one sense to add drama to a scene. One playwright, when writing about a dispute between a husband and wife, added the sound of a garbage truck outside their window. As they argued, the truck noises slowly became so loud that the characters could no longer hear each other. The playwright used the sound outside to make the audience notice the couple's growing inability to communicate with each other.

EXERCISE 5: Using Your Senses to Remember

You will use your senses—hearing, sight, touch, taste and smell—to add detail to your selected event to help it come alive.

STEP 1. Title a sheet of paper SENSE SHEET and list the five senses: *Touch, Taste, Smell, Hearing* and *Sight.* Then take a look at your outline. Taking one sense at a time, list some words that describe your event as you remember it. For example, *Touch*: I was nervously crunching a ball of paper in my hand. *Taste*: We ate hot buttered popcorn. *Smell*: There was perfume in the air. *Hearing*: My favorite song was playing on the radio. *Sight*: The Christmas decorations were still hanging up.

List as many ideas as you can come up with.

STEP 2. After you are done, look back at your outline of the scene and then look at your sense sheet. Close your eyes for a few minutes and think about your sensory memories of the event. You will probably remember more to add to your lists.

The Setting

Many of your sense memories will help you picture what the scene looked like and details of what was going on. They will tie in with the *When* and *Where* of your outline by giving you more details of time and place. They will help you describe the play's *setting*.

A playwright has to tell an audience where and when the scene is taking place. It helps people understand a scene better if they know the type of place where it's happening and the year, time of year and time of day it's happening. How can you help the audience discover when and where your scene is happening?

The playwright usually writes a description of the time and place at the very beginning of each scene. From this description, the production team uses its imagination and talent to make the setting real. The audience sees the finished result of the production team's work: the *set*, and understands the time and place the playwright had in mind for the scene.

Playwrights describe settings in many different ways. Some descriptions are long and detailed, and include props and furniture to be placed on the stage. Others simply give the place and time during which the scene takes place and leave the rest up to the imagination of the production team.

EXAMPLE

Read the setting descriptions at the beginning of "The Odd Couple" and "Driving Miss Daisy" in *Selected from Contemporary American Plays*. Notice the various ways that different playwrights write about place and time.

EXERCISE 6: Creating a Setting

You will now expand on the *Where* and *When* of your outline and create your setting.

STEP 1. Title a new page in your notebook SCENE SETTING. Below this, put the season and year in which your scene took place. For example: Spring 1985.

STEP 2. Next, write the place where your scene happens. Look at your outline. Your scene could be indoors or outdoors, in a specific building or place, or in a city or deserted town. Think about what is important for people to know. Describe the place from an outsider's point of view. This general description might read: Outside an apartment building in a neighborhood in Brooklyn.

STEP 3. Take out your sense sheet. Look over the things you listed under *Sight* and add more things that will give the production team a clearer picture of what the setting could look like. For example, small buildings, laundry hanging on lines, a narrow street.

STEP 4. Look back at the other things you have listed on your sense sheet. Check off the sensory experiences that give important information about your event. Think about which can help provide the audience with clues about the time and place of the event. For example, if you listed that you saw leaves starting to come out on the trees, this will help the audience see that the event is happening in the spring.

All these details will help the production team know what information the setting must convey and what mood it must set for the audience. For example, if it was summer and hot, you may want to put a fan in your set or have the sun beaming through a window. If a love song is playing, you may want to put a radio or stereo in your set. The fan, stereo and radio help "dress" the set; they are the details that help the audience know when and where the scene takes place.

STEP 5. On your SCENE SETTING sheet, below the time and the general setting, write sentences that include the important details of the setting that you got from your sense sheet and your outline. This is your setting description. What you write might look like this:

SCENE 1: Early spring 1985. Outside an apartment building in a neighborhood in Brooklyn. It is evening. There is a row of small apartment houses on a narrow street. Laundry lines full of drying clothes hang from the apartments above. A rap song from a radio plays in the distance.

You have completed the section, "Using Your Own World." You have decided on an event and outlined it. You have created characters and a setting. Make sure all your notes and exercises are in your notebook. You may want to reread them or add to them before you go on to the next section of this book. You will need all of these exercise sheets to continue. The next section will help you develop your outline into a dramatic scene.

3

DEVELOPING YOUR SCENE

Characters are the most important element in a scene. It is through each character's words that we begin to discover exactly who that person is. Playwrights refer to their characters' words as *dialogue*.

The Importance of Listening

Listen carefully to how different people speak. Everybody has a distinct way of communicating and expressing themselves. There are many differences such as the words we choose, our accents, the slang that we use, our tone of voice and what language we speak.

We might learn something about where a person lives from the way he or she talks. People who live in different parts of the United States have different accents. A person who lives on a farm often uses different words than someone in a city. Playwrights listen carefully to differences in language and use those differences to give their characters individual personalities.

When you go to places where many people come and go, try listening for these differences. A restaurant or a movie line is a perfect place to overhear conversations. How do people sound the same? How do they sound different? What exactly makes them different?

A character's words can also give us a good idea of when the scene is taking place. If your scene takes place in the 1930s, your characters would not use words like "rap" or "yuppie." If your scene takes place in the 1960s, you might use words like "groovy" or "hippie." Slang words change with time. By using the language of the time in which your scene takes place, your characters seem more real and believable.

Notice the differences between the way you speak and how your parents or grandparents speak. Do you speak differently from your brothers or sisters? What about your children?

For many playwrights, listening becomes a habit. They search for new words and speech patterns. They think about how each person's speech gives insight into the speaker. Often, playwrights take notes on what they have heard.

EXAMPLE

In *Selected from Contemporary American Plays,* read the selections from "The Trip to Bountiful" and "for colored girls who have considered suicide/when the rainbow is enuf." Notice the differences in the language of the characters. What does their speech tell you about each of the characters?

EXERCISE 7: Writing Dialogue

You are now going to write dialogue for the characters in your scene.

STEP 1. Look at the outline of your event from Exercise 3. You are going to describe the scene again, but this time it will be through dialogue.

STEP 2. On a new page titled DIALOGUE, write what the two characters say. Write only the dialogue, no directions or other description.

Of course, some of the dialogue from your event may contain a description of the time or place. For example, if the event took place in a restaurant, the characters may have talked about how the place looked or smelled or what food was on the menu.

It's all right to include this kind of description of where the scene takes place; it provides clues for the audience.

STEP 3. Let's look at an example that shows how to put dialogue on a page. We will use the *script* form because it clearly shows who is talking.

<u>TONY</u>
Julie, I want you to stay.

<u>JULIE</u>
No, it's getting late.

In this example, you see that the name of the character is in the center of the page with a line under it. The name is in capital letters so it is easy to see. Under the name is the dialogue the person speaks.

STEP 4. Continue through the scene writing dialogue this way. Look at your outline when you need to. It doesn't matter if you don't remember exactly what your real-life people said. Dialogue should tell the important parts of the story, reveal the characters' personalities and keep the action moving. You can leave out dialogue that is not important to the story. You can make up dialogue that will make the action clearer. Be sure each person's words are true to that person's personality and style.

Your first page might look like this:

TONY
Julie, I want you to stay.

JULIE
No, it's getting late.

TONY
That's what you said last night. It's only eight o'clock.

JULIE
My kids worry about me after it gets dark.

TONY
So bring them along next time.

JULIE
You'd want to see me and my kids?

TONY
Sure.

STEP 5. Look over the example. It tells the same story we described in the outline—only it tells it through dialogue. We find out something about when the story takes place because Tony tells us it is only eight o'clock. We begin to understand who these characters are through their dialogue. We sense Julie's shyness by her surprise that Tony would want to see her kids. We get the feeling that Tony is a nice guy because he makes this suggestion. We also discover a conflict—Tony and Julie want to be together but she has to get home to her children. And we learn how this conflict might be resolved—by the kids visiting Tony with Julie. Notice how there is no unnecessary dialogue, only what is necessary to tell the important parts of the story, reveal the characters' personalities and keep the action moving.

STEP 6. Reread your scene. Make any changes in the dialogue that make the characters more real. Take out unnecessary dialogue. Read it over again and see if it tells your story as you want it told.

EXERCISE 8: Reading Your Dialogue

STEP 1. If you are working in a group, take turns reading the lines to each other. If you are working alone, ask a friend to read with you. You read one character's lines and your friend reads the other's lines. Read only the dialogue, not the character's name. The names are there only to tell you who is to speak. If you have a tape recorder, record the scene as you read it.

STEP 2. Listen to the tape, or talk with others about the reading.

Does it sound like two people talking? Does the dialogue give the information about what is happening clearly? Are there any changes needed? Do the words that you have put in each character's mouth show their personalities and backgrounds? Does everyone have a clear idea of who the characters are?

STEP 3. Have other people listen to the tape of your scene. Ask them to tell you what they think about the characters. What do they think is happening in the scene? Ask for specific answers because they can help you make changes in the scene.

STEP 4. Write down the suggestions in your notebook and save the dialogue to be used later.

4

PREPARING A SCRIPT

A script is the written form of a play. It includes
not only the dialogue but all the other information
needed by the production team. The script con-
tains all the elements of the play. It has 1) a
description of the *setting*, or where and when the
play takes place; 2) a description of the people in
the play, or the *cast of characters*; 3) the dialogue
for the actors to say; 4) the instructions for the
actors on how to move around the stage, or
stage directions; and 5) explanations for the actors of how the characters are feeling at certain
times.

If you've completed Exercises 2 to 8, you're
ready to put these pieces together in script format.

A script is written in a special format. A play in a
book such as *Selected from Contemporary American Plays* is no longer in the script format. The
format has been changed to make it easier for a
reader. The script format is designed to make it

easy for the production team to work with when putting on a play.

The Script Format

As you discovered when you wrote dialogue, plays look different on paper than novels or newspaper articles. You placed the characters' names over the dialogue to indicate who speaks the line. This is part of the script format.

A script must be clear and concise. Only the most important information should be included. The script must give the technical director and his team everything they need to know. It describes the setting, props and sometimes the costumes. The technical team will use its talents to add detail to this information.

The actors refer to the script during rehearsals. Because the characters' names are centered on the page and underlined, the actors can locate their lines easily.

The script may also tell the actors where on stage they will be and where and how they will move—the stage directions. The actors take this information—character descriptions, lines and stage directions—and use their own talents as guided by the director to create real and interesting characters.

EXERCISE 9: Step by Step Through a Sample Script

In this exercise, we will create a first draft of a scene in script format. We will take all the pieces you've already written—character description, setting and dialogue—and add one more thing—the stage directions—to complete a draft script of your scene.

STEP 1. The Character Description: A script begins with a page describing the characters in the play. This page stands alone in the script. Look at this example of a character description and notice how the lines are written. It is based on the characters we described in Exercise 4.

CHARACTERS:

TONY TAYLOR is twenty-nine years old. He is tall and thin. Tony is very straightforward and kind. He is sure of himself, yet seems self-conscious.

JULIE CLARK is twenty-two years old, shy
and reserved. She is very pretty but does
not seem to know it.

Take a clean sheet of paper and title it DRAFT
PAGE 1. Copy your character descriptions from
Exercise 4 onto this new page, so that they look like
the sample above.

STEP 2. Setting the Scene: The actual scene
begins on the next page of a script. The setting for
the scene is described in detail, including any
props. You already developed the setting for this
scene in Exercise 6. You can take the setting you've
already written and remove this page from
your notebook and write DRAFT PAGE 2 at
the top.

STEP 3. The Opening Stage Directions: There is
one thing you need to add to your setting to
complete the description of what we see at the
moment the play begins—where your characters
are and what they are doing. Where are they when
the scene starts? If they are not onstage at the
beginning, you must have them come on. This is
known as their *entrance*. Their entrance and their
first actions before speaking are added to the end of
the setting description. The whole thing would
look like this:

SCENE 1: Early spring 1985. Outside an apartment building in a neighborhood in Brooklyn. It is evening. There is a row of small apartment houses on a narrow street. Laundry lines full of drying clothes hang from the apartments above. A rap song from a radio plays in the distance. JULIE and TONY come out the front door of one of the apartment buildings. TONY sits down at the top of the stoop. JULIE continues down a few steps and then turns back to TONY.

Add stage directions to your setting description for any character who appears onstage before the dialogue begins.

STEP 4. Stage Directions in the Scene: You will also need stage directions during the scene. Often the characters will move as they talk. The playwright needs to tell the actors when and where to move.

These stage directions usually begin at the left margin of the paper and are put in parentheses. This tells the actor that this is something he must *do* and not something he must say.

Try to keep the stage directions simple. Characters should move from one place to another for a reason. The stage directions for the movements of the characters can help the actors (and the audience) understand the feelings or the reactions of the characters as much as what they say out loud.

For example, in our scene Julie is leaving because she must, but she doesn't really want to go. We have to show her going away, and we can also show her feelings about leaving Tony. She could start to walk away but stop to talk to Tony, hoping he will say something. The stage directions would read:

(JULIE continues down the steps and stops on the sidewalk.)

The actor needs to know this information. She may not need information such as "smile" or "wave good-bye." This is left up to the creativity of the actors. But if a character suddenly has an emotional change, you would want to tell the actor to "cry," for example.

Reread the dialogue you wrote for your scene (Exercise 7). Think about what stage directions you will need to add to explain the action as the characters talk in the scene. You will always need a stage direction when a character comes on stage, or *enters* and when a character goes off stage, or *exits*.

STEP 5. Putting the Scene Together: After the setting description and opening stage directions for Scene 1, the dialogue begins. The stage directions are inserted into the dialogue where necessary.

This is what the whole scene would look like when the setting for the scene, the dialogue and the stage directions are put together:

SCENE 1: Early spring 1985. Outside an apartment building in a neighborhood in Brooklyn. It is evening. There is a row of small apartment houses on a narrow street. Laundry lines full of drying clothes hang from the apartments above. A rap song from a radio plays in the distance. JULIE and TONY come out the front door of one of the apartment buildings. TONY sits down at the top of the stoop. JULIE continues down a few steps and then turns back to TONY.

TONY
Julie, I want you to stay.

JULIE
No, it's getting late.

TONY

That's what you said last night. It's only
eight o'clock.

(JULIE continues down the steps and
stops on the sidewalk.)

JULIE

My kids worry about me after it gets
dark.

TONY

So bring them along next time.

JULIE

You'd want to see me and my kids?

TONY

Sure.

(JULIE walks down the sidewalk. After
she has taken a few steps, she stops.)

JULIE

Okay. Me and the kids will see you
tomorrow night.

(JULIE walks away and exits. TONY goes
back into the building.)

On the same page where you described the setting for your scene and the opening stage directions (DRAFT PAGE 2), skip a few lines and start writing the dialogue. Insert the stage directions where they are necessary as you go along. Take your time and remember this is only a draft—it can be changed later.

STEP 6. When you finish the first draft of your scene, put the date on the top of the pages and keep them in your notebook. You've completed your scene.

5

EDITING YOUR SCENE

Even though you've already done a lot of work writing your scene, it is quite rare that a scene is written perfectly the first time. Going through the editing process helps you to get your scene just the way you want it. The amount of editing needed differs from scene to scene and from person to person. Some scenes go through many drafts before they are exactly right. Your scene may only need some fine tuning or it may need a complete tune-up.

When editing, you look at many elements of your script. You need to correct spelling mistakes. You want to be sure the characters sound real. You want the story to be believable. You want the time and place of the scene to be clear.

You can use the editing process to begin to try making fiction out of fact. Sometimes you will need to change some of what really happened to make the meaning, or *theme,* of your story clearer and more dramatic. This does not take away from the importance of your real experience. It is adapting, or changing, it for the stage.

In editing, you will work with comments that you and your friends have made. Editing will help you gain playwriting skills.

EXERCISE 10: Reading Your Scene

When you read your scene aloud, you can often hear what information is missing or what needs to be changed. If you're able to get some other people together, it is helpful to hear your script read aloud by others. It will give you a chance to see how it sounds to an audience.

STEP 1. Take your script and read it aloud to yourself. How does it sound? Does it tell your story well? Are there any changes you would like to make?

STEP 2. Ask two people to read the scene aloud. Have them read the script silently to themselves before they read it aloud.

STEP 3. Ask them to act out the stage directions. They may want to rehearse the scene before they perform it for you.

Don't give the actors directions on how to read or perform the scene. You want to find out if the script has all the information they need.

STEP 4. You might ask some other people to watch the performance with you. Have one of the actors read the character and setting descriptions aloud. This is necessary because they don't have costumes, makeup, a set or props.

STEP 5. When you watch their performance, you will begin to see two things. One, the actors add something of themselves to the characters. Two, you will learn if the dialogue and action tell your story the way you want it told.

STEP 6. After the performance, write down ideas about any changes you would make.

STEP 7. Talk to the performers and the other people who watched the scene. Be sure to ask them specific questions so you will get helpful comments. For example, did they understand who was in the scene and where and when it took place? Did they understand the story? How did they feel about the characters? What did they think about the scene? What did they have difficulty with? Listen to them with an open mind.

STEP 8. Add a new page in your notebook of these COMMENTS, writing down what people have told you. It will be helpful to you later if you put the person's name next to his or her comment.

EXERCISE 11: Deciding on Changes

You will have to make decisions about how to edit your script. As a playwright, you will need to think about all the elements of your scene: the characters, the setting, the dialogue, the story, the conflict and its resolution.

Playwrights think about ways to add interest for the audience. They often create a turning point in the story at the end of a scene or an act. This is called a *climax*. It is a moment when something is said or something happens that the audience understands will affect the characters and the story. But the audience doesn't know how it will affect them or what will happen next. This keeps the audience eager to find out what will happen in the next scene or act. Does your scene have a moment of excitement or mystery like this? Does it have a climax?

Another thing to think about is your scene's meaning, or *theme*. The theme is different from the story. The theme is the main point you want the audience to understand. The theme of our example might be "patience and understanding are essential to love." Try describing your theme in one sentence. You want the action of your scene to illustrate your theme to the audience. This is what they will take home and think about. Keep it in mind when you write and edit.

STEP 1. Take a new piece of paper and title it EDITING LIST. Put the date at the top of the page. Use the list to write down all the changes you decide to make to the draft of your script.

STEP 2. Write down the correct spelling of any words that are misspelled. Write down new information you want to add and where you will put it in the script. Also note anything you want to take out or change.

STEP 3. Look over the comments you and your friends have made. Think about what information they give you. Has more than one person made the same comment? If so, you need to consider carefully what they have said.

Ask yourself, Do I agree with this comment? If your answer is yes, think about how you could change the script to improve it. If your answer is no or I don't think so, just go on to the next comment.

Comments and suggestions can be very useful, but your scene belongs to you. Be sure that the changes you decide to make help tell the story you want to tell.

STEP 4. Write down further ideas for changes on your editing list.

Sometimes you will have to change some part of the real-life event that your scene is based on to make things clearer. You will be using your creativity and imagination to make the scene *more* believable, even if it's different from what really happened.

Some examples of comments and editing solutions:

- You have comments such as "I don't get the point of the scene." Perhaps you need to change your real-life event a little. Maybe there is too much dialogue that doesn't have anything to do with the meaning of your scene. Keep in mind that the problem might not be in the scene— sometimes people in an audience just don't tune in. Decide if there is a problem and if so, how to solve it. Perhaps you need more or less dialogue.

- You have a comment like "I don't understand why a character did what she did." Maybe you left something out that would explain the action of the character—the character's *motive* for doing what he or she did in the scene. Think about how you could give this information. Perhaps you need some more dialogue or action. Perhaps the setting is unclear.

- Two people commented that "I thought the character was much younger than I found out he was." How did you describe the character in the character description? Does the way the character talks make him sound like a teenager rather than an older man?

STEP 5. Read over your editing list to make sure the changes won't create confusion. Sometimes, if you make one change, you will need to make others. Add any further changes to your editing list. For example, if you have taken out dialogue, you may have to add new dialogue for the scene to make sense and move smoothly. Or you may have two ideas for changes that are contradictory. Decide which way you want to go and cross the other change off your list.

STEP 6. Make the changes you want on your script.

STEP 7. Reread your script after you've changed it. Ask yourself if the story and its meaning are clearer. Are the characters more believable? Are you satisfied with your changes?

STEP 8. When you have made all the changes you want, write a clean second draft of the script and date it for your notebook.

Don't think of your edited draft as permanent. In a few days or weeks, you may read it again and decide to make new changes or get rid of changes. Reading your edited scene aloud may also give you different ideas. A play is a constant work in progress.

6

TURNING YOUR SCENE INTO A PLAY

Now that you've worked on your scene, you may want to see it performed (see Chapter 7, "How to See Your Play Performed"). Your scene can stand on its own, but you may also find that there are other scenes you want to write to go with it. You might want to develop these scenes into a one-act play.

A one-act play usually takes twenty minutes to an hour to perform. It might have many scenes or just a few. It probably would not have a lot of characters or settings.

EXERCISE 12: Creating More Scenes for Your Play

STEP 1. Look at your scene. Ask yourself, What happens next? and, What, if anything, happened before? You can add scenes to your play before or after the time of the scene you have already written. Your play can take place over hours, days or years—*there are no rules.*

STEP 2. Try making a LIST OF SCENES that came before and/or after your scene. Right now, you only need to write a short description of what happened. You will develop the ideas and action in the next exercise. Here is an example of a scene that comes before the one we created and one that comes after it:

Before example: (Early spring 1985) Julie and Tony meet for the first time.

Existing example (already written): (Three days later) Julie visits Tony. She has to get home because of her kids. Tony invites Julie to bring her kids over the next night.

After example: (The next night) Julie and her kids come over to Tony's apartment. Julie's son, Sam, won't talk to Tony and sits in the corner. Julie tries to get Sam to behave. Sam starts crying and screams that no one is going to take his father's place. Julie is upset and wants to leave but Tony talks to the boy. He tells Sam about his own life and how he misses his own father. Julie says it is time to go home. Sam asks Julie if Tony can come to their house to-morrow.

STEP 3. Think about your characters and the events in the new scenes. Are the situations real? Are the characters believable? Make sure you have scenes where the audience gets to know and care about the characters.

STEP 4. Look at your list of scenes. Does one scene lead into the next? Does your play have conflict? Does this conflict build to a climax? And is the conflict resolved for better or worse? In our example, there is conflict between Tony and Sam. It reaches a climax when Sam gets mad. It is resolved when Sam asks Julie if Tony can come over. If your play doesn't have conflict, it may not hold the audience's interest. And if the conflict is not resolved, the audience will not be satisfied at the end.

Think about using conflict, climax and resolution to make your scenes dramatic.

STEP 5. You may have to change the things that really happened before or after your event to give your play more dramatic interest. Make any changes to your list of scenes that will clarify the theme, make the characters more real or add conflict.

EXERCISE 13: Developing Your Play

You can use your list of scenes as the outline for your play. Write one scene at a time, using the same steps you did before.

STEP 1. OUTLINE

Outline each new scene on a separate piece of paper as you did in Exercise 3.

STEP 2. NEW CHARACTERS

Describe any new characters as you did in Exercise 4.

STEP 3. CREATE A SETTING

Make a sense sheet for each new scene, as you did in Exercise 5.

Create the setting for each new scene as you did in Exercise 6. Keep down the number of different settings. You might try to make the scenes fit into the same general setting. In our example, the setting is outside an apartment building. If we have Tony and Julie meet for the first time outside this building, then our first two scenes can take place in the same place.

Much of the setting description for the new scene may be the same as your first scene. However, if time has passed from scene to scene, you may

want to change a few details of the setting to show
the passage of time.

For example, maybe Tony and Julie meet on the
first warm day of spring. We might add to the
worksheet for our new Scene 1: The sun is shining
brightly. Because our original scene takes place in
the evening, people will understand some time has
passed.

In our example, Scene 3 takes place inside
Tony's apartment. We need to describe this new
setting completely. You will need to follow Exercise 6 for any new settings you may have.

STEP 4. DIALOGUE

Write the dialogue for each new scene as you did
in Exercise 7. Be sure the dialogue is true to the
character. For example, Sam would talk differently
if he were five years old or if he were ten.

STEP 5. READ YOUR DIALOGUE

Read through all the dialogue as you did in
Exercise 8. Make any changes you want based on
this reading.

EXERCISE 14: Scripting Your Play

After you have developed your new scenes, you will
need to write the new scenes in the script for-

mat. Reread Exercise 9: Step by Step Through a Sample Script if you want to refresh your memory. When these new scenes are combined with your original scene, your play will be written.

STEP 1. NEW CHARACTERS

Using your characters pages, add any new characters and their descriptions in script format to the first page of your draft script.

STEP 2. SETTINGS FOR EACH SCENE

Set the scene in script format for each new scene. Be sure to add the opening stage directions for each new scene to the setting description.

STEP 3. ADD DIALOGUE

Put each scene together, adding the dialogue and stage directions after each scene setting. Be sure to include exits and entrances. Look at your sense sheet again to see if it gives you any ideas you could put in the stage directions to make the time and place clear.

For example, when our new first scene opens, Tony could be sitting on the apartment house steps, listening to a baseball game on a radio and drinking a soda. This would help the audience know it is warm and baseball season. Julie could enter, carrying a bunch of daffodils. This would help people know it is spring.

STEP 4. PUT SCENES IN ORDER

Put all the scenes in order (your draft plus the new scenes). In our example, we would have to change the scene number on our draft since it is now Scene 2 instead of Scene 1.

STEP 5. EDIT YOUR SCRIPT

Read through your script. Is there enough information for the audience to understand the story? Do the characters sound real? Do they stay true to their personalities? Is there conflict, climax and resolution?

Edit your script as you did in Exercises 10 and 11 and make sure it is as good as you want it to be.

STEP 6. CHOOSE A TITLE FOR YOUR PLAY

Now that you have a complete draft of a play instead of a scene, you need to choose a title for your play. Take a clean sheet of paper and put the title at the top of the page with your name under it. This is the first page of your script, standing alone in front of the character page.

STEP 7. A SUMMARY OF SCENES

This title page should also have a summary of

when and where each scene of the play takes place. Read back over your setting descriptions and see what are the most important things about the time and place of each scene. The summary will contain only a general description; the details are saved for the setting descriptions. For example, our summary would look like this:

TIME: Early spring 1985

SETTING: Outside and inside an apartment building in a neighborhood in Brooklyn

SCENE 1: On the street, one afternoon

SCENE 2: On the street, three days later

SCENE 3: In Tony's apartment, the next night

Add a summary of your play to the title page. Now you have completed your one-act play.

7

HOW TO SEE YOUR PLAY PERFORMED

Now that you have completed your scene or written several scenes as a one-act play, you may want to see it performed or read aloud before an audience. Many playwrights produce their scripts themselves. You need to find a space for the play and the audience. A church or community center might be good. If you are in school, perhaps the auditorium or gymnasium could be used.

You need to put together a production team. Some people could work on the costumes. Others could work on the sets and props. (Watch expenses for these things!)

You also need actors. Pick people who are similar to your characters and who are not embarrassed to act in front of an audience.

Let the actors read their parts at home until they are comfortable with their lines. Then organize rehearsals. This will give everyone the chance to interact with one another.

You will need a director. You may want to do it yourself. Or you might pick someone who is less personally involved.

Sometimes playwrights have a reading of their play. There are no costumes, sets or props used in a reading. The cast stands or sits and each person reads his or her part. Readings also need rehearsals.

Decide on your performance date. Send invitations to friends or post flyers in your neighborhood. You may want to charge a small admission price to cover your production costs or to give to charity. One playwright charged a can of food per person to give to the local food bank.

Have a program printed or photocopied. It should have all the information from the title page of the play: the title, your name and the summary. Then list the name of each character and the name of the actor playing that part. Also list the other members of the production team and their jobs.

Congratulations! You have accomplished a great deal. We hope you have found that writing a play is an exciting way to express your ideas and creativity.

GLOSSARY

Act. One of the major divisions in a play. "To act" means to perform onstage.

Actor. A person who plays a character in a play

Cast. All the actors in a play are the cast.

Character. A person portrayed in a play

Climax. The turning point in a play

Conflict. The struggle between characters resulting from differences in interests, ideas or expectations or from actions and circumstances

Costume. The clothes that an actor wears onstage

Cue. A signal given to a member of the production team to begin an action, such as dimming the lights, or to an actor to begin a speech

Dialogue. The lines the actors speak

Director. The person who instructs and supervises the production team

Edit. To change and improve writing

Motive. The reason for a person's actions

Play. A story written to be acted

Playwright. The person who writes a play

Producer. The person responsible for raising the money and making the business arrangements for a play

Production team. The group of people who work to present a play

Prop (short for "property"). An item used onstage by an actor

Rehearsal. A practice session before a public performance of a play

Resolution. The point where the conflicts are worked out

Scene. The smaller divisions within acts of a play

Script. The written text of a play

Set. The scenery and other onstage elements (like furniture and props) that show where the play takes place

Setting. The description of the time and place of the play

Stage directions. Descriptions of where and how the actors move onstage

Theme. The central meaning of the play

DIAGRAM OF THE PRODUCTION TEAM

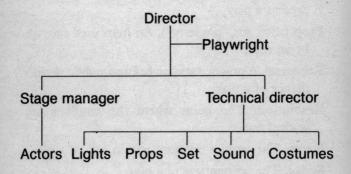

PRAISE FⱯ ⟨✧⟩ SO-ALN-188

Redemption: Hunters ✓

"James Reasoner creates a terrific air of tension . . . His pacing is excellent and his prose believable . . . a first-class series . . . nearly a year between books is far too long to wait for those of us eager to see what troubles befall the town of Redemption next."   —Western Fiction Review

"*Redemption: Hunters* proves, once again, why James Reasoner's name is synonymous with superior Western storytelling . . . After the strength of both *Redemption, Kansas* and *Redemption: Hunters*, I hope that Reasoner keeps his Bill Harvey series going for a long time. I'm already eager for a third book."   —*Fires on the Plain*

PRAISE FOR

Redemption, Kansas

Winner of Western Fictioneers Peacemaker Award

"A Western novel with characters you care about and a crackerjack plot. If anybody asks you who's carrying on the heritage of fine traditional Westerns in the vein of Louis L'Amour and Elmer Kelton, tell 'em James Reasoner's the man."   —Bill Crider, author of *Murder of a Beauty Shop Queen*

"A wonderful book, wonderfully told. James Reasoner has the gift of words, telling a fast-paced story that reaches into the hearts of his characters . . . and his readers."
                                        —Frank Roderus, author of *Ransom*

"A fast-paced cowboy tale written with the flair of a master. If you've never read a Western by James Reasoner, pick this one up. You won't put this novel down until you've finished it, and you'll be ready for more."
                                        —Larry D. Sweazy, Spur Award–winning author of
                                        The Coyote Tracker

Berkley titles by James Reasoner

REDEMPTION, KANSAS
REDEMPTION: HUNTERS
REDEMPTION: TRACKDOWN

LOVELAND PUBLIC LIBRARY

000482868

Withdrawn

REDEMPTION:
Trackdown

James Reasoner

BERKLEY BOOKS, NEW YORK

THE BERKLEY PUBLISHING GROUP
Published by the Penguin Group
Penguin Group (USA) Inc.
375 Hudson Street, New York, New York 10014, USA

USA / Canada / UK / Ireland / Australia / New Zealand / India / South Africa / China

Penguin Books Ltd., Registered Offices: 80 Strand, London WC2R 0RL, England
For more information about the Penguin Group visit penguin.com

REDEMPTION TRACKDOWN

A Berkley Book / published by arrangement with the author

Copyright © 2013 by James Reasoner.

All rights reserved.
No part of this book may be reproduced, scanned, or distributed in any
printed or electronic form without permission. Please do not participate in or encourage piracy
of copyrighted materials in violation of the author's rights. Purchase only authorized editions.

Berkley Books are published by The Berkley Publishing Group.
BERKLEY® is a registered trademark of Penguin Group (USA) Inc.
The "B" design is a trademark of Penguin Group (USA) Inc.

For information, address: The Berkley Publishing Group,
a division of Penguin Group (USA) Inc.,
375 Hudson Street, New York, New York 10014.

ISBN: 978-0-425-25060-0

PUBLISHING HISTORY
Berkley mass market edition / March 2013

PRINTED IN THE UNITED STATES OF AMERICA

10 9 8 7 6 5 4 3 2 1

Cover illustration by Dennis Lyall.
Cover design by Diana Kolsky.
Interior text design by Kristin del Rosario.

This is a work of fiction. Names, characters, places, and incidents either are the product
of the author's imagination or are used fictitiously, and any resemblance to actual persons,
living or dead, business establishments, events, or locales is entirely coincidental.
The publisher does not have any control over and does not assume any responsibility for
author or third-party websites or their content.

If you purchased this book without a cover, you should be aware that this book is
stolen property. It was reported as "unsold and destroyed" to the publisher, and neither
the author nor the publisher has received any payment for this "stripped book."

For Tom Roberts

Loveland Public Library
300 N. Adams Ave.
Loveland, CO 80537

Chapter 1

The tinny strains of music from a player piano drifted over the batwings, mingled with raucous laughter. Folks were having a fine old time in the Prairie Queen Saloon this evening, Bill Harvey thought as he paused on the boardwalk outside the establishment.

He pondered pushing the batwings aside and going in to have a look around, then decided not to. The saloon was loud but otherwise peaceful enough at the moment. No need to put a damper on the festivities by showing up with a marshal's badge pinned to his shirt.

Bill walked on past the entrance, limping a little on his left leg, the permanent result of an injury suffered back when he was still a Texas cowboy helping to push a herd to market here in Kansas. A spooked steer had gored him in that leg, and he could have easily died if not for Eden Monroe taking such good care of him.

She was still taking care of him as his wife now, since he'd given up cowboying, pinned on the marshal's star, and settled down here in Redemption.

Bill glanced at the horses tied up at the hitch rails in front of the Prairie Queen. Those rails were just about full. As the new saloon in town, the place was doing a booming business, while Smoot's Saloon, well established and on the other side of the street on the next block, was suffering a mite as many of Fred Smoot's regular customers flocked to the Prairie Queen to try it out.

It didn't help matters for Smoot that the Prairie Queen was owned by a woman, and a good-looking one at that. Annabelle Hudson, she called herself, and for all Bill knew, that was her real name. Blond, about thirty, with some hard edges about her that said she knew a lot about the world, though still very attractive. Naturally her presence was going to lure most of the thirsty hombres in town.

That was none of Bill's concern, of course. His job was to keep the peace, not worry about business rivalries. As long as they didn't lead to shooting, those things would have to sort themselves out.

He had reached the alley between the Prairie Queen and the hardware store, which was closed and dark for the night, when a shot blasted from the saloon, and a woman screamed.

Bill wheeled around and moved fast, limp or no limp. Some nights he carried a shotgun with him when he made his evening rounds, but tonight he flat out hadn't thought to bring it along.

He had a Colt holstered on his right hip, though, and he drew the revolver as he reached the batwings. His keen brown eyes peered over them.

Customers yelled and scrambled to get out of the way as a man in range clothes stood next to the bar swinging a gun back and forth in a threatening manner.

"Everybody back off!" he shouted. "I'll shoot the next man who lays a hand on me!"

Behind the bar were Glenn Morley, a balding man with graying red hair who wore a bartender's apron, and the Prairie Queen herself, Annabelle Hudson. Annabelle's long-sleeved, high-necked blue gown didn't reveal much skin, but it was tight enough to show off the generous curves of her body.

Bill saw Morley start to reach under the bar and figured he was trying for a weapon of some sort. Annabelle moved up and put a hand on his arm to stop him. She wouldn't want that cowboy shooting up her saloon, but clearly she didn't want Morley to risk getting hurt, either.

Instead she said, "Take it easy, mister. Nobody's going to hurt you."

The cowboy grimaced as he jerked his head around to look over his shoulder at her.

"Damn right they ain't, lady. I'll blow a hole in the first man who gets near me."

Bill saw a big wet patch on the cowboy's faded blue shirt. He could make a pretty good guess what had happened. Somebody had gotten a mite too boisterous and spilled a beer on the cowboy, who'd taken offense, whipped out his gun, and let off a shot at the offender.

The fact that the cowboy was obviously drunk was probably the only reason a body wasn't stretched out on the floor, leaking blood. He had missed . . . but he might not the next time.

At one time, Redemption had had an ordinance prohibiting cowboys from entering the town. Bill had come along, rescued the settlement from a bad fix, and then taken the marshal's job. That had led to the easing of the prohibition against cowboys. Most of the time that had worked out fine, but not always.

Like tonight.

Bill was reasonably fast on the draw but no gunslick. However, he nearly always hit what he aimed at, and he knew he could put a bullet in that drunken troublemaker from here.

But if he did that, there was a good chance he would kill the man, and he wasn't sure the fella deserved to die just for getting liquored up and crazy.

Instead Bill took a deep breath, pouched the iron, and pushed the batwings aside to step into the saloon.

Some of the frightened customers looked at him, and that drew the attention of the gun wielder. He swung the revolver in his hand toward Bill, who was ready to dive to the floor if he thought the man was about to shoot.

"Hold it right there!" the cowboy yelled. "Don't come any closer, you damned star packer, or I'll ventilate you!"

Bill held his hands up in plain sight so the man could see he wasn't holding a gun.

"Settle down, amigo," he said. "Texas, right?"

The cowboy frowned owlishly at him and said, "That's right. How the hell did you know?"

Bill put a grin on his face.

"You think one Texan don't recognize another Texan?" he asked. "Whereabouts you from?"

Still frowning, the cowboy replied, "Little place called Lockhart. You know it?"

"Shoot, yeah," Bill said. "I'm from down around Hallettsville and Victoria."

"Then what in blazes are you doin' all the way up here in Kansas, and wearin' a badge, at that?"

"Came up here on a cattle drive and decided to stay." Bill moved closer as he spoke, not getting in any hurry. He was deliberate enough about it that he hoped the cowboy wouldn't even notice. "It's really a nice place."

"I don't know about that." The man glared around the room. "I don't think they like Texans."

A year earlier, that would have been true, but not anymore. Bill didn't want to go into all that history while the man was still waving a gun around.

The cowboy's stance wasn't quite so threatening anymore. The barrel of his revolver drooped a little, pointing more at the floor than the frightened customers. Bill eased a little closer and hoped that he could get the man to holster the gun.

Then he'd haul the fella down to the jail and lock him up overnight to sleep it off. He had done that before with other cowboys who'd had too much to drink. It sure beat having to kill somebody.

Keeping his voice calm and steady, he said, "You just got off on the wrong foot, amigo, that's all. I promise you, Redemption is a nice, friendly place. Folks around here took right to me, and I'm as Texan as they come."

That was stretching the truth some—when his trail boss Hob Sanders had brought him into town, badly injured by that bull, there had been plenty of citizens who didn't want him to stay—but things had changed. If this hombre would just put his gun up and go along peacefully . . .

Glenn Morley snatched a bungstarter from under the bar and swung it at the cowboy's head.

Bill couldn't stop his eyes from jerking wide in surprise. The cowboy saw that reaction, ripped out a curse, and whirled around. His gun came up again and flame spouted from the muzzle.

Chapter 2

Several things happened at once. Annabelle Hudson cried "No!" too late to stop her bartender from attacking the cowboy. The bungstarter missed, zipping past the cowboy's head with four or five inches to spare. The bullet from the cowboy's gun went wide and hit a bottle of whiskey on the back bar. Glass and liquor sprayed in the air as the bottle exploded.

A split second later, Bill crashed into the cowboy as he tackled the man from behind. The impact drove the cowboy against the bar and bent him over the hardwood. Morley had lost his balance from the missed blow, but he recovered and brought the bungstarter around again in a backswing that cracked across the cowboy's forearm and sent the revolver flying from his fingers.

The man's hat had fallen off when Bill tackled him. Bill grabbed the back of the man's head, tangling his fingers in thick sandy hair, and bounced the hombre's forehead off the bar. He rammed into the man again, which drove the cowboy's belly against the edge of the bar and knocked the wind out of him. The cowboy was stunned and gasping for breath when Bill hauled him around and walloped him in the jaw.

That put the cowboy down and out, sprawled in the saw-dust that littered the floor in front of the bar.

Morley extended the bungstarter and asked, "You need this, Marshal?"

"No, there's not any fight left in him," Bill replied. "Where'd his gun go?"

"It's back here," Annabelle Hudson said. She reached down behind the bar and retrieved the weapon from the floor. Bill took it from her as she held it out to him.

Three rounds were still in the Colt's cylinder. As Bill was emptying the cartridges into the palm of his hand, Annabelle went on, "Thank you for stopping him, Marshal. I was afraid he was going to kill somebody."

"He might have," Bill admitted, "but it would have been sort of by accident."

"They'd be just as dead," Morley said.

Bill shrugged and nodded.

"Can't deny that." He put the bullets in his shirt pocket and shoved the empty revolver behind his waistband. "Sorry about the bottle of whiskey he busted. If he's got any money in his pocket, I'll take out for it and see that you get it."

Annabelle shook her head.

"There's no need for that. I'm not worried about one bottle of whiskey. I'm just glad that no one got killed."

"Me, too, ma'am," Bill said. This was the most he had talked to Annabelle since she and Morley had showed up in town a couple of weeks earlier and moved into the vacant building to set up the Prairie Queen. He found himself liking her. She seemed pretty levelheaded.

He turned toward the crowd of customers, who were starting to relax now that the drunken cowboy was out cold.

"Who spilled beer on this hombre?" Bill asked.

"That was me, Marshal," a man said as he moved half a step forward. Bill recognized him as Jed Abernathy, a freight wagon driver who passed through Redemption from time to time. Abernathy went on, "But it was an accident, I swear. I didn't mean to cause no trouble. I started to apologize to the fella, but he whipped out that gun and dang near blew a hole in me."

Abernathy swallowed hard at the memory of how close he had come to maybe dying.

"It's all right, Jed," Bill told him. "You've never started a ruckus before, and I don't see any reason you would have on purpose tonight."

"You're not gonna arrest me, then?"

"Nope." Bill looked down at the unconscious man at his feet. "But if you and your pards want to help me out, you can carry this fella down to the jail for me so I can lock him up. Reckon Judge Dunaway will want to levy a fine on him in the morning for disturbin' the peace."

Abernathy and several of his friends were eager to lend a hand. They took hold of the senseless cowboy's arms and legs and picked him up. As Bill followed them out of the saloon, he heard Annabelle tell Morley that he should have done like she told him and not reached for that bungstarter.

Bill left them to work that out between themselves and went down the street with the men carrying the unconscious cowboy. He got ahead of them and opened the door of the marshal's office.

As he did so, he heard the loud snores coming from the back room where his deputy Mordecai Flint had a cot. Mordecai was a wiry, bearded little frontiersman, a former fur trapper and army scout who had been serving as Bill's deputy ever since some Indian trouble had trapped him in Redemption a few months earlier.

He could have left once that scrape was over, but as he told Bill, he had been drifting pretty much his entire life and wanted to see what it was like to settle down for a while. So far he had done a fine job as Redemption's deputy marshal.

He was a mighty sound sleeper, which explained why he hadn't heard those shots from the Prairie Queen and come to find out what the commotion was about. Bill didn't hold that against him. Mordecai would be holding down the fort here in the marshal's office later tonight while Bill was home sleeping in a nice, warm bed with a nice, warm wife.

The door to the cell block stood open since there were no other prisoners at the moment. Bill gestured toward it and told Abernathy and the other men, "Just take him in there and put him in the first cell. The door should be open."

He followed them into the cell block and watched as the men lowered the cowboy onto the bunk in the first cell on the right. There were four cells, two on each side of the center aisle.

As the men filed out of the cell, Bill nodded to them and said, "I'm much obliged for the help."

"We're grateful to you for what you did, Marshal," Abernathy said. "If that locoweed emptied his Colt, there's no tellin' how many innocent folks he would have killed."

"I think he was probably too drunk to hit anybody except by accident," Bill said, "but it's better not to take that chance."

He grasped the iron-barred cell door and slammed it with a clang.

The noise must have roused Mordecai from his slumber, because the old-timer came out of the storage room scratching at his bristly, salt-and-pepper beard as Bill went back into the office part of the building.

Mordecai frowned in confusion at Abernathy and the other men as they left the office.

"What's goin' on here?" he asked.

Bill jerked a thumb over his shoulder at the cell block door, which he had closed behind him.

"We've got company in there," he said. "Some cowboy had too much to drink down at the Prairie Queen and threatened to shoot up the place."

Mordecai grunted and asked, "Kill anybody?"

"Not so's you'd notice," Bill said. "He shot the hell out of a bottle of whiskey, though."

"Waste of a perfectly good bottle o' who-hit-John," Mordecai said with a sigh and a shake of his head. "Don't reckon you can blame that yaller-headed gal who owns the place. We've had drunks get feisty in Smoot's Saloon, too."

"That's right," Bill said as he took off his flat-crowned brown hat and set it on the desk. He sat down and ran his fingers through his shoulder-length brown hair. He was tired and ready to go home, but he frowned as he remembered something. "Aw, hell. I didn't finish makin' the rounds."

"Let me do it," Mordecai said. "I'm awake anyway. Once I get woke up, I have a devil of a time gettin' back to sleep."

Bill thought about it for a second and then nodded.

"All right, thanks." He put his hands on the desk and pushed himself back to his feet.

"Prisoner got a name?" Mordecai asked.

"I reckon he does, but we didn't get around to introductions. We can find out who he is in the morning."

"That'll do," Mordecai said. He took down one of the shotguns from the rack on the wall behind the desk, got a couple of shells from a drawer, and slid them into the barrels. He wasn't as good with a handgun as Bill, but he was a crack shot with a rifle and could handle a scattergun just fine.

The two lawmen left the office together, Mordecai setting off to finish the evening rounds and Bill turning toward the side street where he shared a big old house with his wife Eden and her father Perry Monroe, who owned Redemption's biggest and best general store. Living with your father-in-law maybe wasn't the best arrangement in the world, but Bill got along well with Perry Monroe.

One of these days, though, he and Eden were going to have to start giving some thought to getting a place of their own. Especially once kids started arriving. Bill had been thinking about that more and more lately, too.

Redemption was quiet behind him as he quickened his pace, the limp barely noticeable now.

Chapter 3

The alley behind a residential street near the edge of the settlement was thick with darkness. The windows in most of the houses along here were dark as well, as the hour was late enough that most people were asleep.

Then the yellow glow of lamplight sliced across the alley like a knife blade as a back door opened. Only for a moment, though, as someone inside blew out the lamp. Shadows closed in again.

A deeper patch of darkness moved in the gloom, drawing closer to the house where the rear door still stood open. The shadow stopped and stood motionless in a tense, listening attitude.

The moon was only a sliver in the sky overhead, but enough light filtered down from the stars for the watcher to make out the shape of a man that appeared in the doorway. The man turned his head and said quietly to someone inside, "It's all right, there's nobody out here."

Ah, but he was wrong about that, the watcher thought.

The man in the doorway moved aside to let another figure slip past him. The watcher heard the rustle of skirts and

knew the second person was a woman. She paused and said
something to the man, but the words were too low for the
watcher to make them out. The timbre of the woman's voice
was familiar, though.

The man in the doorway whispered something in return.
The two figures moved toward each other as silently as fog
drifting. They seemed to merge and stayed that way for a
long moment before breaking apart again.

How tender, the watcher thought. How touching. A good-
night kiss shared between lovers.

The woman turned from the door. The man who had just
kissed her stood there watching as she crossed the small rear
yard and turned down the alley. Her path took her right past
the frozen figure lurking in the shadows. The man in the
doorway kept an eye on her until he couldn't see her anymore, then went back in the house and closed the door softly
behind him.

The watcher in the shadows still hadn't moved, even when
the faint scent of perfume drifted tantalizingly through the
night air. She passed so close that the smell of her was a tor-
ment, but an even worse torture was knowing that her scent
clung to the man inside the house.

Something had to be done about this. It was intolerable.

And something *would* be done . . . soon.

But not tonight. Tonight the charade would continue. The
watcher had to think about everything and decide what to do.
Once that decision was reached . . .

Preferring not to think about that just yet, the figure
moved again, taking a different route through the streets and
alleys of Redemption, hurrying now.

Places to go, things to do.

Vengeance to be taken.

Three riders sat their horses atop a slight rise . . . which was
the only sort of rise to be found in this part of Kansas. Even
so, it was enough for them to be able to see several miles
across the dark prairie to a scattering of lights.

The man on the left of the trio took a cigarette from his

mouth, pinched out the butt, and snapped the quirley away into the darkness.

"That's it?" he asked.

"That's it," replied the man in the center, whose name was Caleb Tatum. "Redemption, they call it."

The third man said, "Place is full of churches, is it?"

"Not that I know of," Tatum said. He was a man in his thirties, slightly barrel-chested, handsome enough to have a touch of arrogance to his features. His black hat was thumbed back on crisp black hair. "Why would it be full of churches?"

"Well, with a name like Redemption, I just figured—"

"I don't know why whoever founded the place called it by that name, but when I rode through last week to take a look, I didn't see but two or three churches. I don't think the name has anything to do with religion."

"I ain't interested in churches," the first man said, "just banks."

"It's got one of those," Tatum said. "A pretty prosperous one, too, from the looks of it. There are a lot of successful farms and ranches around here, plus the cattle drives from Texas still come through these parts and pump some money into the town. It'll be a good haul."

Tatum hoped he was right about that. He had heard that some fellas had tried to rob the bank in Redemption a while back and gotten killed for their trouble.

But those hombres were rank amateurs compared to the hardened gang of owlhoots who rode with him, Tatum thought. He had nine men, and every one of them knew how to ride and shoot and didn't mind killing if it was necessary.

A few of them, he had to admit, liked killing a little too much. But he could ride herd on them and keep them in line. He had done it so far and would continue to do so, because no matter how tough they were, they all knew that he was tougher.

"They have a lawman there?" the first man asked.

"A marshal," Tatum said. "Some Texas cowboy who decided to put down roots."

The third member of the trio said, "Those Texans are all gunslingers."

Tatum grunted and said, "That's what they'd like you to believe. I got a look at this fella. He's just a gimpy kid. He won't give us any trouble, and neither will his deputy, who's some stove-up old geezer. Those two aren't fit for anything except breaking up bar fights and wrangling drunks."

"I hope you're right, Caleb," the first man said.

"I haven't steered you wrong so far, have I?" Tatum snapped.

"No, I reckon not."

Tatum turned his horse and said, "Let's get back to camp. We'll ride into Redemption tomorrow, and we'll be a hell of a lot richer when we ride out."

Bill stopped and took his boots off downstairs so he wouldn't make as much noise when he went into the bedroom. Eden was probably asleep already, and he didn't want to disturb her. He unbuckled his gun belt, too, and coiled it around the holstered Colt.

The stairs creaked a little under him as he went up them, but that was the only sound in the house. When he reached the second-floor hallway, he heard snores coming from behind the closed door of Perry Monroe's room. Monroe was pretty good at sawing logs, but he couldn't hold a candle to Mordecai Flint when it came to sheer volume.

Thankfully, the room Bill and Eden shared was all the way down at the other end of the hall from her father's room. Bill slipped inside, moving by feel as he placed the coiled gun belt on the small table next to his side of the bed. He and Eden had been married long enough now that he didn't need light to find his way around in here. He peeled off his duds, down to the bottom half of a pair of long underwear.

He was about to slip under the covers when Eden said, "You thought I was asleep, didn't you?"

Bill jumped a little, then said, "Dadgummit, Eden, were you just layin' there in the dark waitin' for me?"

She laughed. "That's right. I want a good-night kiss before I go to sleep."

Bill got into bed and reached out for her, drawing her into his arms.

"If I start kissin' you, it's liable to be a while before either of us get to sleep, and I'm tired."

"So am I," she said sleepily, "but I'm willing to risk it."

So was Bill. He found her mouth with his. The kiss had enough passion in it that it might have turned into more, as he had warned, if both of them hadn't yawned at the same time and then broken down laughing.

"Any problems in town tonight?" Eden asked as she pillowed her head on his shoulder.

"Not really. One fella got a mite too liquored up in the Prairie Queen and wound up sleeping it off in a cell."

"The Prairie Queen . . . That Hudson woman's place?"

"Yep. She seems pretty nice."

Eden lifted her head from Bill's shoulder and said, "Oh, really?"

"For a saloonkeeper, I mean. And an older woman."

"Uh-huh." Eden settled back down against him.

Hoping that he had responded correctly, Bill suppressed another yawn and said, "I could probably stay awake a little while longer . . ."

Eden's deep, regular breathing told him that she couldn't, though. She had dozed off.

That was all right, Bill told himself. He was tired, too, and he enjoyed holding her like this while she slept.

Besides, they would both be more rested in the morning and could make up for missed opportunities.

Chapter 4

When Bill woke up, he was alone in the bed, tangled in the sheet from thrashing around, as he sometimes did. The gray light of dawn came in around the curtains over the bedroom window. He smelled coffee and bacon and knew that Eden had gotten up early to fix breakfast.

Although he was disappointed that she wasn't still here beside him in bed so they could make love, he wasn't going to complain about coffee and bacon. He grinned and stretched for a minute before sitting up and swinging his legs out of bed.

By the time he was dressed and downstairs, he was even hungrier. He detoured by the living room to hang his gun belt on the hat rack next to his hat, then went into the kitchen.

Eden was at the stove. She wore a robe over her nightgown, and her short blond hair was still a little tousled from sleep as it curled around her ears and jaw. Bill thought she looked mighty pretty and said so.

"You'd say that to any woman who was cooking bacon for you," she told him with a smile.

"Not hardly," he insisted as he came up behind her and put

his arms around her waist. He pressed himself against her and planted a kiss on the side of her neck.

"Go sit down and I'll bring you some coffee," she ordered, although she didn't seem displeased by his attenton. "My father will be stirring any minute now, if he's not already."

"Sure," Bill said. He let go of her and turned to the table, where he pulled out a chair and sat down. She set a cup of steaming coffee in front of him a moment later, followed soon by a plate full of flapjacks, fried eggs, and bacon.

Perry Monroe came in while Bill was digging into the food. The storekeeper was burly and had a long white beard. He had been one of those opposed to Bill staying in Redemption at first, but as a widower with only one child, he was powerless to deny Eden anything she wanted. She had insisted that she would nurse the injured cowboy back to health, and she had gotten her way.

And thanks be to the Good Lord for that, Bill had thought many times since. Getting gored by that steer had been the luckiest thing that had ever happened to him. If not for that cantankerous steer, he'd still be a shiftless cowpoke, or lying dead in some trail-town boot hill.

"Mornin'," Monroe said as he sat down across the table from his son-in-law. "Any trouble in town last night?"

"Not much. One little ruckus in the Prairie Queen."

"I'm not sure why Redemption needed another saloon," Monroe said with a frown. "There's already Fred Smoot's place and a couple of others."

Those other places Monroe mentioned weren't really saloons, more like hole-in-the-wall taverns. One of them had a billiard table, and that was all they sported in the way of entertainment.

"Redemption is growing," Bill said. "You've got to expect more businesses to come in, and there'll be saloons among 'em."

Monroe snorted.

"The town council could outlaw liquor," he said, then added, "Although I wouldn't really want to run Fred Smoot out of business. The man's had enough hard luck already."

That was true. Due to an injury, Smoot was confined to a wheelchair that had been built for him by Josiah Hartnett, the livery stable owner. Bill wasn't sure he'd be able to stand that. It had been hard enough when he had to use crutches for a while because of his bad leg.

"I don't think you'd have much luck turnin' the place dry," Bill said. "Too many folks like a drink now and then. I don't mind a little nip myself."

Monroe said, "Hmmph," and turned his attention to the breakfast that Eden set in front of him.

Yeah, Bill thought again, sooner or later he and Eden would have to start thinking about moving out. Maybe sooner.

The rest of the meal was pleasant enough, though, and when Bill was finished he stood up so he could go down to the office and relieve Mordecai. Eden followed him into the living room, leaving her father in the kitchen.

She came into his arms and kissed him, then whispered, "Sorry I woke up early. I couldn't get back to sleep."

"Mordecai's the same way."

"Yes, but Mordecai didn't have the same sort of plans I had for this morning."

Bill chuckled and said, "Probably not." He kissed her again, this time on the forehead. "See you at lunch?"

She generally brought him his midday meal at the marshal's office, sometimes one that she prepared, sometimes a tray that she picked up at Gunnar and Helga Nilsson's café.

"Of course," she said.

Bill buckled on his gun belt, put on his hat, and left the house. It was still early. The air held a definite chill. In a few weeks it would be fall, and after that winter. He had heard about Kansas winters but had never experienced one. Being from the southern part of Texas where snow and freezing temperatures were uncommon, he wasn't sure he was looking forward to the change in the weather.

For now, though, it was mighty pleasant, and he enjoyed his walk to the marshal's office. Business owners were sweeping off the porches and boardwalks, and housewives were doing some early shopping. Redemption was waking up to a new day.

Mordecai had the office door open and stood there with his shoulder propped against the jamb. His floppy-brimmed plainsman's hat rested on the back of his balding head.

"Quiet night?" Bill asked.

"Until about an hour ago," the deputy answered. "That's when that prisoner woke up and started raisin' holy ned."

"I don't hear anything now."

"He's just takin' a break. Cussed and hollered so much he must've run outta breath."

"That's not a very good way to get turned loose."

"You weren't gonna turn him loose anyway, were you? Not until after the judge sees him?"

Bill shrugged and admitted, "No, I don't reckon I was. If he'd just made a jackass of himself, I might've let him sleep it off and then told him to get out of town. But he fired off two shots, nearly ventilated a couple of citizens, and did a little damage in the saloon. If that's not disturbin' the peace, I don't know what is."

He went into the office with Mordecai following him. Taking the ring of keys from their hook, Bill unlocked the cell block door and went inside.

The prisoner was sitting on the bunk. He lifted his head and turned bleary eyes toward Bill. He glared and demanded, "Damn it, Marshal, let me outta here!"

"Hold on," Bill said. "Do you even remember what you did last night?"

"Damn right I remember. I didn't kill anybody."

"Not for lack of tryin'."

The man got a cunning look on his narrow face.

"I remember you said you was a Texan, too," he went on. "You know good and well that down in Texas a man can let off a little steam without gettin' hisself locked up."

"This isn't Texas," Bill pointed out, "and firing off a gun inside a crowded saloon isn't quite the same as lettin' off a little steam. You're gonna have to sit there until the justice of the peace comes by. It'll be up to him to decide what we're gonna do with you."

The cowboy held his hands to his head and groaned.

"Aw, hell! Can I at least get some coffee?"

"That we can do," Bill said. "Mordecai?"

"I got the pot boilin' already. How about some breakfast, mister? You want a big plate full o' greasy eggs?"

The prisoner groaned again, closed his eyes, and let himself fall over onto his side on the bunk.

Bill grinned and told his deputy, "Now you're just bein' cruel to a poor, hungover hombre."

"He's got it comin'," Mordecai said. "I'll get that coffee."

Bill's bad leg was starting to get tired and he wanted to sit down. But before he did, he asked, "What's your name, mister?"

The man cracked an eye open at Bill and said, "It's Overstreet. Jesse Overstreet."

"Well, Jesse, in a little while I'll go let the judge know he's got a legal matter to deal with this morning. Until then you just take it easy."

"I'm not goin' anywhere, am I?" Overstreet muttered.

"No, sir," Bill said. "You're sure not."

Chapter 5

Thomas Gentry let fly with the lasso and watched with satisfaction as it settled over the horse's head. The big gray stallion reared and slashed angrily at the air with its hooves. When the horse came down, Tom quickly took up all the slack in the rope and snubbed it around a sturdy post buried in the ground. The gray stood there glaring at him.

"You'll learn," Tom muttered as he returned the glare. "By God, you'll learn. Or you'll be sorry. It's up to you."

His father, Burkhart Gentry, leaned on the fence around the horse pen and watched with a keen, critical eye. Burk Gentry was a heavyset, bulky man with a mostly bald head under his hat and a tuft of white beard on his chin. Some days Tom felt a grudging affection for him. Other days he hated his father with a deep and abiding passion. It had been that way for as far back as Tom could remember.

"Don't mollycoddle that horse today," Burk rasped. "It ain't a pet."

"I don't intend to," Tom said. He got the saddle that was hanging on the fence and approached the horse carefully. He knew how the gray liked to twist around suddenly and kick with no warning.

"You shoulda been at this sooner," Burk said.

"I've been busy with other things."

"No, I mean half the mornin's gone. You could get started on chores like this earlier if you didn't have to ride out here from town ever' damn day. Don't know why you have to live in town, anyway."

"Because Virgie likes living in town," Tom said. "She wanted to be closer to her folks."

Burk snorted in obvious disgust.

"No offense to that gal you married, but I wouldn't give you two cents for those folks of hers. I don't care how much money he's got, Walt Shelton's the biggest bag o' hot air I ever did see."

Talk about the ol' pot calling the kettle black, Tom thought. He didn't know why his father bothered saying things like "no offense" when Burk Gentry didn't give a damn whether he offended anybody and never had.

Certainly he had never hesitated when it came to telling Tom that he shouldn't marry Virginia Shelton. She was weak and pampered and not a fit wife for a Gentry, according to Burk, and Tom would be a fool to get hitched to her.

As much as he disliked his father most of the time, Tom had to admit that sometimes Burk had a point.

He got the saddle on the gray, which stood calmly at first and then exploded into frenzied motion when Tom started to tighten the cinches. He had to jump back to get out of the horse's way. The saddle slipped and then fell off. The stallion started kicking at it and raising a cloud of dust.

"By God, that's enough," Tom said. He went over to the fence and picked up the long quirt he had left there. The gray was still capering around as Tom dashed in and laid the quirt across its nose in a vicious swipe.

"That's it, boy!" Burk said. "Beat some sense into that jughead!"

The gray was far from a jughead. It was a fine animal, just too high-spirited. Tom wished sometimes there was another way to break it, but he didn't know of any.

Anyway, when the anger welled up inside him like it was today, laying into the bastard with the quirt felt good, mighty good. He slashed at the gray again and again, leaving bloody stripes on the sleek hide, until the horse finally calmed down and stood there quivering slightly. The stallion's nostrils flared wide, and Tom would have sworn he saw an almost human hatred in its eyes.

"That's the way," Burk said. "You got to make 'em afraid of you. That's the only way to get what you want in this world. Make the varmints who're in your way afraid of you."

Tom wasn't sure the horse was afraid of him. It was more like the animal had realized the best thing to do was just bide its time.

Tom was doing sort of the same thing where Virgie was concerned. The time was coming for him to let her know that he was aware of what she was up to. Then she'd be sorry.

But not yet.

Tom tossed the quirt aside and picked up the saddle and blanket. He got them on the gray again, and this time the horse stood for having the cinches tightened.

"There. You can stand there for a while and get used to it," Tom told the horse. He turned toward the gate.

"You might break that horse one of these days, if you stay with it long enough," Burk said as Tom left the corral. "If I was you, I'd handle that woman of yours the same way. Make her do what you want. There's plenty of room in the house. Ain't no reason you should live in town instead of out here."

"It's what Virgie wants," Tom said dully.

Burk's disgusted snort was all the response he needed to make.

The Gentry horse ranch was five miles southwest of Redemption. Burk and his sons Tom, Thurmond, and Tobias Gentry raised the finest horses in this part of the state. Thurm and his wife Sue lived here on the ranch, as did Toby, the unmarried youngest of the Gentry brothers. Tom was the only one who had left home, much to his father's displeasure.

Six months earlier, when he was getting ready to marry Virginia Shelton, he had assumed that he would just move her into the sprawling Gentry ranch house as Thurm had done with Sue. As Burk said, there was plenty of room.

But Virgie had sprung a surprise on him, saying that there

was a really nice little house in Redemption they could buy, and it was only a couple of blocks from her parents' house. Her father, who had a bushel basket of money because of the successful furniture stores he owned in Topeka and Wichita, would help them buy the house, Virgie said.

Why somebody who was rich would want to live in a little town like Redemption, Tom didn't know. Walter Shelton hadn't grown up here or anything like that, nor had his wife Clarissa. But they built one of the biggest, fanciest houses in Redemption and moved in with their beautiful blond daughter, and from the first time Tom Gentry laid eyes on her, he knew he wanted to marry her.

It had taken a few months to get Virgie to feel the same way, but once Tom set his sights on something, he usually got it.

He and Burk climbed onto the porch and sat down in the shade. Tom took one of the cane-bottomed chairs, but Burk had a specially made rocker that would support his weight.

Going after the gray with the quirt like that had caused Tom to work up a sweat. He took his hat off and ran his fingers through his thick, damp, wildly curling dark hair.

There was a time when Virgie had liked to run her fingers through his hair, Tom thought . . . before she had turned cold and hostile and stopped touching him at all.

And that was right after Ned Bassett came to town.

Tom shoved the thought of Bassett out of his mind. He had already let his temper get the best of him once this morning, and he didn't want it to happen again. He told himself not to even think about how he had followed Virgie to Bassett's house the night before, after she thought he was sound asleep in the spare bedroom where he'd taken to spending his nights. He had beaten her back to the house and was in bed pretending to be asleep when she slipped past the door of his room. She thought she was getting away with it.

She would find out differently . . . once he'd figured out what he wanted to do.

"Well, how's things in town?" Burk asked.

"How the hell would I know?"

"You live there."

"Yeah, but I'm either out here, riding back and forth, or sleeping. Virgie runs the house. I don't have much to do with the folks in town." Tom paused. "Although there is a new saloon, just been open a couple of weeks. Owned by a woman."

"A woman, you say?" Burk shook his head. "Mark my words, no good'll ever come of lettin' a woman own a business. It just ain't proper."

"Well, I guess it's not too bad if it's a saloon or a whorehouse."

"Hmmph. What would you know about whorehouses?"

More than you think I do, old man, Tom thought. Since Virgie'd turned her back on him, he had visited Miss Alvera Stanley's house a few times, when the need was too strong to ignore.

"Anyway, the place is called the Prairie Queen," Tom said. "I've heard it's nice, but I haven't been there."

"Good. Keep your mind on business, I always say."

Tom would try, but more and more these days, his business was figuring out how he would take his revenge on Ned Bassett and his own cheating trollop of a wife.

Chapter 6

Judge Kermit Dunaway, Redemption's justice of the peace, was a thick-bodied man in late middle age, with a beefy, jowly face and thinning, rust-colored hair. He wore a brown tweed suit and a brown vest that stretched tight over his ample belly, and an old-fashioned beaver hat perched on his head. He peered through the bars at Jesse Overstreet and asked, "What are the charges against this miscreant, Marshal?"

"Well, he fired off a couple of shots in the Prairie Queen Saloon, Your Honor," Bill said.

"In self-defense?"

"Not unless you figure he was tryin' to fight off the bellyful of whiskey he'd guzzled down."

"Was anyone injured?"

Bill shook his head.

"He came close to Jed Abernathy, that teamster, and Glenn Morley, Miss Hudson's bartender, but the only damage was to a bottle of whiskey that got broke by a bullet."

Overstreet had been standing on the other side of the bars as Bill and Judge Dunaway discussed his case. His eyes were downcast, but they came up now as Bill spoke.

"Maybe I lost my head when I took a shot at the fella who

spilled beer on me, but that damn bartender tried to stove in my head with a bungstarter, Judge," he said. "If tryin' to plug him before he could take another swipe at me ain't self-defense, I don't know what is."

Dunaway frowned and asked, "Was the other shot fired first?"

Overstreet licked his lips. He still looked hungover and sick.

"Well, yeah," he admitted.

"Then the bartender was simply trying to protect his employer's customers and property, thus mitigating any claim of self-defense on your part because of your prior actions."

Overstreet looked confused.

"Once you pulled the trigger the first time, whatever else happened was on your head," Bill explained.

Looking at the floor again, Overstreet muttered, "That don't hardly seem fair."

"I'd advise you not to question my rulings, young man," Judge Dunaway said. "I could find you guilty of contempt of court, as well as disturbing the peace."

"Sorry, Judge."

"Very well. Are there any more pertinent facts to add, Marshal?"

Bill shook his head and said, "Nope, that's about the size of it."

"Then I find the defendant guilty as charged and levy a fine in the amount of twenty dollars, his release pending the payment of said sum."

"Twenty—" Overstreet looked stricken. "What if I can't pay, Judge?"

"Then I'll sentence you to thirty days in jail, the standard sentence for disturbing the peace."

Overstreet put his hands to his head and groaned.

"I can't sit in here for thirty days," he said. "I'll go loco!"

"I don't want you sittin' here, either," Bill told him. "The town's got to feed you as long as you're locked up. If you've got the twenty dollars, I think you should pay it. And I happen to know you've got it, because we cleaned out your pockets and all your belongin's are locked up in my desk."

"All right, all right," Overstreet said with a surly glare. "It don't seem right, though. I didn't even get a trial."

"This was a fair and legal hearing, all that's required for a misdemeanor charge," Judge Dunaway said.

"If I say to take the twenty bucks outta my poke, I can get out of here?"

"Right away," Bill said.

"Do it, then."

Bill and Dunaway left the cell block. Bill unlocked the desk drawer where he'd put Jesse Overstreet's belongings, which included a gold double eagle, six dollar bills, a handful of smaller change, a Barlow knife, tobacco and papers, a dozen .45 cartridges, a turnip watch with a dented cover, and a woman's gold ring attached to the other end of the watch chain. Bill wondered idly if the ring had belonged to Overstreet's mother or sister or somebody else.

He picked up the double eagle and handed it to the judge.

"I'll add this to the town coffers," Dunaway said. "You can release the boy."

Bill picked up the key ring from the desk and returned to the cell block as Dunaway left the office. Mordecai was off doing something else; Bill didn't know exactly what. But the old-timer would be back to take a nice long siesta during the afternoon.

The key rattled in the lock as Bill turned it. He swung the cell door open and told Overstreet, "You're free to go."

The cowboy said, "You know, there was somethin' else damaged in that ruckus that you didn't say nothin' about, Marshal." He touched the bruise on his forehead. "You bounced my head off the bar pretty good. And my arm hurts where that bartender hit me with the bungstarter, too."

"You could have it a lot worse, Jesse." Bill used his thumb to point toward the office. "Let's go get your stuff."

Overstreet picked up his belongings from the desk and stowed them away in his pockets. He checked everything carefully as he handled it.

"Don't worry, nobody stole anything," Bill assured him. "I'm not that kind of lawman."

"Can't blame me for bein' suspicious. Everybody knows most Kansas lawmen are crookeder'n a dog's hind leg."

That was the prevailing attitude among Texas cowboys, Bill knew, since he'd shared it for a long time. There was some justification for it, too, he supposed, recalling the two star packers who'd caused so much trouble in Redemption when he first came here.

"What about my gun?" Overstreet asked.

Bill opened another drawer in the desk and took out a coiled gun belt and holstered revolver.

"It's unloaded," he said as he set the gun on the desk. "Keep it that way as long as you're here in town. I wouldn't mind knowin' how long that's gonna be."

"Are you runnin' me out of town?" Overstreet asked with narrowed eyes.

"Not officially, but I don't reckon you have any friends in these parts, which means there's not really any reason for you to stay, is there?"

"You came up from Texas and stayed here. Maybe I want to do that same. There are spreads around here where a good hand could get a ridin' job. I can drive a wagon, too, or maybe ride shotgun on the stagecoach."

Bill had a hunch that Overstreet was just being contrary, but he said, "If you're really thinking about settlin' down around here, you'd be smart not to get drunk again. You get too touchy and proddy when you're drunk."

"Yeah, yeah." Overstreet sneered as he buckled on the gun belt. "You're startin' to make me ashamed of bein' a Texan, Marshal. What the hell happened to you, anyway? You forget what it's like to be a real hombre?"

Bill pointed at the door.

"Get out."

"I'm goin'."

Overstreet turned toward the door. Before he got there, it opened. Mordecai started to step inside the office but stopped and moved back so that Overstreet could go past him. The cowboy gave him a glare, too, then stalked off.

"Judge Dunaway fine him for disturbin' the peace?" the

deputy asked as he came into the office and closed the door
behind him.

"Yep. A double eagle's worth."

"You tell him to light a shuck outta here?"

"Not in so many words," Bill said, "but I strongly advised
that he move on."

"Huh. Hardheaded galoot like that, best advice mighta
been a good swift kick in the butt. You think he'll leave or
hang around and cause trouble?"

"Only one way I know of to find out," Bill said. "Wait and
see."

Chapter 7

Caleb Tatum rode into Redemption just past the middle of the morning, along with Dave Belton and Chico Flynn. They brought their horses to a stop in front of a big building with a sign on the front proclaiming it to be Monroe Mercantile. As the three men swung down from the saddles, Tatum glanced along the street and spotted a trio of familiar figures lounging in front of the hotel.

Whit Cook, Ben Hanley, and Lou Price had ridden into town about half an hour earlier. Later, Roy Keene and Andy Jordan would show up, followed by Russ Garwood and T. J. Evans.

Ten hard-faced, gun-hung strangers riding in together would attract a lot of attention and arouse suspicion. Tatum didn't want that. Redemption was a growing community, so strangers weren't that unusual as long as they weren't in large groups. By midday, all ten outlaws would drift toward the bank, ready to strike as soon as Tatum gave the word.

For now, Tatum, Belton, and Flynn went into the general store, looking like grub-line riders who had stopped to pick up some supplies. That was exactly what Tatum wanted people to think.

With spurs jingling, the three men walked along an aisle between shelves full of assorted goods and approached the counter at the back of the store. An old man with a long white beard stood behind the counter waiting on a couple of women. Tatum barely gave them a glance.

His attention was focused on the other person behind the counter.

The woman was in her early twenties, he figured, with a shining cap of fair hair that curved around her face. She had blue eyes and a little dimple in her chin, and she was so wholesomely pretty that Tatum felt the impact of it like a punch in the gut.

She smiled and asked, "What can I do for you?"

There were a lot of answers to that question, Tatum thought, none of them particularly proper but all highly exciting and appealing. He made sure his face didn't reveal what he was thinking as he replied, "My pards and I need some flour and coffee. Pound of each, I reckon."

"All right, I can get that for you."

Her hands were resting on the counter. Tatum glanced at the left one and saw the wedding ring on her finger.

So she was married. That was just as well. He already had a woman back at the hideout they'd been using, and Hannah was the jealous sort.

Besides, he sure as hell hadn't come to Redemption to go courting. He was here for the money in the bank, and that was all.

The old-timer finished with the two ladies, and as they left the store, he strolled over and gave a friendly nod to Tatum, Belton, and Flynn.

"Morning," he said. "You fellas just passing through? I don't recall seeing you around here before."

"That's right," Tatum said easily. "We're on our way to Colorado. Thought we might try to get in on some of those gold strikes out there."

The mouth wreathed in a long white beard curved in a smile as the storekeeper nodded again.

"Just between us, if I was thirty years younger I might give it a try myself," he said.

"If you're gonna settle down, though, this looks like a nice place to do it."

"That it is," the old-timer agreed. "Redemption has had its troubles, but it's pretty peaceful now."

That was liable to change pretty soon, Tatum thought. He and his men wouldn't shoot up the town unless it was necessary, but if anyone got in their way, it would be just too damned bad for whoever it was.

"Maybe if the prospecting doesn't work out, we'll come back here," he said.

"You do that. Good citizens are always welcome."

Flynn laughed. Tatum shot him a sharp glance. Sure, it was pretty funny for anybody to refer to them as good citizens, but they didn't want to act like that.

The storekeeper didn't seem to notice. He kept talking, shooting the breeze as old men had a tendency of doing, while the blonde weighed and bagged the flour and the coffee. When she was done, she set the bags on the counter in front of Tatum and toted up the price. He paid her, handed the flour to Belton and the coffee to Flynn, and said, "Let's go."

He couldn't stop thinking about how pretty that woman was as they walked out of the store.

He wasn't the only one. When they reached the high porch, Flynn let out a low whistle and said, "Lord have mercy. I'd give a lot to spend some time with that gal."

Flynn was the product of an Irish father and a Mexican mother. He was young and handsome and considered himself irresistible to women. For the most part he was right.

Belton said, "Yeah, she was pretty sweet."

"Forget it, both of you," Tatum snapped. "That's not why we're here, and you know it."

He wasn't going to let on that the blonde had affected him the same way. He was the leader of this gang, and he didn't want his men knowing that he was thinking about anything except cleaning out that bank.

He slipped his watch from his pocket, flipped it open, and checked the time.

"We'll give it another half hour," he said. "Then it'll be time to make our move."

* * *

Roy Fleming, mayor of Redemption and president of the bank, had a habit of working at his desk through lunch. That was even more common these days, because several months earlier his head teller, Mason Jones, had been killed during an attempted robbery. The would-be thieves hadn't gotten away, but they hadn't been stopped until it was too late to save poor Mason's life.

After that, Fleming had promoted one of the other tellers, but the man just wasn't as good at the job as Mason had been. So Fleming wound up being nervous about leaving the bank in anyone's hands other than his own.

Today, however, he was thinking about going over to the café for lunch. This was the day they served pot roast, and Helga Nilsson's pot roast was the best Fleming had ever eaten. It would be a shame not to indulge in it.

He left his office and strolled out into the bank's lobby. All three tellers had customers, with two more waiting at a couple of the windows. One of the customers was Walter Shelton, Fleming realized.

Shelton was fairly new in Redemption, having moved here about a year previously. The man kept only a small amount on deposit, but Fleming knew from talking to banker friends of his in Wichita and Topeka that Shelton had much larger accounts there, where his businesses were. It seemed to Fleming that it would make sense for Shelton to transfer some of that money here.

When Shelton finished his transaction at the teller's window and turned to start toward the door, Fleming moved to intercept him.

"Hello, Walt," Fleming said with a big smile on his round, florid face. "How are you today?"

Shelton was a thin, sallow man with iron gray hair. Spectacles rested on his nose. He never smiled much, so the faint twitch of his mouth counted almost as a grin.

"Mr. Fleming," he said.

"Now, I've told you to call me Roy. We're doing business together, aren't we?"

"I have some of my money in your bank," Shelton said dryly.

"Well, that's almost the same as us being partners. How are you doing today?"

"Fine, I suppose."

"How are that beautiful wife and lovely daughter of yours?"

"Fine."

Fleming kept smiling even though he was wondering what in blazes he had to do in order to drag more than a few syllables out of Shelton.

"You know, my wife and I really should have you and your wife over for Sunday dinner some week. We'd love to get to know you better . . ."

Fleming's voice trailed off as he realized that Shelton wasn't paying attention to him anymore. Instead, the man's eyes had narrowed behind those rimless spectacles as Shelton peered out through the bank's front window.

Several men were tying up their horses at the hitch rack in front of the bank, Fleming noted. He didn't recognize them, but seeing strangers in Redemption was nothing unusual these days. Lots of people were passing through. Some of them stayed and opened bank accounts. Those were the ones Fleming liked.

These men didn't look like the sort to open accounts, though. In fact, apprehension stirred inside Fleming as he saw how two of the men stayed with the horses and the other eight stepped up onto the boardwalk and headed for the bank's front door.

Shelton must have leaped to the same conclusion as Fleming. He exclaimed, "My God, they're going to rob the bank!"

Then Shelton did something that Fleming wouldn't have expected in a thousand years.

He reached under his coat and pulled out a hogleg that was damned near as big as he was.

At that moment, the door burst open and the eight men came in fast, bristling with guns of their own. Shelton pointed his revolver at them, said with surprising power in his normally reedy voice, "Eat lead, you sons of bitches!" and pulled the trigger.

Chapter 8

Just about the last thing Caleb Tatum expected to see when he charged into the bank was some spindly, middle-aged townie pointing a gun at him.

Tatum hadn't lived as long as he had by being slow to react, though. He jerked his Colt toward the man threatening him and fired.

The guns roared so close together it sounded like one shot. Neither bullet found its target because the red-faced fatso standing next to the skinny gink with the gun tackled him just as both men pulled trigger. The slug from the townie's gun went into the ceiling while Tatum's bullet whistled harmlessly through the air and thudded into the bank's rear wall.

The townie lost his gun when he hit the floor. The impact jostled it out of his hand.

All this was unexpected, but Tatum knew they could deal with it. No job ever went off perfectly. Keene and Garwood wheeled around to cover the windows and door, while Cook, Belton, and Price rushed the tellers' windows. Flynn and Hanley threw down on the customers, while Tatum went for the fatso, who had to be the bank president, and his gun-toting friend.

Tatum kicked the gun out of reach before the townie could make a grab for it. He pointed his Colt at the men on the floor and ordered, "Don't move!"

By now Cook, Belton, and Price had the tellers emptying their cash drawers into canvas sacks they had brought along for that purpose. Flynn and Hanley made sure none of the customers tried anything funny and grabbed a few wallets and watches while they were at it. No point in wasting time when you could be making a little extra profit.

From the front window, Roy Keene called, "A few people are lookin' around like they might've heard those shots, but nobody's headed this way yet."

"Good," Tatum grunted. He reached down and bunched his free hand in the banker's vest. He pointed his gun at the man's nose and went on, "Get up."

The banker obeyed, clambering awkwardly to his feet as Tatum half-dragged him up.

"You shouldn't have stopped me, Fleming," the skinny hombre still on the floor said. "I would have taught these owlhoots a lesson."

"The only lesson you could teach is how to die quicker," Tatum said. Knowing that the stubborn old coot would cause more problems if he got the chance, Tatum hauled off and kicked him in the head, knocking him out.

"Oh, dear Lord . . ." the banker breathed in horror.

"You'll get worse if you don't cooperate." Tatum shoved him toward the safe. "Open it."

The banker opened his mouth and for a second Tatum thought he was going to argue, but then the man said, "All right. Just don't hurt anyone else."

He stumbled over to the massive safe, which was painted green—the color of money, Tatum thought—and worked the combination, spinning the dial with trembling but relatively confident fingers. Then he gripped the handle, twisted it, and swung the door open.

Bundles of cash were stacked on the shelves inside. Tatum

pulled his own canvas sack from under his shirt and tossed it to the banker.

"Rake 'em in there," he ordered. Over his shoulder he asked, "How's it looking out there?"

"People are still lookin' over here," Keene reported, "but nobody's—Hell! There goes somebody runnin' up the street. Must be going for the law."

"More than likely," Tatum said. The banker was still putting money in the sack. "Hurry up."

The man reached in the safe again, but when his hand came out this time it had a small-caliber pistol in it. Tatum had been waiting for something like that. He struck swiftly, chopping down with his gun on the banker's head. The man dropped the pistol, groaned, and fell to his knees, blood welling from the gash that Tatum's gunsight had opened up in his scalp.

Tatum holstered his gun, reached into the safe, and scooped up the last few bundles of greenbacks. There were some papers in the safe as well, but he left them and wheeled around as he cinched the top of the sack closed.

"Got it?" he called to the men at the tellers' windows.

"Got it," Price confirmed.

"Then let's go."

The bank robbers started toward the door, ready to shoot their way out of Redemption if they had to.

Even though it wasn't quite noon yet, Mordecai had already gone over to the café for lunch. Or supper, as he sometimes called it, because he would sleep most of the afternoon before getting up to take over the night shift in the marshal's office.

Bill was sitting in the office going over a new batch of wanted posters that had just come in. He tried to keep up with such things, because you never could tell when some wanted owlhoot might drift into Redemption.

To tell the truth, such studying reminded him a little too much of schoolwork. He'd had enough book learning that he could read and write and cipher just fine, but he had never cared for being cooped up in a schoolhouse.

So he was almost glad for the interruption when he heard running footsteps outside the open door and Benjy Cobb suddenly appeared with a wide-eyed look of excitement on his weathered old face.

Benjy worked mostly as a swamper for Fred Smoot over at the saloon, although he helped out sometimes at Monroe Mercantile, too, when he could stay sober long enough in his continuing battle with whiskey. He seemed to be sober now, just all worked up about something.

"What is it, Benjy?" Bill asked as he pushed the reward dodgers aside and stood up.

"I ain't sure, Bill," the swamper replied, "but I'd swear I heard some shootin' a couple of minutes ago inside the bank."

Bill stiffened in alarm. There had been an attempt to rob the bank several months earlier, during all that Indian trouble, but he'd been able to stop the robbers before they got away.

"Why'd you wait to come tell me?" he asked as he came out from behind the desk in a hurry.

"Well, I wasn't sure . . . the bank's got pretty thick walls, you know . . . but then some other folks said they thought they heard somethin', too . . ."

Bill didn't wait to hear any more. Without pausing to grab his hat, he rushed past Benjy out of the office. He flung an order over his shoulder.

"Go find Mordecai at the café!"

The bank was a couple of blocks away. Bad leg or no bad leg, Bill could move pretty fast when he had to. He did now, running toward the bank.

Behind him, Benjy scurried across the street toward the café. People started to yell questions, sensing that something was going on.

Bill was still more than a block away when he spotted two men standing by a bunch of horses tied in front of the bank. Those men appeared to see him coming at the same time. They twisted toward him, clawed guns from their holsters, and opened fire.

With his heart hammering wildly in his chest, Bill threw himself down and to the right, landing behind a water trough.

The range was too far for accurate shooting with handguns, but the men at the bank might get lucky. The bullets they sent toward Bill kicked up dust from the street in a wide swath.

He rolled closer to the boardwalk and looked through the gap between it and the water trough toward the bank. More men spilled from the building now, all of them brandishing guns. It was a robbery, all right, no doubt about that. Bill drew his revolver, aimed high so the shots might carry better, and triggered two rounds toward the outlaws.

That drew more fire from them. He didn't have time to see if his shots hit anything before bullets began coming uncomfortably close to him. He scooted back to his right as slugs thudded into the water trough.

Some of the townspeople were still yelling, but they weren't asking questions now. Those cries were shouts of alarm and warning. People scurried for cover as the battle continued in the street.

It was a pretty one-sided battle, Bill thought. There were nine or ten of the robbers and only one of him.

A rifle cracked behind Bill and to his right. He twisted his head around to look and spotted Mordecai crouched behind a barrel on the boardwalk on the other side of the street. The deputy had gotten hold of a Henry rifle somewhere and used it to open fire on the outlaws as they tried to get mounted. Men and horses milled around now in a confused mass.

Monroe Mercantile was only a few doors away. Bill cast an anxious glance toward the store. At this time of day, Eden might be in there, or she could be over at the café or even back at her father's house. Bill just didn't know.

He hoped that if she was in the store, she would have the good sense to stay behind the counter in the back, where she ought to be safe from any of the bullets flying around wildly in the street.

He needed to get closer, he realized. His Colt would be more effective at shorter range. The shots from Mordecai's rifle had the outlaws roiled up right now, so this might be his chance.

He pulled three cartridges from the loops on his gun belt and thumbed them into the empty chambers in the revolver's cylinder. Then, snapping it closed, he lunged to his feet, leaped to the boardwalk, and started running toward the bank.

Before he had gone more than three steps, something knocked his right leg out from under him. He fell off the boardwalk and toppled into the street. At first he thought a bullet had struck him, but he didn't feel any pain other than that of crashing to the planks and getting the wind knocked mostly out of him.

He didn't have time to figure out what had happened because at that moment, the door of the mercantile was flung open and Eden ran out, crying, "Bill!" She must have been watching from inside the building and had seen him go down. She leaped off the boardwalk and started running toward him.

Fifty feet separated them. Bill shouted, "Eden, go back!" but she might not have heard him over the sudden thunder of hoofbeats. The outlaws had made it into their saddles and now they charged along the street, guns still blazing.

Bill's eyes widened in horror as he saw one of them veer his horse straight toward Eden. His gun was still in his hand, but he couldn't fire because she was between him and the outlaw.

At the last second she must have realized her danger, because she jerked her head around and screamed. She was too late as she tried to twist away.

The man didn't ride her down, though. Instead he turned his horse a little, leaned down from the saddle, and threw an arm around her, scooping her right off the ground in one smooth movement.

Then he sent his horse pounding right at Bill.

Chapter 9

In desperation, Bill scrambled to his hands and knees and threw himself into a roll toward the boardwalk. The hoofbeats were so loud they sounded like cannon shots as the outlaw's horse raced past him, missing him by mere inches. He would have sworn he felt the animal's hot breath against his face.

Eden screamed again as Bill rolled and came up on one knee. He could see the top of her head and her thrashing legs in a long gray skirt, but the outlaw's broad back shielded the rest of her from his sight.

Bill lifted his gun and started to fire, but his finger froze on the trigger before he squeezed off a shot. It was possible the bullet would go all the way through the outlaw's body and hit Eden, too. He couldn't take that chance.

Maybe Mordecai could stop the man.

But as he looked past the rider who had grabbed Eden, Bill saw one of the other bank robbers thrust his pistol in Mordecai's direction and pull the trigger. Flame gouted from the gun muzzle, and Mordecai was driven backward by the slug's impact, away from the barrel where he'd been crouching. The deputy landed on the boardwalk in a limp sprawl.

"Mordecai!" Bill shouted as he surged to his feet. The

wild thought that this couldn't be happening racketed through his brain. In the span of only a few seconds, he had seen his wife kidnapped and his friend and deputy gunned down. He had to stop this somehow, he told himself as he started to run after the escaping outlaws.

Several of them twisted in their saddles and fired back at him. Bill had to hit the dirt again as bullets whistled through the air just above him. That hail of lead would have cut him down if he hadn't thrown himself to the ground.

The riders were a full block away from him now, he saw to his dismay as he looked up. He couldn't hope to catch them on foot, nor could he empty his Colt after them without running the risk of hitting Eden.

But if he had a horse . . .

He leaped to his feet again and headed for the nearest hitch rack. His own horse was down at Josiah Hartnett's livery stable. He didn't have time to fetch it. He would just have to take one of the saddle mounts tied up along the street and return it to its owner later on, after he'd rescued his wife and brought the bank robbers to justice.

He wasn't going to even entertain the possibility of some other outcome.

He was even more hobbled than ever as he hurried along the street, and after a second he realized it wasn't because of his limp. A glance down at his feet told him that the heel of his right boot was gone. A stray bullet must have caught it and knocked it off as he was running along the boardwalk. That was why he had fallen into the street.

And it was him falling into the street that had drawn Eden out of the mercantile and put her in a position to be swooped up by that damned bank robber, Bill thought bitterly. He had to get her back before she was hurt. He just had to.

He grabbed some reins, jerked them loose, and swung up into a saddle. He didn't know whose horse he had and didn't care. He jerked the animal around and kicked it into a run after the fleeing bank robbers. They had reached the western edge of Redemption by now and were galloping out onto the prairie, strung out in a line. Bill tried to find the one who had taken Eden.

A flash of bright hair caught his eye. He raced after that rider. Buildings flashed past him on both sides. The citizens were running out into the open now, and some of them carried rifles they had fetched from their homes or businesses. They started firing after the outlaws, their bullets streaking through the clouds of dust raised by the hooves of the galloping horses.

"Hold your fire! Hold your fire!" Bill bellowed the order and hoped they would follow it. He didn't care how many of the outlaws they killed, but he didn't want anything to happen to Eden.

The settlement fell behind him. He was riding full tilt over the prairie now, leaning forward over the horse's neck and urging every bit of speed out of it that he could. The animal responded gallantly. Bill didn't know if he could cut into the lead that the outlaws had, but he was sure going to try.

He never got the chance. He heard a sharp crack, followed instantly by a scream from the horse, and he barely had time to kick his feet free of the stirrups before he flew through the air above the head of the falling animal.

Once again Bill crashed to the ground, but this time the landing was hard enough to knock all the breath from his body and all the awareness from his brain. Oblivion swallowed him up whole.

Tatum wasn't sure what had possessed him to grab that pretty blond clerk from the general store. Sure, sometimes a hostage came in handy, and a pretty girl or a kid were the best ones. A posse wouldn't crowd you too close if they thought they might stumble over the body of a slain prisoner.

On the other hand, a hostage could put up a fight and slow you down, too, and the members of a posse might be more determined than ever to keep going if you snatched one of their own. It was easier to give up when money was all that was at stake.

So there were pros and cons to the whole thing, but even so, when he'd seen her there in the street, ripe for the taking, he hadn't hesitated. He didn't regret that decision, at least not yet.

The blonde seemed to have yelled herself out for the time being. She wasn't screaming in his ear anymore.

But she hadn't stopped struggling. She still twisted and fought, trying to get free from his grip. She must not have given any thought to the fact that they were galloping across the prairie at top speed. If he let go of her now, she'd fall off the horse and probably break her neck.

"Settle down!" he shouted as he tightened his arm around her. "Stop it! You're gonna get hurt!"

"Let me go, damn you! Let me go!"

Tatum glanced back over his shoulder. The members of the gang were spread out and a haze of dust a hundred yards wide hung in the air. He wasn't sure how far they had come, but Redemption was far behind them. He didn't see any pursuit yet, but it was inevitable.

Other than the young marshal, who hadn't appeared to be hurt bad, that old-timer with the rifle was the only townsman Tatum had seen go down. Chico was a good shot; he'd drilled the old bastard. But they had thrown plenty of lead around elsewhere during their getaway. Some of the other citizens could have been hurt. The gang had made a good haul at the bank, too. Tatum was experienced enough at this sort of thing to know that.

So the townspeople would have plenty of reason to get a posse together and come after them, even if he hadn't scooped up the blonde, he told himself.

Anyway, he was the boss. The others knew better than to question his decisions.

They would have a good lead. The trick would be to maintain it.

And the first thing to consider was the strength and stamina of their horses. They made sure they had good mounts. In this line of work, that was vital. Not only that, they had spare horses stashed in a little canyon about ten miles from here. Hannah and the old man were watching them.

Tatum slowed his horse, knowing that the others would

see what he was doing and follow his example. It wouldn't do them any good to ride their horses into the ground before they reached the canyon where they could make the switch.

The blonde finally managed to twist around enough that she could throw a punch at his face. Tatum moved his head aside and laughed.

"You're wasting your time and energy, honey," he told her.

"Damn you!"

"Too late. I reckon the Devil's already got a corner of Hades all picked out for me, so it doesn't really matter all that much what I do in this world, now does it?"

She was smart enough to understand the veiled threat in those words. She didn't try to hit him again, and she stopped writhing in the circle of his arm.

"What . . . what are you going to do with me?" she asked.

"You're going to ride with us for a little while," he said. "Just long enough for us to make sure no posse is on our trail. Then we'll let you go."

That was a lie, and she probably knew it. Tatum wasn't sure what he was going to do with her, but he wasn't going to be letting her go anytime soon.

In a part of his mind, he wondered if he had actually known that as soon as he laid eyes on her in the mercantile. Had he realized even then that somehow she was going to wind up in his arms?

Maybe, if you wanted to believe in fate . . . and Caleb Tatum was starting to.

Chapter 10

The first thing Bill saw when he regained consciousness was the flushed, gray-bearded face of Josiah Hartnett, the burly liveryman and one of his best friends in Redemption.

"Praise be," Josiah said. "For a few minutes there I was worried the fall had killed you, Bill."

"Wh . . . where . . ."

"I brought you back into town in my wagon. You're laying on the bar in Fred Smoot's place."

The smell of stale beer in the air was enough to tell Bill that much. As he struggled to sit up, he finished the question he had tried to ask.

"Where's . . . Eden?"

Hartnett rested a big, strong hand on Bill's shoulder and held him down.

"Take it easy for a minute. You had a really nasty spill. We've got to make sure that you're all right."

Bill ached from head to toe, but he knew that other than that, he was fine. There had been dozens, if not hundreds, of bullets flying around in the street as the bank robbers found their getaway, but the closest any of them had come to him was blowing the heel off his boot.

"Damn it, Josiah, what about Eden?"

The horrible fear that the outlaws had already killed her and left her body behind as they fled suddenly gripped him.

With a grave expression on his face, Hartnett shook his head.

"We don't know, Bill," he said. "We purely don't. They took her with them when they got away."

A second of relief went through Bill, followed instantly by an even greater surge of fear. There was a chance that Eden was still alive, but there was no telling what was happening to her now . . . or would happen to her in the future as long as she was in the hands of those outlaws.

"I gotta get a posse together," he muttered as he tried to sit up again. "Go after 'em . . ."

This time Hartnett allowed him to rise, and as soon as Bill was upright, the saloon started spinning crazily around him. He saw that the room was crowded with concerned citizens, but he didn't have time to recognize any of them before he groaned and felt himself falling. He would have toppled off the bar if Hartnett hadn't been right there to catch him and lower him gently to the hardwood. Somebody had folded a bar towel and stuck it under his head as a pillow.

"Now, blast it, lay there and rest for a minute," Hartnett told him. "You won't be doing anybody any good by falling on your face again."

Bill supposed he was right. He didn't want to pass out again. If he did, it would be that much longer before he set out in pursuit of the outlaws who had taken his wife.

Fred Smoot rolled closer to the bar in his wheelchair and said, "There's a bottle of brandy in my office, Josiah. It might do the marshal some good if you want me to fetch it."

"Yeah, that's a good idea," Hartnett said. "Damn, I wish we had a doctor here in Redemption."

That reminded Bill of how Eden had stepped in to take care of him when his leg was injured. She had patched him up as well as any sawbones could have, he thought, and she had tended to other people's ills, too. She was as close to a doctor as the town had.

But now she was gone. That thought made him feel hollow, as if fear had whittled away all his insides.

Smoot came back with the brandy. Hartnett lifted Bill's head and helped take a drink from the bottle. The stuff burned all the way down Bill's throat and lit a fire in his belly. He tried to draw strength from it.

After a few more sips of brandy, he felt stronger. Knowing that the feeling might not last, he said, "I gotta get up, Josiah. I got things to do."

"Yeah, I know. Just take it slow and easy."

With Hartnett's arm around his shoulders, Bill sat up. He still felt pretty wobbly, but the room didn't go to spinning this time. He swung his legs off the front of the bar and let them dangle.

Something occurred to him, and he felt sick that he hadn't thought of it earlier.

"Mordecai—" he began.

"He's wounded, but he's alive," Hartnett said. "I don't know how bad it is. He was on the boardwalk in front of the newspaper office, so they carried him in there."

"Somebody go see about him."

Hartnett nodded to the crowd in the saloon, and a couple of men hurried out.

Bill sat there on the bar taking deep breaths until he felt himself growing steadier. He asked Hartnett, "Was anybody else hurt?"

"Not that I know of. It's possible, though."

Bill nodded. It might be a while before everybody in town was accounted for.

The crowd in the saloon parted to let a couple of people through. Bill was surprised to see Annabelle Hudson and Glenn Morley. So was Fred Smoot, judging by the way his eyes narrowed. Even under the circumstances, he didn't seem happy to have the competition in his place.

"We heard that the marshal was hurt," Annabelle said. "Glenn's had some medical training, if he can help."

"You're a doctor?" Smoot asked the bartender.

"I never said that," Morley replied with a shrug. "But I worked in a field hospital during the war."

Hartnett scowled and said, "Most of those surgeons were no better than butchers."

"They did the best they could with battles going on around them," Morley said. "But if you don't want my help—"

"Nobody said that, Mr. Morley," Bill told him. "I'm all right, though. What I'd appreciate is if you'd go over to the newspaper office and see if there's anything you can do for my deputy. One of those outlaws shot him."

Morley nodded. "I'll take a look at him, Marshal, if you're sure there's nothing I can do for you."

"I'm sure. Go check on Mordecai."

Morley turned and hurried out, but Annabelle lingered.

"I also heard that the robbers carried off your wife, Marshal," she said. "I'm sorry. If there's anything I can do—"

"There's not," Bill said. "I'm feeling better now. I need to put a posse together." He looked around the room and realized that someone else was absent who should have been there. "Where's Mr. Monroe?"

Hartnett looked uncomfortable again, and that made a bad feeling go through Bill.

"That's another thing," Hartnett said. "Perry went down to my stable, threw a saddle on a horse, and lit out after those bandits. He said they had his daughter, and he wasn't going to wait for any posse."

"Damn it! He should've had more sense than that. Even if he caught up to them, there'd be one of him and ten of them, and all of them hardcase killers, to boot! Why didn't somebody go with him?"

Nobody answered that question. Bill glared around the room. Most of the townspeople refused to meet his angry gaze. Clearly, they were embarrassed that they had let an old man like Perry Monroe gallop off after those ruthless outlaws by himself . . . but that didn't change the fact that no one had volunteered to go with him.

Bill wasn't really surprised. Twice before he had rallied the citizens of Redemption when violence and destruction threatened the town. They had risen to those occasions, fighting bravely to defend their homes and families and businesses. Some of them had been hurt in those battles, and some had died.

But they were like most people, Bill supposed. Their backs

had to be against the wall before they would fight. Up to that point, they would do everything they could to avoid risking their lives. He couldn't blame them for that. It just made them human.

"I need a posse," he said, his voice grim. "Any man who can ride and shoot and stick with me is welcome to come along." He glanced down at his feet. "And I need a pair of damn boots that aren't missing a heel, too!"

"Bound to be some at the mercantile," Hartnett said. "Let's go over there and gather up some ammunition. We're liable to need plenty."

"You're comin' along, Josiah?"

"You bet I am." Hartnett looked around the room. "Who's with me?"

A number of men spoke up, indicating their willingness to join the posse. Fred Smoot said, "I would if I could, Marshal."

"I know that," Bill told him. He leaned against the bar to pull off both boots so he could walk without falling over. The crowd moved aside to let him pass. The men who had volunteered followed him out.

Bill glanced to the west along the street. The dust kicked up by the outlaws' horses had long since settled. But they had left tracks, and he was going to follow them. His wife was out there somewhere, and so was her father.

Bill was going to do everything in his power to see to it that nothing else happened to either of them.

Chapter 11

Tom Gentry knew something was wrong as soon as he rode back into town. People were scurrying around on Main Street and gathering in small groups to talk loudly and excitedly. Men strode along purposefully, leading saddled horses. Tom hadn't seen the town this worked up since that Indian attack a few months earlier.

He had stayed out at the ranch, working with that stubborn gray stallion, until he couldn't stand his father's constant carping anymore. He'd told Burk that he would be back tomorrow, and he headed for Redemption.

"You're wastin' half a day!" Burk had called after him as he'd ridden off. "Is that the way I taught you to be?"

Tom hadn't answered. There was nothing he trusted himself to say. He didn't even look back. His father would brood about being ignored like that, but it didn't really matter. If Burk wasn't angry and resentful about one thing, he'd be angry and resentful about something else.

Spotting a horse trader he sometimes drank and played cards with, Tom reined in his chestnut saddle horse and called, "Hey, Harry, what the hell's going on?"

The man came over, looked up at him, and said, "The bank's been robbed."

"Again?" Tom said with a wry smile, remembering the incident a few months earlier.

"Yeah, but this time they got away with it. There were fifteen or twenty of 'em, I heard, and they kidnapped the marshal's wife while they were at it."

Tom frowned. He knew Eden Monroe—Eden Harvey, now—and a few years back he'd even been a mite smitten with her for a while. She was beautiful, smart, levelheaded . . . everything that Virgie wasn't, aside from the beautiful part. He couldn't help but think for a second about how different his life might have been if he'd married Eden instead of Virginia Shelton.

Of course, Eden hadn't returned those feelings. When he'd hinted around that he might be interested in courting her, she'd slammed that door in a hurry. He found out later from gossipy mutual friends that she thought he was too quick-tempered.

Well, it was true he had a temper, but he never lost it without good reason.

"I'm really sorry to hear that about Eden," he said now to the horse trader. "I guess that explains all the commotion."

"Yeah, the marshal's putting together a posse to go after them. Perry Monroe already took off."

Tom frowned.

"By himself?"

"Yeah."

"That crazy old man's gonna get himself killed," Tom said with a shake of his head. "Did they clean out the bank?"

"That's what I heard."

Tom's frown deepened. Burk Gentry had never really trusted banks, so he kept most of his money in a safe in his office at the ranch. But he'd had some cash deposited at the bank in Redemption.

Tom supposed that money was gone now, and they might not ever get it back. That wouldn't break the family, of course, but Burk would be hopping mad about losing it, anyway.

"That's not all that happened," Harry went on with a worried look on his face. "Your father-in-law was right in the middle of that bank robbery, Tom."

Tom's eyes widened, and for a second he didn't know what to think—or to hope for. If Walter Shelton had gotten himself killed, that might distract Virgie from her lover for a while. In her grief, she might even turn back to her husband for comfort.

Tom supposed he should feel bad about letting those thoughts cross his mind, but somehow he couldn't.

"Is he all right?" he asked, not knowing what he wanted to hear in reply.

"Yeah, but from what I heard, he pulled out a gun and took a shot at those outlaws while they were robbing the bank. Can you believe that?"

Tom couldn't. He could no more imagine dry, dour Walter Shelton blazing away with a six-gun than he could flap his arms and fly to the moon.

"They didn't kill him?"

"No, Roy Fleming tackled him and knocked him down to save his life. It wasn't much of a gunfight."

"Where is he now?"

"At home, I guess," Harry replied.

"Thanks," Tom said. He turned his horse and started toward the Shelton house.

If Virgie had heard about the robbery and her father's involvement in it, and it seemed likely she had, she would have headed for her parents' home to see about Shelton. She might not be very good at following the commandment about adultery, but she damn sure honored her father and mother.

The house was two stories, one of the biggest in town, and it had been expensive to build out there on the Kansas plains where lumber had to be freighted in. The place even had a picket fence around it, with an iron gate set into it.

Tom brought his horse to a halt in front of that gate, swung down, and looped the reins around one of the pickets. He went up a flagstone walk to the columned porch and knocked on the door.

His mother-in-law opened it a moment later. Clarissa

Shelton was what some people called a handsome woman with graying blond hair that was worked into tight braids and wound at the back of her head. As far as Tom was concerned, she was as dumb as a post, but she didn't get on his nerves as much as his father-in-law did.

"Tom!" she exclaimed when she saw him. "Thank God you're here. Come in."

Her reaction to seeing him confirmed her stupidity. She had no idea what her daughter had been doing. She believed that Virgie and Tom were still happy in their marriage.

"You heard what happened?" she went on as Tom stepped into the foyer.

"Something about Walter shooting it out with some bank robbers?"

"That's right! He was so brave. Foolish, but brave. He's in the parlor with Virginia."

Clarissa never called her daughter "Virgie." Shelton did, sometimes. Tom always did, because it didn't sound as high-falutin as Virginia.

Shelton was sitting in an armchair in the parlor. Virgie perched on a stool that was drawn up next to his right knee. She held his right hand in both of hers. When Tom came into the room, she glanced up at him and said, "There you are." She didn't sound nearly as glad to see him as her mother had.

Shelton had a big bruise on the side of his forehead. Tom didn't know if he'd gotten it when Roy Fleming knocked him down or if something else had happened. He never would have expected to see Shelton looking like he'd gotten into a fight.

"Hello, Walter," Tom said. "I hear you had some excitement today. Are you all right?"

"I'm fine," Shelton snapped, "and one of those blasted bandits would be dead now if Roy Fleming hadn't butted in."

"You'd be dead, too," Virgie said. "The other outlaws would have shot you."

Shelton snorted and said, "Maybe, maybe not. Criminals like that are cowards. They might've turned tail and run once somebody stood up to them."

Tom didn't believe that for a second. Judging by what

he'd heard so far, those outlaws would have blown Shelton full of holes. He supposed he was glad that hadn't happened.

"Where'd you get a gun?" he asked. "I didn't know you packed iron."

Shelton looked at him with narrowed eyes and said, "There's probably a lot you don't know about me, Tom."

That might be true. Right now, Tom didn't care. He had missed the excitement, and the money his father had lost didn't really matter that much to him, so as far as he could see, today's events didn't affect him at all. He could go on with what was really important to him.

Plotting his revenge on his wife and Ned Bassett.

"Is the marshal putting together a posse?" Shelton continued.

"I'm pretty sure he is. His wife was kidnapped."

"We heard," Clarissa said. "That poor woman. Carried off by bandits like that." Her voice grew hushed. "There's no telling what's going to happen to her."

"She'll probably be all right," Tom said. "Even outlaws won't mistreat a decent woman too much."

That was usually true, he thought, but he would have hated to bet money on it if he was Eden's husband.

"I think I should get my horse and go with the marshal," Shelton said, proving that this day held no end of surprises.

"You most certainly will not," Clarissa said, and her tone made it clear that she wouldn't put up with any argument. "You're injured. One of those brutes kicked you in the head. You're in no shape to go chasing after outlaws."

That explained the bruise.

Virgie looked at Tom and asked, "What about you? Are you going with the posse?"

Tom hesitated in answering. Actually, the thought had entered his mind. He was a good rider, able to stay in the saddle for long hours at a time, and a decent shot with both pistol and rifle. He didn't have any lingering affection for Eden Monroe, but he didn't want anything bad—anything *else* bad—to happen to her.

But when he looked at Virgie, he realized how much she would like it if he accompanied the posse. If he was gone for several days, she could spend that time with Bassett. He knew she was cheating on him, but he was damned if he was going to *help* her do it.

"No, I think I'd better stay here," he said.

"The marshal wanted every able-bodied man who can to go with him."

"It looked like he'd already got plenty of volunteers. Anyway, they may have left by now. I think it's more important that I stay here to look after all of you."

Clarissa smiled and said, "Isn't that nice?"

Shelton just gave him a hawk-like stare. The old man might not know exactly what was going on, but he wasn't as gullible as his wife. He knew that Tom had some other reason for staying behind.

He probably thought that his son-in-law was just a coward.

Shelton would find out differently soon enough, Tom told himself. Once he'd figured out exactly what he was going to do, everybody would know about Virgie. She'd be exposed for what she really was: a whore.

Tom felt a sudden qualm as he looked at her. She was his wife, after all. When they were first married, he had loved her, genuinely loved her. That had to be worth something.

But she had changed, and what she had become was unforgivable. His resolve strengthened.

He might not be going along with the posse in pursuit of those bank robbers, but he had some justice of his own to deal out.

Chapter 12

By the time Bill emerged from the general store wearing a new pair of boots, with a couple of boxes of .44s in his pockets, he felt considerably stronger. He still experienced a touch of dizziness from time to time, but he was confident that he would be all right.

Josiah Hartnett was with him. The liveryman said, "I'll go saddle my horse and yours, too, Bill. I imagine you'll want to check on Mordecai before you leave."

"I do," Bill said, "but I'm going back to the office first to get my rifle."

While he was there he picked up his hat, too, and settled it on his head. He felt even better as he walked out of the office. As long as a fella had his hat, his boots, and his guns, he could start to deal with his problems.

Fear for Eden and her father and worry over Mordecai's condition gnawed at his guts as he walked across the street to the newspaper office, though. The door was open and several men were standing around on the porch.

They moved aside quickly as Bill stepped up onto the planks. One of the men said, "The deputy's still alive, Marshal."

That was good to know. Bill gave the man a curt nod of thanks and went inside.

Mordecai was stretched out on an old sofa that sat against one wall of the office. Bill knew that Phillip Ramsey, the editor and publisher of the Redemption *Star*, sometimes slept on it when he'd been putting in late hours at the paper. Ramsey stood to one side now while Glenn Morley knelt next to the sofa and swabbed blood away from Mordecai's upper left arm. Several other people were in the room as well, including Jeffrey McKenna, the Methodist preacher, and Charley Hobbs and Leo Kellogg, two local businessmen and members of the town council.

Mordecai had been propped up with some pillows behind him, and he was awake but obviously woozy. He looked up at Bill and said, "Howdy, Marshal. Sorry I . . . I got . . . plugged. Happened so fast . . . there wasn't a durned thing . . . I could . . . I could do about it."

"Is he drunk?" Bill asked. He was mighty glad to see that Mordecai was alive, but that wound on his arm was an ugly one.

"He'll need to be even drunker before I start digging around after that bullet," Morley said. "If I had anything to knock him out, I would."

"Can't knock . . . knock me out," Mordecai said. "Ol' skull o' mine's . . . too damn thick."

"I don't think he means—" Bill stopped and addressed Morley instead. "How bad is he hurt?"

"The bullet hit the bone. It's bound to be cracked, but I don't think it's a clean fracture. The problem is that the bullet skidded up the bone and is lodged somewhere higher in his arm. I have to find it and get it out, otherwise he'll stand a good chance of losing that arm." Morley paused, then added, "Of course, there's a chance he'll bleed to death while I'm working on him, too."

Mordecai didn't seem to hear that. He said, "I'll be fixed up here . . . in a jiffy, Bill. Then we can get after them . . . damn bank robbers."

Morley glanced at Bill and shook his head.

"You're not goin' anywhere, Mordecai," Bill told his deputy. "You're hurt too bad for that. You've got to stay here and let these folks look after you."

Mordecai blinked and said, "But you're gonna need my help!" He seemed to be making an effort to be more coherent. "I'm the best damn tracker in these parts! If anybody can follow those owlhoots, it's me."

Unfortunately, Mordecai was probably right about that, Bill thought. The old frontiersman likely was the best tracker around here.

"I can follow a trail just fine," Bill told him, hoping that was true. "We'll find 'em, don't worry."

"Thought I saw . . . thought that one of the varmints . . ." Mordecai's voice grew hushed and solemn. "Bill, did I see that one of 'em had your missus with him?"

"That's right," Bill said, trying to keep the emotion out of his voice. "But we'll find her and bring her back. She'll be just fine."

He hoped that was true, too.

"You're gonna need another few shots of redeye now, Deputy," Morley said. "I've got work to do."

"Ain't that . . . just like a bartender?" Mordecai said. "Always tryin' to . . . pour hooch down a fella's throat."

Bill couldn't wait any longer. The delay was already chafing at him. He reached down, grasped Mordecai's good shoulder, and squeezed for a second.

"I'll see you when I get back," he said.

"Bill." Mordecai lifted his head. His eyes were bleary from pain and whiskey, but he was dead serious as he said, "You just get Eden. Don't worry about the town. I'll look after things around here."

"I know you will," Bill said, even though he wasn't confident of that at all.

Redemption might just have to get along without a lawman for a while, because he wasn't coming back without Eden, no matter how long it took.

"I need the sharpest knife you can find, and heat it up over a flame until it's red-hot," Morley was saying as Bill left the newspaper office.

When he stepped out onto the porch, the first thing he saw

was a familiar but surprising face. Jesse Overstreet stood there blocking his path.

It seemed like days since Judge Dunaway had fined the cowboy and Bill had released him from jail, instead of only hours. So much had happened since then, all of it bad.

"What do you want?" Bill snapped.

"To go with you," Overstreet said.

That brought Bill up short.

"You want to join the posse?" he asked. "Why?"

"I heard those outlaws took your wife with them. That ain't right. Besides, lookin' back on it now, you treated me halfway decent, Marshal, especially considerin' that I'm from Texas and you're a Kansas lawman."

"I'm from Texas, too, remember?"

"Still and all, you've could've been a lot harder on me. I reckon I owe you somethin' for that." Overstreet smiled faintly. "Anyway, you know how it is. When somebody asks a Texan why, he just naturally says why the hell not."

Even under these bleak circumstances, Bill couldn't help but return the young cowboy's smile for a second. Overstreet still looked a little hungover, but if he could stay in a saddle, that was all that mattered right now.

"Is your horse ready to ride?"

"Yes, sir, he sure is," Overstreet answered with a nod.

"Then come on. We need to get on the trail."

Josiah Hartnett had assembled the posse in front of his livery stable. As Bill walked up, he did a quick head count. Sixteen men, counting him and Overstreet. That wasn't bad. They would outnumber the bank robbers. Some of the faces were familiar and some weren't, but they all looked determined, if a mite nervous at the same time. What they were setting out to do could easily be dangerous.

Bill took the reins of his horse when Hartnett handed them to him. He mounted, then faced the members of the posse.

"I don't know how long or how far we'll have to chase those outlaws, but we're gonna chase them until we catch up to them," he said. "And then we're going to kill them or capture them. If any of you feel like you're not up to that job, you can fall out now and nobody will think any worse of you."

None of the men budged.

"We're all bound and determined, Marshal," Hartnett said. "I've got a couple of packhorses loaded down with ammunition and enough supplies to last us at least a week."

"Thanks, Josiah. You've done a good job getting ready for this." Bill turned his horse. "Let's go."

A lot of people were still on the street. They stopped talking and turned to look as the posse rode out. Somebody started to let out a cheer, but when nobody else joined in, the voice trailed off.

This wasn't a moment for cheering. These men were setting off on a mission of blood and death.

And there was no way of knowing if any of them would come back alive.

Chapter 13

It took every bit of strength and determination Eden possessed to keep herself from giving in to her fear and screaming hysterically.

She didn't want to give this bastard the satisfaction of seeing her react like that.

His name was Caleb; she knew that because she had heard some of the other outlaws address him that way. He was also the leader of the gang, giving the orders that made them speed up and then slow down to rest the horses.

He had his left arm around her as she rode in front of him. His forearm sometimes pressed against the underside of her breasts, but at least he hadn't groped her as blatantly as he could have. At this point, Eden supposed she should be grateful for small favors . . . such as being alive and still relatively unharmed.

The worst part about it, other than the fear she felt for her own future, was not knowing whether Bill was all right. She had seen him pitch head-first off the boardwalk into the street as if he'd been shot. She hadn't had a chance to see how badly he was hurt. Before she could, this bank robber had grabbed her and ridden off with her.

The hope she clung to was that she hadn't seen any blood on Bill's clothes in that brief second when Caleb galloped past him. Eden kept telling herself that he was all right, he had to be all right, and he would be coming after her.

"How are you doing?" Caleb asked her, breaking into her thoughts as they loped along, heading northwest now, Eden thought. This was the first time he had actually talked to her, other than yelling at her and telling her to stop fighting and settle down.

"How do you think I'm doing?" she asked icily. "You *kidnapped* me."

He chuckled.

"I'd rather think of it as taking you along for the ride," he said, "although I guess if you want to get down to brass tacks . . . Anyway, I don't have any interest in hurting you. You're a lot more valuable to us if you're safe and sound."

"As a hostage, you mean?"

"That's right."

Without looking back at him, she shook her head.

"That won't do you any good," she said. "My—"

She'd started to say "my husband," but she stopped herself in time. If Caleb knew that she was married to Redemption's marshal, that would give him even more reason to think that he could use her as a hostage.

Instead she said, "The marshal is going to come after you and kill you. He's a gunfighter from Texas, you know."

"That's not what I heard. I heard he's just a kid cowboy."

"He's fought outlaws and Indians," Eden insisted. "You're no match for him."

That drew an outright laugh from Caleb.

"We'll see, we'll see." He paused, then asked her, "What's your name?"

"You don't need to know my name," she snapped.

His arm tightened around her. Not painfully, just enough to remind her that she was in his power.

"I don't like talking to a lady without knowing her name," he said. "There's no reason we can't be polite to each other."

"You call it polite to grab a woman off the street—"

"Just tell me your name."

It wasn't worth making him angry, she decided. She said, "My name is Eden . . . Eden Monroe."

She left off her married name, just in case he knew what Bill's last name was. That seemed possible, since judging by what he had said earlier, he had checked to see who the law was in Redemption.

"Eden," Caleb repeated. "That's a mighty pretty name. It suits you."

"Are you trying to pay me a compliment?"

"Like I said, there's no reason we can't be polite to each other."

Something about the way he spoke struck her as being more educated than she thought of most outlaws as being. On the other hand, what did she really know about outlaws? Nothing, really. She had been acquainted with another cold-blooded killer, and he had been fairly well-spoken, too.

They were riding toward a line of low bluffs that rose from the prairie in an irregular line maybe thirty feet tall. As they came closer, Eden realized they were heading for a gap in the bluffs that led to a small canyon. That canyon formed a little pocket hidden from the view of the surrounding plains.

The gang had been pretty spread out, but they converged on the gap with Caleb in the lead. As he trotted his horse into the canyon, Eden spotted movement up ahead. A dozen horses were picketed at the far end of the canyon.

Someone stepped out from behind a clump of brush. At first Eden thought the person was a man, because of the boots, whipcord trousers, and flat-crowned hat. Also, the figure held a rifle ready for use.

But no man was shaped like that, and when the sentry pushed her hat back so that it hung by its chin strap behind her head, long, fiery red hair spilled down past her shoulders.

"Who the hell is *she*?" the woman demanded as she glared at Eden.

Caleb reined his horse to a stop and grinned.

"A hostage," he said. The other outlaws came to a halt behind him.

One of them, a darkly handsome youngster with obvious Spanish blood, called, "Yeah, Caleb picked himself up a play-pretty in Redemption, Hannah."

The redhead continued to scowl.

"Since when do you take hostages?" she asked.

"I thought it would be a good idea." Caleb's voice hardened as he went on, "And I don't cotton to having to explain what I do, Hannah. You ought to know that."

Hannah sniffed. She lowered the rifle.

"You got the money from the bank?"

"Cleaned it out," Caleb told her.

"Then I guess that's all that really matters." She jerked her head toward the picketed mounts. "Eugene and I brought the horses."

"Where is he?"

"Up on the rim, checking your back trail."

"Good idea." Caleb turned his head to look at the others. "Let's get these saddles switched. I want to put a lot more miles between us and Redemption by nightfall."

This made sense to Eden. The gang had stashed fresh horses here. Switching mounts like that would give them an advantage over any posse that came after them, unless the pursuers had extra horses as well. She didn't know if Bill would have thought of that in his hurry to get started after the outlaws.

Assuming, of course, that Bill was still alive . . .

Eden banished that thought. She wasn't going to allow herself to believe anything except that Bill was alive and coming after her.

"Stay where you are," Caleb ordered her. He dismounted, then reached his hands up toward her. "I'll help you."

"She looks like she can get off a horse by herself," Hannah said. Eden could feel the dislike in the way the redhead looked at her.

But it wasn't just dislike, she thought. It was jealousy, too. Maybe even a little hatred. It wasn't hard to guess that Hannah was Caleb's woman, and she didn't appreciate even a potential threat to that position.

"She's right, I can dismount," Eden told Caleb. She had

felt his hands on her body enough already. She didn't want any help from him.

He shrugged and stepped back.

"Suit yourself."

Eden grasped the saddle horn to steady herself and swung down, acutely aware that her dress was hiked up because of the way she'd been riding and she was showing a considerable flash of leg to these men.

But given her circumstances, she thought, a little minor embarrassment wasn't really much to worry about. With the redhead giving her a cold, baleful, narrow-eyed stare, she moved aside to get out of the way as the men began switching their saddles to the fresh horses.

With a rattle of rocks, a man slid and jumped nimbly down the sloping wall of the canyon. He had a spryness that belied his age, because as he approached, Eden saw the lined, leathery face of an old-timer.

"Anybody on our trail, Eugene?" Caleb asked as he started loosening his saddle cinches.

"Nope," the lookout replied in a raspy voice. "You know these ol' eyes o' mine are still pretty keen. No dust as far back as I could see."

Caleb nodded in satisfaction.

"That's good. Those folks back in Redemption won't give up, though. Some of them will be coming after us. You can bet all that bank money on that."

"We headed for Castle Rock?"

"That's right. If we can get there, a posse will have a damned hard time rooting us out."

Eden had heard vaguely of Castle Rock. It was part of an area of badlands somewhere in the northern part of the state. A long way from Redemption, and she had never been there. It would probably take several days to reach that destination.

Good, she thought. That would give Bill time to catch up to them.

For a second she considered trying to get away, since all the men were busy switching mounts and weren't paying attention to her. Hannah was still watching her, though, and from the look on the redhead's face, if Eden made a break for freedom, Hannah might just shoot her.

Besides, where could she go? They were in the middle of nowhere, and on foot she would stand absolutely no chance of getting away from outlaws on horseback.

No, Eden told herself, she would just have to be patient and hope that nothing too bad happened in the meantime. She would do everything in her power to stay alive until help arrived.

Because help was on its way. She was sure of that.

She just wished she could quiet that nagging voice of fear and despair in the back of her head.

Chapter 14

Bill had to admit, being on horseback and moving fast over the prairie made him feel better. He didn't know if it was the wind in his face or the familiar sensation of sitting in a saddle, but whatever the cause, his head was clearer and he felt less like he was on the edge of panic. Ever since he'd seen that outlaw grab Eden and jerk her off her feet to ride away with her, it had seemed to him like he was on the edge of losing control.

Now that he was taking action, he had reason to hope again.

Those optimistic feelings lasted for a couple of miles as the posse followed the welter of hoofprints left by the bank robbers' horses.

Then Bill spotted something lying on the ground several hundred yards ahead of them and his insides were suddenly clenched hard with ice-cold fear again.

Could the outlaws have killed Eden and dumped her body this soon, he asked himself? Surely not. If they were going to do that, what was the purpose of taking her along in the first place?

But that sure looked like a body. As Bill slowed his horse and pointed it out to Josiah Hartnett, the liveryman agreed.

"But it couldn't be Eden, Bill," Hartnett argued. "They wouldn't have grabbed her like that and then killed her so soon."

"Yeah, I thought the same thing," Bill said. "But what if she fought 'em so hard they didn't have a choice? She might've gotten her hands on a gun—"

"Let's just go see," Hartnett suggested.

That made sense. The body lay in the direction they were headed anyway.

Bill had been trying to pace them starting out, so the posse's horses wouldn't get worn out too soon. The outlaws already had a good lead, so catching them wasn't going to be a matter of speed as much as it was of persistence.

Faced now with this grim discovery, Bill kicked his horse into a run and pulled out slightly ahead of the others. This wasn't a trap, so he wasn't worried about that. On these plains, a man could see for a mile or more in every direction, so there was no place for bushwhackers to hide.

As he came closer, a mixture of relief and apprehension flooded through him. The person lying sprawled on the ground was too bulky to be Eden, he realized. But Bill recalled now that Perry Monroe had galloped out of Redemption ahead of the posse, and so far they hadn't seen any sight of him.

Until now. Bill saw something white moving and recognized it as Monroe's long beard fluttering in the wind that sighed almost ceaselessly across the prairie.

He hauled his horse to a halt and was out of the saddle almost before the animal stopped moving. After running the last few feet, Bill dropped to his knees beside the still figure. Monroe lay on his back with his eyes closed. Bill looked for blood or other signs of a wound but didn't see any.

"Is he breathing?" Hartnett called as he reined in. The other members of the posse were right behind him.

Bill thought his father-in-law's barrel chest was rising and falling, but he laid a hand on it to be sure. When he felt definite movement against his palm, he glanced up at Hartnett, who had dismounted and come over to lean above them with his hands on his thighs.

"Yeah, he's alive, thank God," Bill said. "Looks like he's just out cold."

"Where's his horse?"

That was a good question. Bill looked around and didn't see the animal.

"I don't know. Maybe Perry can tell us if we can bring him around. Anybody have any whiskey?"

Bill had told the members of the posse to bring guns, ammunition, and a good horse, but he suspected some of the men had slipped a flask or a bottle into their saddlebags as well. He wasn't disappointed. Jesse Overstreet was actually the first one to speak up.

"I, uh, grabbed a bottle at the saloon before we started out, Marshal . . ."

"Get it," Bill told the young cowboy.

Overstreet took the bottle from one of his saddlebags and brought it over. He pulled the cork from the neck with his teeth and handed the bottle to Bill.

Hartnett knelt on the other side of Monroe and lifted the storekeeper's head. Bill put the mouth of the bottle against Monroe's lips and tilted it so that some of the whiskey spilled into his mouth. More of it dribbled down the front of Monroe's shirt.

"Uh . . ." Overstreet began.

Bill glanced up, figuring that Overstreet was going to say something about being careful with the whiskey and not spilling so much of it.

"Never mind," Overstreet said hurriedly when he saw the look Bill gave him.

Monroe hadn't responded so far, but when Bill got more of the whiskey in his mouth and Hartnett held him up so the fiery stuff went down his throat, he began to cough. His eyelids jerked and tried to open.

"Maybe we should have given him some water," Hartnett suggested.

"Wouldn't have brought him around as fast," Bill said. "I want to find out what happened."

After a minute or so, Monroe was able to open his eyes. He

looked up in confusion, squinting because the sun was in his face. Bill said, "Somebody hold a hat so it shades his eyes."

One of the possemen complied. Monroe blinked a few more times, then his gaze settled on Bill.

"Wha . . . what happened?" he asked.

"That's what I want you to tell me, Mr. Monroe," Bill said. "We found you out here in the middle of the prairie, and your horse is nowhere around."

Monroe coughed again, then said, "That . . . that damned nag! A snake spooked him . . . and he ran off with me! I tried . . . to stay in the saddle . . . Couldn't do it . . ."

"You fell off?"

"Yeah. That's . . . the last thing I remember."

Bill wasn't surprised. Perry Monroe was a townsman, seldom budging from Redemption, and the few times he had gone anywhere while Bill was around, he had taken a buggy. Bill wasn't sure if he had ever seen Monroe on horseback. He had known right from the start, though, that it was a mistake for Monroe to charge off after those outlaws by himself like that. Some mishap was bound to occur.

Actually, thought Bill, Monroe getting thrown from a runaway horse wasn't nearly as bad as some of the things that could have happened.

"Did you see the outlaws?" Bill asked. "Did you see Eden?"

"No. Never came . . . within sight of 'em."

"How bad are you hurt?"

"Don't know. Guess it knocked me out . . . when I fell. I don't even know . . . how long I've been lyin' here."

It had been a while, Bill figured, since they weren't really that far from the settlement. The accident must have occurred not long after Monroe left Redemption.

And they were wasting time now, Bill reminded himself. Now that Monroe had regained consciousness, he appeared to be all right for the most part, just shaken up. There was no telling where his horse was. Spooked like that, the animal could have run for several miles before stopping.

Bill looked around at the other members of the posse and said, "We need somebody to take Mr. Monroe back to Redemption."

Monroe struggled to sit up and said, "Take me back! I . . . I'm goin' with you boys—"

"No, you're not," Bill told him. "For one thing, we don't know how bad you're really hurt, and for another, your horse is gone and we don't have time to look for him. I hate to lose a man so soon, but we don't have any choice." Bill faced the posse again, ignoring his father-in-law's sputtered protests. "How about it?"

For a long moment, none of the men said anything. Then Leo Kellogg spoke up.

"I hate to say it, Marshal, but I came along because I was so angry at those outlaws I couldn't hardly see straight. But now that I consider it, I'm not sure how much of an asset I'd be. I've never ridden much, and I'm not a very good shot. I was already thinking that maybe I made a mistake . . ."

"I appreciate you bein' honest enough to say that, Mr. Kellogg," Bill told the tailor. "And I'm mighty glad you came along because now you can see to it that Mr. Monroe gets back to town all right. The two of you ought to be able to ride double on your horse for that far."

"Yes, of course," Kellogg agreed.

"And when you get there, have that fella Morley check him over."

"The bartender from the Prairie Queen?"

"I reckon he's the closest thing Redemption's got to a doctor right now."

Bill glanced around at the other men and started to ask if it was all right with them for Kellogg to take Monroe back to town, but then he caught himself. He didn't need to ask their permission. He was the leader of this posse, and he had to remember that. There might come a time when hard decisions had to be made, and he was going to be the one to make them.

"I still say I could come with you fellas," Monroe said as Bill and Hartnett got him on his feet and helped him climb into the saddle on Kellogg's horse.

"No offense, sir, but you'd just slow us down," Bill told him.

Monroe frowned, and Bill knew he'd offended his father-in-law, no matter how he'd prefaced the remark.

Well, better that than risking catching up with the outlaws too late to save Eden, Bill thought. He would offend anybody if it meant saving his wife.

Hell, he'd go right through anybody if it meant saving Eden . . .

Kellogg climbed onto the horse behind Monroe and took the reins when Hartnett handed them to him.

"Good luck," he said. "I hope you find them."

"We'll find them," Bill said. "You can count on that."

And if anything happened to Eden, he would kill every last son of a bitch who'd had anything to do with it.

You could count on that, too.

Chapter 15

Virgie didn't want to leave her parents' house. She would have been content to stay there and fuss over her father all evening.

Tom was tired and hungry, though, and eventually he persuaded her to return home with him and prepare some supper for them.

Their house was only a couple of blocks away, much smaller than the ostentatious dwelling where her parents lived but still a nice, neat frame home with whitewashed walls. Tom led his horse as he and Virgie walked toward it through the dusk.

"I still think you should have gone with the posse," she said without looking at him.

"That wouldn't be a good idea," Tom told her. "I'm needed here."

"For what?"

Tom looked over at her then, and she went on, "I didn't mean that the way it sounded. I just meant that there's no reason you couldn't be gone for a couple of days."

"I'm working with that gray stallion out at the ranch."

"It would still be there when you got back."

"And it might be for more than just a couple of days," Tom said. "I've heard of posses chasing outlaws for a week or more. Maybe as long as a month."

"That would be all right, if it was necessary."

"You wouldn't miss me if I was gone that long?"

"Of course I would," Virgie said, but Tom didn't think she sounded like she meant it at all.

She wouldn't have a chance to miss him if he was gone for a month. She'd be busy with her lover the whole time.

"Anyway, there's no point in talking about it," he said. "The posse's already gone, and by now they're a long way from Redemption. I couldn't catch up to them, and I'm not going to try. I'm afraid you're still stuck with me."

"I wouldn't put it that way."

He shrugged, making it clear that he didn't care how she would put it.

When they reached the house, Tom led the horse around back to the shed, unsaddled it, gave it a good rubdown, and made sure there was grain and water for the animal. When he went through the back door into the kitchen, he saw that the stove was still cold and Virgie was nowhere to be seen.

Unlike her parents' house, this one had only one story. Tom went through the kitchen, along a corridor, and into their bedroom. The lamp wasn't lit, but enough gray light remained outside for him to see Virgie as she pulled a night-gown over her head and let it drop around her body.

He caught a glimpse of the clean, sleek lines of her figure and felt an instant reaction inside himself. He didn't want to react that way to her—things would a lot simpler if he just didn't give a damn—but he still did and he couldn't help it.

"After everything that's happened today I'm just worn out," she said. "I think I'm going to bed."

"What about supper?"

"I'm not hungry."

"That's not what I—"

Tom stopped short. What was the point in explaining what he'd meant? It wouldn't make any difference to her.

"All right, go ahead and turn in," he said. "I'll see you in the morning."

She didn't say anything. He turned, closed the bedroom door behind him, and went back to the kitchen. There were some biscuits left over from breakfast. They might be a little dry, but he could wash them down with whiskey from the bottle he kept in the spare bedroom where he slept most nights.

As suppers went these days, it wouldn't be too bad.

He just needed to be careful not to drink too much. If he sank too deeply into a stupor, he wouldn't hear Virgie when she went to sneak out.

And then he couldn't follow her to her latest rendezvous with Ned Bassett.

Mordecai Flint shifted a little on the cot, trying to get comfortable. He knew that wasn't going to be possible, but instinct made him try anyway.

The whiskey he'd drunk earlier in the day had dulled the pain in his arm to a certain extent. That apron from the Prairie Queen who'd patched him up had said that he ought to have some laudanum and even hinted that he could supply it, but Mordecai had turned that down flat. He was the only law in Redemption right now, and he couldn't afford to be doped up.

Morley had located the bullet lodged in Mordecai's arm, dug it out, and cleaned and bandaged both wounds, wrapping the strips of cloth tightly. In addition, he had splinted Mordecai's upper arm to keep the cracked bone from moving around, and the short lengths of wood he had used for splints were bound tightly in place, too. Then he had fashioned a sling for the arm and lashed the whole thing down so that Mordecai couldn't move it.

"If you don't get blood poisoning, the wounds should heal and the arm ought to be all right in a few weeks," Morley had told him. "I'll have to change the dressings a couple of times a day and you'll need to be careful not to use the arm. Other than that we'll just wait and see."

Mayor Roy Fleming had offered to have Mordecai moved from the newspaper office to the extra bedroom in the mayor's house. Fleming was still mighty upset about the bank robbery, of course, but he said that as the leader of the town council and the community, it was his responsibility to see to it that Mordecai was taken care of.

"You and Marshal Harvey are the town's only actual employees, Mr. Flint," as Fleming had put it.

"Maybe so, but I still got a job to do," Mordecai insisted. "I'll sleep in the marshal's office the way I always do."

Glenn Morley said, "You're in no shape to do anything except rest, Deputy. You need to forget about law enforcement for a while."

That drew a disgusted snort from Mordecai. Folks just didn't understand. When a man had a job to do, he did it, by God, no matter what.

"The way you got me wrapped up like one o' them goldang Egyptian mummies, this bad arm can't go nowhere," he'd said. "I can stand on my own two feet, and there ain't a blamed thing wrong with my other arm or my gun hand. So as far as I can see, I'm the law in Redemption right now, and that's the way it's gonna stay until Bill gets back."

Eventually Fleming, Morley, and everybody else quit arguing with him. As he left the newspaper office, walking on his own, he'd heard Morley mutter something about him being a stubborn old pelican, but that was nothing new. He'd been called a lot worse.

Somebody had found his old, floppy-brimmed hat where it had fallen off his head when he'd been shot, and they gave it to him as he headed for the marshal's office. With his hat on his head and his gun on his hip, he felt mostly human again. A mite drunk, maybe—Morley had been pretty free about pouring the hooch down his throat—but Mordecai's reflexes were just as good drunk as sober. Sometimes he even thought he was a little sharper once he had a few drinks in him.

He walked around town for a while, letting people see him so they would know there was still law in Redemption.

While he was doing that, Leo Kellogg, who had gone with the posse earlier, rode back into town with Perry Monroe on the horse with him. Mordecai hurried out into the street to meet them, as did several other people.

Kellogg had explained about them finding Monroe several miles out of town, where he had been thrown by his horse. Monroe had insisted that he was all right, but Charley Dobbs, probably his best friend in town, had taken Monroe back to his house so that he and his wife could look after the storekeeper. Mordecai thought that was a good idea.

Then he went into the marshal's office and sank gratefully into the chair behind the desk, wincing a little when his arm twinged as he leaned back.

He knew he would have to get used to the pain. The arm was going to hurt, that was all there was to it. Dulling the pain with whiskey was one thing; he could get away with that and still function. Laudanum might take the pain away, but it would knock him out, too, and that was unacceptable.

Anyway, Mordecai thought now as he tried to catch a few winks despite being uncomfortable, he had it a lot better than Bill did. Bill was somewhere out there in the dark prairie night, wondering if his wife was all right or even still alive. That worry would be eating the young lawman's guts away from the inside out.

Mordecai had never been much of one for praying, but if he had been, tonight he would have been asking *el Señor Dios* to see to it that both Bill and Eden returned safely to Redemption.

Chapter 16

"Marshal, I don't think this is a good idea," Josiah Hartnett said.

Bill knew by the way Hartnett called him "Marshal" instead of by his name that the liveryman was trying to make his comment sound more serious.

"I can still see the trail, Josiah," he said.

"I don't see how. It's too dark to see much of anything."

Bill didn't think that was true. In fact, there was still a thin line of fading rose on the western horizon, the last vestiges of the setting sun.

However, the shadows *were* getting pretty thick over the prairie. Bill thought he could still see the tracks left by the outlaws' horses, but it was difficult to be certain.

He had known all along that it was unlikely they would catch up to the bank robbers today. He had known as well that sooner or later they would have to stop and make camp for the night.

But he hadn't wanted to think about that, because it meant thinking about Eden spending the night with those ruthless men, with God knows what happening to her. He was torn between hoping that the outlaws would make camp, too, so they wouldn't get any farther ahead of the posse during the night, and hoping that they would keep moving because if they were still in the saddle they couldn't be hurting Eden.

Hartnett was riding just behind Bill and to the right. Jesse Overstreet was in the same position to the left. The young cowboy said, "I sure can't see much, Marshal. I'm a mite worried that my horse might step in a prairie dog hole or somethin' like that."

Bill started to snap a response, telling Overstreet that if he was worried, he could damned well stop if he wanted to. He could even turn around and go back if he didn't want to be part of the posse anymore.

Bill didn't say either of those things. He knew Hartnett and Overstreet were right. If he asked the other members of the posse, no doubt they would agree, too.

Tightening his grip on the reins, Bill pulled his horse to a stop. Like it or not, they couldn't go on. If they did, they would be running too great a risk of losing the trail completely in the dark. Picking it up again in the morning would cost them even more time.

"All right," he said. "We'll stop and make camp for the night."

"That's the smart thing to do," Hartnett said.

"But we'll be on the move again as soon as it's light enough to see in the morning."

"Sure."

Out here on these mostly featureless plains, one place to camp was just about as good as another, so the men dismounted right where they were.

"Should we have a fire?" one of the men asked Bill.

He thought about it for a moment. The glow of a campfire could be seen for a long way. The outlaws might be within sight of it, so a fire would announce that the posse was back here behind them.

On the other hand, they had to know that already. They had cleaned out the bank and taken a hostage. Of course a posse was going to come after them.

"Yeah, build a fire," Bill decided. "Keep it small, but some hot coffee and food will be good for all of us."

"Sure thing, Marshal."

There was no wood to be found, but the prairie was littered with dried buffalo chips from the vast herds that moved through here over the years, millions upon millions of the great shaggy beasts leaving their droppings behind. First the Indians and then later plainsmen had been using those chips as fuel for as far back as anybody could remember.

One of the men soon had a small fire burning. He set a coffeepot over the flames and got some Arbuckles brewing. Another man fetched a frying pan from one of the packhorses and got to work cooking biscuits and frying bacon.

The other members of the posse tended to the horses, picketing and unsaddling the animals. There was enough grass for them to graze but no water along here, so the men would have to pour water from their canteens into their hats and let the horses drink from those.

After Bill had tended to those chores, he found himself standing at the edge of the camp with the fire behind him, staring out into the darkness in the direction the bank robbers had been going. That was north by northwest, Bill judged. He had never been where they were headed.

Hartnett moved up beside him and asked, "Thinking about Eden?"

"Thinking about where we're going," Bill lied. Eden was always in his thoughts. But he had forced a part of his brain to remain cool and calculating. That was going to be important. "Do you know what's up there in that direction, Josiah?"

"Well, if they keep going the same way, they'll get into the Blue Hills."

"Are those like most of the hills in Kansas? They don't amount to much?"

Hartnett let out a grim chuckle.

"Well, I reckon that's true. There's a little bluff or a plateau or whatever you want to call it that runs along there and separates the plains from some higher plains. But believe it or not, there's some pretty rugged country in those parts, too. The Chalk Bluffs, the Castle Rock badlands . . . it's not all just prairie."

"How well do you know it?"

"Hardly at all," Hartnett admitted. "I went on a hunting trip up there once. You've got to remember, it hasn't been that many years since there were Indians roaming in those parts pretty regular-like. They might not have been on the warpath all the time, but they weren't hardly what you'd call safe company, either."

"Any settlements?"

"A few," Hartnett said with a shrug. "Little places that grew up around trading posts. A few ranchers have moved in here and there, or so I've heard. It's not fit country for farming. Mostly it's just big and empty."

"A good place for a gang of outlaws to hole up."

"Yeah, I'd say so." Hartnett paused. "But maybe we'll catch up to them before they get there. If we don't . . . we'll follow them wherever they go."

Bill nodded and said, "All the way to hell and back if we have to."

Eden hurt. She had ridden horses before, but never for this far or this long. Her legs and back ached, and the insides of her thighs felt like they were rubbed raw. When the outlaws finally stopped to make camp and she was able to dismount, her legs tried to fold up underneath her like those of a rag doll.

Caleb was right there beside her to take hold of her arm and steady her. He said, "Take it easy. You'll get your bearings in a minute."

"I'm fine," she said as she tried to pull her arm away from his grip. She had already felt his hands on her plenty of times today. Enough was enough.

Hannah came over and said, "I'll take her."

Caleb shrugged and let go of Eden's arm.

"I don't want her hurt," he said.

"I'm not gonna hurt her. But there's no need for you to keep fussin' over her, either." She took hold of Eden's other arm. "Come on."

They had stopped beside a mostly dry wash. A thin trickle

of water ran in the bottom of it. A few stunted cottonwoods grew along the bank, an indication that the creek ran better at other times of year.

Hannah led Eden over to one of those trees. Eden's steps were pretty unsteady at first, but they strengthened as she went along. When they reached the tree, Hannah told her, "Sit down." She turned to one of the outlaws and added, "Dave, bring your rope over here."

"What're you gonna do, Hannah?" asked the man called Dave.

"Tie this prisoner up so she can't get away, of course."

Dave hesitated.

"Hadn't you better ask Caleb about that?" he suggested.

For a second Eden thought Hannah was going to shoot the man. She looked that angry. But then she snapped, "Forget it. Eugene!"

The old-timer hurried over.

"What do you need, Hannah?"

"Some rope to tie up this prisoner."

Eugene didn't argue. He just said, "Sure. I'll get it right now."

"Sit," Hannah told Eden again.

Eden didn't think there was any point in arguing with the redhead. Anyway, after those long hours in the saddle, it might feel good to rest for a while, even if it meant sitting on the ground. She leaned against the tree to brace herself as she sat down.

Eugene came back with a lariat. Hannah took it and wrapped it around Eden's body and the tree trunk several times before knotting it on the other side of the tree, well out of Eden's reach even if she could move her arms.

Caleb stalked up in the gathering darkness and said, "What in blazes are you doing?"

"You don't want her getting away, do you?" Hannah challenged him, an obvious note of defiance in her voice. "Hell, she won't do us any good as a hostage if she runs off."

"That's no reason to mistreat her."

"I didn't tie her that tight." Hannah's tone was surly now. "She's fine."

"All right. Just don't get any ideas. She might turn out to be important to us."

Hannah just snorted, as if to say how unlikely she considered that possibility.

Hannah was worried about *Caleb* getting ideas, Eden thought. The redhead didn't like the way he had been treating the prisoner, didn't even like the fact that Caleb had grabbed Eden and brought her along. Eden had a feeling that if she gave Hannah even the slightest excuse, the redhead would shoot her and claim that she hadn't had a choice.

So she was going to do her best to cooperate for now and stay alive until Bill had a chance to rescue her. She wouldn't try to escape, and she wouldn't pay any attention to Caleb.

But all she could do was hope that he wouldn't try to pay too much attention to her, at least while Hannah was around . . .

Chapter 17

Exhaustion—and, he supposed, the whiskey—finally caught up to Mordecai Flint and he dozed off sometime during the night. His wounded arm hurting woke him up early, though, and when he wasn't able to get back to sleep he clambered up off the cot, stumbled into the main room of the marshal's office, and stirred up the embers in the stove. At this time of year, the mornings were just cool enough to need something to take the chill out of the air.

When the stove had heated up enough, he put coffee on to boil. He would go over to the Nilssons' café in a little while for breakfast, he decided, but before that he needed something to perk him up. He didn't want to admit it, even to himself, but he was a mite hungover.

Thank goodness the night had been a quiet, peaceful one in Redemption, he thought.

It *had* been quiet and peaceful, hadn't it?

Mordecai hoped so. Nobody had come looking for the law, so that was encouraging.

The coffee wasn't ready yet when the office door opened and Glenn Morley came in. Mordecai, sitting behind the desk, frowned at him and said, "You're a bartender. What the hell are you doin' up and around this early in the mornin'?"

"I came to see how you're doing and change those dressings," Morley replied. "And I'm up because I haven't been to bed yet."

Mordecai grunted.

"Busy night at the Prairie Queen, eh?"

"Yeah. People are upset and worried about that bank robbery, and a lot of people drink when they're worried. Some of them lost their life's savings."

Mordecai scratched at his beard and said, "I never did hold much with banks for that very reason. And o' course I was always movin' around a lot, so it seemed to make more sense to keep whatever I had with me. Not that I ever had enough for a banker to want my business." He used his good arm to gesture toward the stove. "Want a cup of coffee?"

"That would probably be a good idea," Morley said. "Might keep me awake while I'm messing with that arm of yours."

"Well, help yourself and pour me a cup while you're at it."

Morley smiled wryly.

"I just can't get away from pouring drinks for people, can I?"

The process of changing the bandages and checking the wounds on Mordecai's arm took almost half an hour, but the bartender was pleased with what he found. The injuries were clean so far, with no sign of festering.

By the time Mordecai was bound up and his arm was back in the sling, he was starting to get hungry.

"I'm headin' over to the café for some breakfast," he said. "Care to join me?"

"No, thanks," Morley replied. "I'm going to bed. I'll see you this evening. Be careful with that arm between now and then."

"As careful as this star-packin' job will let me be," Mordecai promised.

Before either man could leave the marshal's office, Mordecai heard an odd, unexpected sound outside. It was similar to bells ringing but lacked the musical quality bells would have. Instead it was more of a discordant clanging.

"Jehoshaphat!" Mordecai exclaimed. "What's that racket?"

He went to the door and stepped out onto the little porch in front of the office. Glenn Morley followed behind him. Both men stood there watching as a big, boxlike wagon rolled slowly past, drawn by a team of four mules.

It was hard to see the wagon itself because the outsides of it were covered with pots, pans, washbasins, tin plates, bowls, cups, shovels, hoes, saws, axes . . . Almost every kind of metal tool or implement a person could think of hung from hooks attached to the wooden sides of the wagon.

The man on the driver's seat of the vehicle was eye-catching as well. He wore a bright red shirt with loose sleeves, a black vest over it, and black trousers. A red bandanna was wrapped around his head, with a black plug hat pushed down on top of it. His hawk-like face sported a gray goatee around his mouth. Beside him on the seat rode a medium-sized, black-and-white, long-haired dog.

At the sight of Mordecai standing there watching him, the driver pulled back on the reins and brought his team to a stop. He lifted a hand in greeting and called, "You are the sheriff, yes?"

"Yes," Mordecai replied, then gave a shake of his head and went on, "I mean, no, I ain't the sheriff. But I'm the deputy town marshal, which means I'm the law in these parts right now, the marshal bein' out of town. What in the name of all that's holy are you?"

"I'm a tinker," the colorful stranger said. "I sell pots, pans, and all these other goods you see hanging on my wagon. Also I sharpen knives, axes, scissors, and anything else that needs a keen edge. My name is Gregor Smolenski."

"You're a gypsy," Glenn Morley said. There was a note of accusation in his voice.

Smolenski's shoulders rose and fell.

"I prefer to think of myself as a citizen of the world. But in point of fact, I was born in England."

"That doesn't make you any less of a gypsy."

"A traveling businessman, that's all I am."

Morley grunted in obvious dislike.

"What brings you to Redemption?" Mordecai asked. "Mr. Smoz . . . Smok . . . Smoltz . . ."

"Call me Gregor," the tinker said. He scratched the dog's ears. "And this is my friend and business associate Tip. He does tricks to entertain the children while I conduct transactions with their parents."

"You mean the dog distracts folks while you pick their pockets," Morley said with a scowl. "I've seen your type before."

Smolenski pressed a hand to his chest.

"You wound me, sir," he declared. "I barely arrive in your town, and already the insults and the suspicions begin." He looked at Mordecai. "I stopped to introduce myself, Marshal—"

"Deputy," Mordecai corrected.

"Deputy, then. I stopped because I always introduce myself to the local peace officers when I arrive in a new town. I'm a law-abiding man, Deputy, who wishes only to do a little business and then be on my way."

"Don't trust him," Morley warned. "I never saw a gypsy yet who wasn't a thief."

"Yeah, some folks say that about Injuns, too, but I've known a heap of 'em who were better men than me," Mordecai said. He fixed Smolenski with a hard stare. "You sure you don't intend to do nothin' except sell those goods you got?"

"That and sharpen blades and do any repair work that needs to be done. I can repair any tool or piece of machinery."

"Reckon I don't see any harm in that. But I'll be keepin' an eye on you, mister. And I won't be in the mood to put up with any tomfoolery."

Smolenski nodded toward the black sling and asked, "What happened to your arm, Deputy?"

"I got winged shootin' it out with a bunch of bank robbers. So let that be a warnin' to you not to cause any trouble. My gun arm still works fine and dandy."

"I hope you recover quickly," Smolenski said. He lifted the reins. "I'll park my wagon down at the end of Main Street, yes?"

"That'll be fine. You can stay as long as I don't get any complaints about you."

"You'll get no complaints, of that I assure you."

The tinker slapped the reins against the backs of the mules and started the wagon rolling along the street again. Mordecai and Glenn Morley watched him go, and the bartender said, "I hope you're not making a mistake by letting that crook stay here, Deputy."

"We ain't got no proof he's a crook," Mordecai pointed out, "and if I am makin' a mistake, it sure as blazes won't be the first one I ever made! Now, I'm headin' for the café. My belly's plumb empty."

Chapter 18

Bill didn't think it would be possible for him to sleep at all, as worried about Eden as he was, but weariness had a way of catching up to a man, no matter what sort of tragedy had befallen him. And having been a cowboy, sleeping in a blanket roll on the hard ground was nothing new for him. So despite the circumstances that might have combined to rob him of slumber, he dozed off and slept for several hours that first night on the trail.

He was still plenty tired the next morning, though, and his eyes felt gritty and raw. He ignored those annoyances, knowing that a couple of cups of coffee strong enough to get up and waltz around on its own hind legs would take care of them.

"Any problems during the night?" he asked Josiah Hartnett. Thinking that he wouldn't be able to sleep anyway, Bill had taken one of the first shifts of standing watch. He didn't know if a guard was necessary, but it seemed like a reasonable precaution this far from town.

"Everything was quiet," Hartnett replied. He had been the last one to stand guard. "Except for that cowboy's snoring. For a young man, he saws more wood than anybody I ever saw."

"That ain't true!" Jesse Overstreet protested from where he hunkered on his heels, sipping from a tin cup of coffee. "I been told I sleep like an angel, with nary a peep."

"Whoever told you that was lying to you, son," Hartnett said.

"Well . . . I got to admit, it was a soiled dove in Dodge City named Flossie, and she might not've been all that truthful. Come to think of it, I believe she stole my watch."

Bill glanced at the eastern sky, where the gray of approaching dawn was growing lighter.

"Let's eat and get ready to ride," he said. "It won't be long until there'll be enough light to pick up the trail again."

Before the sun had even started to peek over the horizon, the members of the posse were back in their saddles. Enough reddish-gold light filled the sky for Bill to see the hoofprints of the horses they were following. That many riders, traveling in a bunch, weren't that hard to follow.

But it wouldn't continue to be this easy, Bill thought. So far it appeared that the bank robbers hadn't even attempted to hide their trail. They had just galloped out of Redemption to the west, then curved north, moving as fast as they could. No doubt they had slowed down from time to time or even stopped to rest their horses, but for the most part they had been concerned only with speed, with putting distance between them and any pursuers.

Today, Bill told himself, today they would start to get tricky.

The sun hadn't been up long when the posse followed their quarry to a low line of bluffs.

"Is this that escarpment you were talkin' about?" Bill asked Josiah Hartnett as they reined in to study the terrain.

The liveryman shook his head.

"No, that's a little taller than this and farther on. This is just a rough spot in the prairie."

"Looks like they headed for that canyon," Bill said, pointing to a narrow gap.

One of the other men asked, "You reckon they're holed up in there waitin' to ambush us, Marshal?"

Bill had already thought about that. He said, "I don't think so. Doesn't look to me like there's enough cover for that. But just in case, the rest of you hang back. I'll go check it out."

"Not by yourself," Hartnett said. "I'm coming with you."

Bill shook his head.

"No, you're not. If anything was to happen to me, you're in charge of this posse, Josiah." Bill looked at the other men. "All the rest of you hear that?"

They nodded in understanding, and Jesse Overstreet said, "Why don't I come with you, Marshal? I ain't fit to be in charge of much of anything, but I can shoot pretty good when I'm sober. Don't go by the other night when I had a snootful."

Bill thought about it for a second, then shrugged.

"Sure, come on, Overstreet. Let's go take a look."

"Be careful," Hartnett called after them as they nudged their horses into motion again. Bill pulled his rifle from its scabbard and laid it across the saddle in front of him.

"Would you look at us?" Overstreet said cheerfully as they rode toward the gap. "A couple of Texas cowboys ridin' for the law in Kansas. Don't that beat all?"

Overstreet's attitude annoyed Bill, but he reminded himself that the cowboy didn't have much at stake here other than his life, and Bill knew from experience that young cowboys often regarded that as pretty trivial compared to the pursuit of adventure and excitement. Less than a year ago, he thought, he had been pretty much the same way.

Now he had a wife and a home, and he realized bleakly how dangerous that situation was. If you cared about something, it could be taken away from you. You could be hurt, in more ways than just physically. The only way to avoid that was to never let yourself get too attached to anybody or anything.

The only true freedom lay in not giving a damn.

Unfortunately, in his case it was too late for that. Never again would he be like Jesse Overstreet, whistling cheerfully as he rode into what might turn out to be a death trap.

And Overstreet was actually whistling, too. Bill glanced over at him and said, "Stop that. You tryin' to tell them that we're coming?"

"If they got eyes, they already know that," Overstreet pointed out.

He was right, of course. Sneaking up on anybody was the next thing to impossible out here on these plains.

As they reached the mouth of the canyon, Bill lifted his rifle and worked the lever to throw a shell into the chamber. The metallic noise echoed back from the earthen walls.

"There's nobody here," Overstreet said.

It was true. A few clumps of brush lined the walls of the canyon, but nothing big enough to hide any bushwhackers. Bill rode forward slowly, studying the ground.

"Lots of horses have been in here recently," he said. "The tracks are all mixed up."

Overstreet pointed and said, "A bunch of them were held for a while over there by that wall, too. You can tell by all the droppin's." He took off his hat and ran his fingers through his sandy hair. "Looks to me like they had extra mounts hidden here, Marshal."

Bill had reached that conclusion at the same time, and he didn't like it.

"If they have enough horses to switch back and forth, they're gonna be able to make mighty good time," he said. "Better time than us."

"Yeah, I'm afraid you're right. Maybe we should've brought extra horses, too."

Bill didn't know whether to curse or groan, so he didn't do either. He was disgusted with himself, though. He had never even thought about bringing extra horses. He'd been in such a hurry to get on the trail of the bank robbers, that urgency and his fear for Eden had consumed all his thoughts.

He was still new to this law business, too. He'd never been in charge of a posse before. He had only ridden with a couple of them, back home in Texas, and somebody else had been giving the orders.

Those posses hadn't caught the men they were after, either, he recalled.

He couldn't allow that to be the case here.

"Marshal, look there," Overstreet said, pointing at something on the ground.

At first Bill didn't see anything except a welter of boot prints, which was to be expected because the outlaws would have had to dismount to switch their saddles to the fresh horses.

But then he spotted what Overstreet must have seen and quickly swung down from the saddle. Holding his reins in one hand, he knelt and reached out with the other, his fingertips stopping just short of some faint impressions in the dirt.

Those weren't boot prints. They were smaller than that, and shaped wrong. They were the prints of a woman's shoes.

Eden had stood right here.

It had to be her who had made those marks, unless the gang had somehow picked up another woman and Bill didn't think that was possible. No, he told himself, his wife had been right here in this place less than eighteen hours earlier. Even though he had known she was with the outlaws, seeing her footprints here like this, mingled with theirs, shook him to his core for a moment.

He got control of himself and straightened.

"Did you see a bunch of tracks leading back out of this canyon?" he asked Overstreet.

"Not so's you'd notice. They must've left out the other end. It ain't too steep, and it looks like there's a trail back there they could've used."

"Go wave the others on," Bill said. He put his foot in the stirrup and swung up into the saddle. "I'll ride up and see if I can pick up the trail."

"Sure thing, Marshal."

Overstreet turned his horse and galloped back to the mouth of the canyon. He took off his hat and waved it over his head, signaling to the rest of the posse that it was all right to advance.

Bill rode toward the far end of the canyon, thinking again about how Eden had been right here in this very place.

He hoped that wherever she was now, she knew he was coming to get her.

Chapter 19

Twenty-four hours earlier, Eden had woken up snuggled next to her husband in a warm, soft bed.

That had been *so* much nicer than this.

She groaned as she shifted slightly on the hard ground. Even though she was awake, she didn't want to open her eyes just yet. As long as she couldn't see her surroundings, maybe she could pretend that she wasn't in as much trouble as she was.

That didn't work. A boot toe nudged her, none too gently, and Hannah said, "I know you're awake. Don't try to fool anybody."

Eden pried her eyes open. The redhead stood over her, hands on hips, glaring down at her with the usual dislike on her face.

"I'm not trying to fool anybody," Eden said. "I . . . I just woke up."

"Uh-huh." Hannah reached down, took hold of Eden's shoulders, and hauled her upright, pushing her back against the cottonwood trunk.

Last night before everyone turned in, Hannah had changed the way Eden was tied, lashing her ankles together and her hands behind her back, but at least she wasn't bound tightly to the tree trunk anymore. She was able to stretch out on the ground. Hannah ran a rope from Eden's wrists to the tree, though, to make sure she didn't try to roll away. Tied up like she was, she certainly couldn't get up and run.

As uncomfortable as she was, her sleep had been restless. She had roused briefly what seemed like a thousand times. As a result, she was still very tired this morning, and the chill from lying on the ground in the open had seeped into her bones and made her ache from head to foot.

"Someone could have at least thrown a blanket over me," she said now.

"You're lucky nobody's thrown a few feet of dirt over you, princess," Hannah snapped.

Eden ignored the threat in those words and looked around. The campsite was even more bleak in the gray light of pre-dawn. A couple of the outlaws were stirring around. One poked at the ashes of last night's fire, trying to bring it back to life, while another had climbed down into the wash and was filling canteens from the creek's trickle. The other men were still rolled in their blankets.

Not for long. Hannah raised her voice and said, "All right, get up, you bunch of loafers! We need to cover some ground today."

Caleb sat up and yawned. He said, "I don't recall putting you in charge of rising and shining, Hannah."

"Somebody's got to do it," she said with a snort. "You're probably too busy dreamin'."

"Somebody has to dream," Caleb said. "Everything worthwhile in the world started with somebody's dream."

"Yeah, and while you're doin' that, somebody else has to get the coffee boilin' and see to the horses."

Hannah turned away and started walking among the outlaws, prodding them with her foot as she told them to get up. Caleb, watching her, smiled and shook his head.

Then he looked over at Eden and asked, "How are you this morning?"

"How do you think?" she asked through clenched teeth. Her jaw was tight from both anger and her effort to keep her teeth from chattering. "I'm cold, I hurt all over, and I want you to let me go."

Caleb shook his head again.

"I'm sorry about the first part of that," he said. "And you know I can't let you go."

"Why not? Just leave me here. When the posse finds me, I . . . I'll tell them you went a different direction than you really did."

Caleb gave her an indulgent smile.

"You don't think I believe that, do you?" he asked.

"You've treated me halfway decent," Eden argued. "I'm grateful for that. I . . . I don't mind if you get away."

"What about that money we took from the bank? Are you saying you don't want the posse to recover it?"

"I'm saying that my life is a lot more important to me than any amount of money."

"Well, that's where you and I are different." Caleb pushed aside his blankets and climbed to his feet. "But I'll do what I can to keep you comfortable as long as you're with us. You should have had a blanket last night. It was such a long day yesterday I just didn't think of it. Sorry."

Hannah came back up in time to hear that. She said, "Don't apologize to her. She's a prisoner. She's lucky we didn't just put a bullet in her head and leave her for the buzzards and the coyotes."

"There's no need to talk like that," Caleb said with a frown.

Hannah just glared at him and turned toward the fire. The cottonwood trees along the bank of the wash, stunted though they were, provided some small branches for firewood, and the outlaw who had been messing with the embers earlier now had flames leaping merrily in the gloom. The coffee was on to boil, and the man soon had salt pork sizzling in a frying pan.

Eden began to feel a pressing need. She felt her face burning hotly with embarrassment as she was forced to say, "I . . . I could use some privacy . . ."

Caleb opened his mouth, but before he could say anything, Hannah said, "I'll take her down in the wash. You men stay here."

Caleb's eyes narrowed.

"I don't want you shooting her and then claiming she tried to get away."

"If I wanted to shoot her, I'd shoot her," Hannah said. "I wouldn't make up some damned excuse."

She bent down and untied the rope connecting Eden's wrists to the tree. Then she untied the one around Eden's ankles.

"What about my wrists?"

"You don't need 'em," Hannah said. She took hold of Eden's arm and hauled her to her feet, seemingly effortlessly.

The rope around Eden's ankles had been so tight that her feet were numb and unresponsive. When she tried to take a step it was like nothing was there at the ends of her legs. She cried out and would have fallen if Hannah hadn't been holding her up.

"Wiggle your damn toes," Hannah ordered.

Eden tried to. The pain was even worse as the blood began to flow freely again in her feet. She bit her lip, determined not to cry out again.

After a few moments, the pins and needles eased. She was able to hobble along with Hannah's help. The side of the wash wasn't too steep, and it was rough enough that there were plenty of places to step as they went down into it. Here below the level of the prairie, shadows still lingered.

For about half a second, Eden considered the idea of lowering her head, butting Hannah in the stomach, and trying to knock her down. If she could do that, she could turn and run along the twisting wash.

And if she did, she would probably get all of ten feet or so before Hannah put a rifle bullet in her back. Caleb would be angry about that, but the outlaw leader's anger wouldn't bring Eden back to life.

Eden didn't want to give Hannah the satisfaction of killing her, either.

So once they were out of sight of the camp, she took care of her personal business awkwardly but the best she could, ignoring the shame she felt about knowing that Hannah was watching her.

When she was finished she staggered to her feet. Hannah smirked at her and said, "You know, for a second there I thought you were gonna make a run for it."

"I have more sense than that," Eden said.

"But not sense enough to keep from gettin' carried off by a love-struck outlaw."

Eden blinked in surprise.

"Love-struck?" she repeated. "Caleb's not . . . He took me to use as a hostage."

"Yeah, that's what he says. Might even be what he thinks is true. But I know better. I've seen him get smitten by some sweet-looking gal. You see, he thinks that because he's had some book-learnin', he's too good for a hillbilly girl like me. But sooner or later he figures out that he's wrong about that. He tries to stray, but he always comes back to me. And when he don't . . ." Hannah shrugged. "Well, when I get through with those gals, they ain't so sweet-lookin', and he don't want 'em no more. So you'd best remember that."

Eden swallowed hard and said, "I . . . I just want this to be over with. I just want to go home."

"Maybe that'll happen." Hannah's cruel grin made it clear she didn't believe there was a chance in the world of that. "As long as you behave yourself, it won't do any harm for you to hope. But if I was you I wouldn't hold my breath waitin' for somebody to come along and save me. Once we get to the badlands, it'd take an army to get us out of there. You got an army comin' after you?"

Eden didn't answer the question, but she knew she didn't have an army coming after her.

But she had the tough Texan she was married to, along with some friends, and she would have to hope that would be enough.

Chapter 20

Roy Fleming came by the marshal's office that afternoon to check on Mordecai.

"You know, a normal man would be laid up in bed for a week or more if he was injured as badly as you are," Fleming said.

"Normal is one thing I ain't been called that often," Mordecai said. "The fellas like me who went west to trap beaver, back when there weren't hardly any white men west of St. Louis, we were a hardy breed. If we got hurt, we might be a hundred miles or more from the closest help, so we learned to take care of ourselves. Learned how to keep goin' and not pay it any mind, too. I'll be fine, Mr. Mayor." Mordecai paused, then added, "But I been takin' it pretty easy today. As long as no more trouble crops up, I'll make my rounds and that's about all."

"Should the town council see about getting some help for you? I'm sure we can afford to hire a temporary deputy." A frown formed on Fleming's face. "Or maybe we can't, come to think of it. Except for a small petty cash fund, the town's money was in the bank, and those outlaws took it."

Mordecai's bushy eyebrows rose.

"You're sayin' you can't pay my wages no more?"

"Now, I'm sure it's not going to come to that," Fleming went on quickly. "Marshal Harvey and the posse will catch up to the thieves and recover the money. Even if they don't, we . . . we'll find a way to carry on somehow."

Mordecai leaned back in the chair and said, "Anyway, I don't need no help. I told Bill I'd handle things here, and that's what I intend to do. Who would I hire, anyway? Is there anybody else in town fit to be a lawman?"

"I'm sure we could find someone . . ."

Mordecai shook his head.

"If I need help, I'll ask for it. Until then, don't worry about it."

"All right. There is one other thing . . ."

When Fleming hesitated, Mordecai said, "Spit it out." He was aware that technically he was talking to his boss, since Fleming was the mayor, but he'd never had much patience for dawdling when there was something unpleasant to say or do.

"Were you aware that there's a gypsy in town?"

"You mean that Gregor Smo . . . Smoz . . . that Gregor fella?"

"That's right. He's parked his wagon down at the edge of town and is selling pots and pans and all sorts of other things. Plus he says he can sharpen blades and repair things."

Mordecai shrugged his good shoulder.

"I reckon he can do that. I ain't seen nothin' to prove otherwise."

"Yes, but people of his . . . ilk . . . have a rather dubious reputation. It's well known that most of them are thieves."

Mordecai cocked an eyebrow and commented, "Some folks say the same thing about bankers."

Fleming's round, friendly face didn't look so friendly for a second. Mordecai thought that maybe he had pushed the mayor a mite too far, especially considering that the man's bank had been robbed only twenty-four hours earlier. Fleming had to be in a pretty bad mood.

"You've obviously spoken to this man."

"Yeah, he stopped by and introduced himself when he got

to town," Mordecai said. "Told me his name and why he's here in Redemption."

"Do you think he could have anything to do with the robbery yesterday?"

"I don't see how." Mordecai frowned. "Seems to me it was just a coincidence that he got here the next mornin'. If he was part of the gang, why would he come *back* here when the robbery's over and done with?"

"I don't know," Fleming admitted. "I just don't trust him, and I don't like having his sort in town. Can't you go down there and run him out?"

"What for? He ain't broke any laws that I know of."

"There must be something . . ."

Mordecai was starting to feel pretty irritated. He had enough on his plate at the moment without Fleming piling on any unnecessary chores. But since Fleming was the mayor, it was sort of Mordecai's job to do what the man said, he supposed.

"Tell you what I'll do, Mr. Mayor," he said. "I'll walk down there and have a look-see, just to make sure Gregor ain't doin' nothin' wrong. If I see anything that strikes me as fishy, I'll tell him it'd be best for him to move on. That do for now?"

"I suppose," Fleming said. "I just know I would sleep easier if that man was gone."

After everything else that had happened, he was going to lose sleep over one lone gypsy? That seemed loco to Mordecai, but he didn't say anything about it. Instead he got to his feet and reached for his hat.

"I'd go with you," Fleming said as they left the office, "but I'm in the process of drafting letters to out-of-town depositors informing them of the robbery and assuring them that everything humanly possible is being done to recover the stolen funds."

"How about ever'thing humanly possible bein' done to get Eden back safe and sound?"

"Yes, well, that, too, of course. The two things go hand in hand, don't they?"

Not exactly, Mordecai thought. If it came down to choosing between saving Eden and recovering the money, he knew which one Bill would pick. That was the same decision Mordecai would have made if he'd been in that position.

Fleming turned toward the bank while Mordecai went the other way. There weren't many trees in this part of Kansas, but there were a few and one of them stood at the end of Main Street. Gregor Smolenski had parked his wagon in the shade of that tree. Part of the vehicle's side folded down to make a table where Gregor could display some of his wares, Mordecai saw as he came closer.

Maybe half a dozen people were gathered around the wagon, examining the things Gregor had for sale. The colorfully clad gypsy stood there talking to them, not really pressuring them to buy but extolling the virtues of the items. The dog Tip still sat on the wagon seat. Gregor had unhitched the mules and tied them under the tree where they cropped lazily at the grass.

"Hello, Deputy," Gregor said as Mordecai strolled up. "What brings you here? You have a knife you need sharpened? Or perhaps you'd like to buy some pots and pans?"

"I already got an old fryin' pan and a coffeepot, and that's all I've ever needed when it comes to things like that," Mordecai said. "I just thought I'd see how you were doin' now that you got set up and all."

"You mean you wanted to make sure I wasn't swindling the citizens of Redemption," Gregor said with a smile.

"I never—"

Gregor waved a hand.

"Oh, don't worry, Deputy Flint, please. I'm accustomed to mistrust from everyone in this world except my friend Tip here. I long since stopped being insulted by that attitude." He nodded toward his customers. "You can ask these people, or anyone else who has done business with me since my arrival this morning. All my transactions have been honest and aboveboard."

One of the women who was examining a pot nodded and said, "Mr. Smolenski's right, Mordecai. I thought he'd be a thief, too, but his prices are very fair."

"You see?" Gregor said, spreading his hands.

"Yeah, I reckon. Just keep things that way."

"Of course." A frown of concern appeared on Gregor's face. "You know, Deputy, I can tell that you're in pain."

"I'll be fine," Mordecai said curtly. "I been shot before."

"I have an herb that's very good for relieving pain. All you have to do is chew it, or brew some tea with it."

"I don't chew plants except tobacco, and I ain't much of a tea drinker. But I'm obliged to you for the thought."

"If you change your mind, come and see me. My people have many cures that are quite effective, just like your Indians in this country. You know, some people actually believe that my countrymen and the Indians are related somehow."

"Is that so?" Mordecai squinted. "You do look a mite like an Injun. You ain't gonna put on feathers and war paint, are you? We already had to deal with that not so long ago."

Gregor laughed and shook his head.

"No, no war paint for me. I'm just a businessman."

"And I'm just a lawman. So you don't want to have any business with me."

Mordecai left it at that. He headed back toward the office, and with each step the throb that went through his injured arm and shoulder made him wonder if he should have taken Gregor up on that offer of the herb.

Probably not, he decided. Who knew what other effects it might have?

Chapter 21

By midday, the tracks left by the outlaws led the posse to a seemingly endless stretch of rocky ground that didn't take hoofprints nearly as well.

"I knew that sooner or later they'd try to throw us off their trail," Bill said as he reined in to study the hard ground.

"I don't know if that's what's going on here," Josiah Hartnett said, "or if the direction they were headed just happened to have a lot of rocks in it."

"Either way, this is going to make it harder. This is where I wish we had Mordecai with us. The tracks would probably still be plain as day to him, even on the rocks."

"We can follow them," Hartnett said. "We just have to be careful."

Bill nodded and said, "Which will slow us down." He heaved a sigh. "But there's nothing we can do about it." He turned to face the other members of the posse. "Unless one of you fellas has a lot of experience as a tracker . . . ?"

All he got back in return were blank looks and a few of the men shaking their heads.

"I'm pretty good at followin' a few thousand head of cattle," Overstreet said. "That's about all."

"All right," Bill said. "We'll see what we can do."

They started forward, moving at a walk now. After a while, Bill had to get down and walk, leading his horse as he searched the ground for fragments of hoofprints, chipped places on the rocks where horseshoes struck them, flat stones with their darker surfaces facing up, indicating that something had overturned them in the past twenty-four hours . . . anything that told him a good-sized group of riders had moved through here.

More than once, he thought the trail was gone completely and had to come to a stop. He hunkered on his heels and studied the ground closely, all too aware that with each passing minute, the outlaws—and Eden—were getting farther away from him.

Each time he was afraid that he had lost the trail, he finally found something that gave him hope they were still headed in the right direction. But they wouldn't know for sure if that was true until after they got out of this stretch and the ground was better suited to picking up tracks.

By that time, he thought grimly, the bank robbers might be so far ahead that the posse would never catch up to them.

All the men dismounted and took advantage of this opportunity to rest their horses by walking. That would keep their mounts fresher, longer, so maybe that was a small silver lining, Bill told himself. But the proverbial clouds were still mighty dark, even though the day was clear and sunny.

Minutes crawled past and turned into hours. The delay ate at Bill until he wanted to scream. Those outlaws would have galloped across these rocks at full speed, more than likely, which meant they were picking up miles on the pursuit.

Then things got even worse. They came to the end of the rocks, and there were no hoofprints anywhere in sight.

Bill stared at the ground in disbelief. He had tried so hard, had been convinced that he was still following the trail.

But now it was gone. Whatever he'd been following, it wasn't the men who had held up the bank in Redemption and kidnapped Eden. Those men were gone.

Josiah Hartnett's hand fell heavily on Bill's shoulder.

"We won't give up," the liveryman said. "We'll backtrack—"

"How can we backtrack when we haven't really been tracking?" Bill asked, his voice raw with emotion. "We took a wrong turn, Josiah. There's no gettin' around that."

"Maybe, but I still say we shouldn't give up. They were headed north, right? They had to leave these rocks somewhere if they kept going. What we should do is split up and ride east and west, searching for the place they came out. When one group finds it, they can signal the others and we'll join forces again. That'll work, won't it?"

Hartnett's words penetrated the despair that gripped Bill. What his friend was saying made sense. That plan was their best option, Bill realized. Unless . . .

"What if they turned around?"

"What?" Hartnett asked with a frown.

"What if they rode across that rocky ground for a mile or two, then turned around and headed back south or southwest? They could be going the opposite direction and we'd never know it."

"Well . . . I suppose that's possible," Hartnett said. "But I think it's more likely they're still headed north, toward the badlands. That's the most likely place for their hideout to be. But it's your decision, Bill. I suppose we could send some men back to search in that direction, too . . ."

"No," Bill said abruptly. "That would be splitting our forces too much. We'd wind up scattered all over the country." Hartnett was right: it was his decision. Bill went on, "Take some of the men and head east from here, Josiah. I'll take the others and go west. If you find what looks like the tracks of that gang, fire three shots in the air. We'll do the same."

Hartnett nodded and said, "Sounds like a good plan." He waved to some of the men. "You fellas come with me."

The posse split up. Overstreet was among the riders who went with Bill, and he moved his horse alongside his fellow Texan to say, "We're gonna find those varmints, Marshal. I know we are."

"I appreciate the confidence, Overstreet," Bill said.

"Oh, it ain't confidence. I got the sight."

Bill looked over at him and said, "The sight?"

"I'm the seventh son of a seventh son. That gives a fella powers. I can tell the future."

"If you can tell the future . . . did you know ahead of time you were gonna wind up in my jail?"

"Maybe," Overstreet said with a grin. "Maybe I figured fate had a good reason for me to get all liquored up and go loco."

"Or maybe you just wanted to get liquored up."

"Well . . . either way it worked out all right, didn't it?"

Bill wasn't sure about that. So far Overstreet hadn't given him any trouble, but this was probably a long way from over.

They were watching the ground closely as they rode, and Bill estimated that they had come about a mile when he spotted something up ahead. His heart slugged in his chest. He told himself not to get his hopes up too much, but that was impossible. He pointed and said to Overstreet, "Are those tracks?"

"Looks like they might be," the young cowboy replied. He spurred his horse forward.

"Hold it!" Bill ordered. "You don't want to mess them up."

Overstreet reined in and grinned sheepishly over his shoulder at Bill.

"Oh, yeah. Sorry, Marshal. Reckon I got carried away."

Bill dismounted and walked forward, unwilling to disturb any of the hoofprints he saw on the ground. During the early part of the chase, he had studied the prints of the outlaws' horses as closely as he could, committing little details about them to memory. Every horseshoe left a slightly different print, and Bill knew that if he saw familiar combinations of nicks and lines and angles, that would be the confirmation he needed.

His pulse hammered in his head as he knelt to study these tracks. After a long moment, he swallowed and turned his head to look up at Jesse Overstreet.

"It's them," he said. "Fire those three shots to signal Josiah and the others."

"Be glad to," Overstreet said with a grin. He pulled his Colt, pointed it into the air, and triggered three rounds. The booming reports rolled over the plains.

By the time Hartnett and the rest of the posse galloped up a quarter of an hour later, Bill had already followed the trail a ways north and then returned.

"It's them, all right," he told Hartnett. "And as far as I can tell, they're all still together. I worried a little that they might have split up while they were in those rocks. That would have been a smart thing to do. They could have rendezvoused somewhere else later."

Hartnett shook his head and said, "I don't reckon any of those boys want to let that money out of their sight. They'll stay together until they get to their hideout and divvy it up."

Bill wondered if there was another reason for the outlaws to stay together. It could be that they all had their eye on Eden, and they didn't want to go their separate ways until they had a chance to divvy *her* up, too.

But he wasn't going to think about that, he told himself. He had known from the start there was a chance bad things might happen, and he was bound and determined that it wasn't going to matter as long as he got her back alive. All he wanted was the chance to make her see that.

"Everybody dismount," he told the newcomers. "We're gonna rest the horses for a while longer."

Hartnett looked confused. He said, "I figured since we've got the trail again, you'd want to move on, Bill."

"We will . . . as soon as the horses catch their breath." Bill gazed off to the north, knowing that Eden was up there somewhere. "Because when we do move out, we're gonna ride like hell."

Chapter 22

Eden wouldn't have thought it was possible that her muscles could hurt even worse than they had the day before, but she discovered that wasn't true. Sharp, jabbing pains each time her horse took a step were mixed with a never-ending ache.

At least she had her own mount today. She didn't have to ride in front of Caleb's saddle with his arm around her. She was thankful for that.

She wasn't sure whose idea it was for her to ride one of the extra horses, but she suspected that Hannah had something to do with it. Hannah didn't like the attention Caleb was paying to Eden, so she wouldn't want him in such close proximity to the prisoner all day.

Caleb had objected at first, saying that it might make it easier for Eden to try to escape, but Hannah said, "We can ride around her so there's nowhere for her to go except where we're goin'."

So that was exactly what they did, surrounding Eden so that her horse had no choice but to go the same direction. If she had tried to make a break for freedom, someone was there to block her no matter which way she turned.

Seeing that it was hopeless, she didn't even try. She rode

with her wrists tied to the saddle horn and her head down. She didn't have to guide her horse; it trotted right along with the others.

She didn't know how far away those badlands that Hannah had mentioned were, or how long it would take to get there. But by late afternoon, they hadn't reached their destination, and Caleb reined in and ordered the men to make camp.

"Lou, you and Andy ride back a ways and have a look," Caleb went on after he'd dismounted. "I want to make sure that posse isn't closing in on us."

"What do we do if we run into them?" one of the men asked.

"If you're careful, you won't run into them," Caleb said. "You'll see them before they have a chance to see you. Think you can manage that?"

Both outlaws looked a little annoyed by his tone, but they shrugged and the other one said, "Sure, Caleb."

"If they're close, though, fog on back here and let me know," Caleb went on. "I'd just as soon give all the horses the chance to rest for the night, but we'll light a shuck and move out again if we have to. I can steer by the stars."

Eden didn't doubt that. She hoped they didn't have to travel at night, though. She needed rest, too. Her body complained constantly that she wasn't accustomed to this.

Caleb started toward her as the two outlaws he had given the job of scouting rode off to the south. She figured he was going to untie her wrists from the saddle horn and help her down from the horse, but Hannah moved smoothly between them.

"I can take care of this," she told him. "You can see to it that camp is set up properly."

Caleb frowned.

"That sounded like you were giving me an order," he said.

"No, just lettin' you know I don't need your help takin' care of the prisoner."

Caleb still didn't look happy about it, but evidently he didn't think the matter was worth an argument. He turned away to supervise the rest of the men as they tended to the horses and got a small fire burning, fed by buffalo chips.

Hannah untied the ropes, which left Eden's hands free for the first time all day. She flexed her fingers to get feeling back in them and then grasped the horn to help her dismount.

"No trees hereabouts to tie you to, so you'll have to be hog-tied tonight," Hannah said.

"Why?" Eden gestured toward the empty, desolate landscape all around them. "Where am I going to go? Even if I escaped, I'd probably starve to death out here."

"Yeah, you might," Hannah admitted. She lowered her voice so that only Eden could hear her. "And it'd be all right with me if you were gone. But I'm not gonna let you escape just to get Caleb's mind off of you. He wouldn't be happy about that. Besides, maybe he's right. Maybe havin' you around will come in handy if that posse catches up to us. So I don't plan on takin' any chances with you." Hannah put a hand on Eden's shoulder and shoved. "Go over there out of the way and sit down."

Eden had no choice but to do as she was told.

The man who had started the fire also boiled coffee, fried salt pork, and cooked biscuits. Eating the same thing for every meal was tiresome, Eden thought, but the food kept them going. She had never lived out on the trail like this. Bill had probably grown used to an existence something like this when he was a cowboy, driving cattle from Texas to the railhead. Eden didn't think she was cut out for it, though.

Darkness had begun to settle down over the prairie by the time the meal was ready. The cook put some bacon and a biscuit on a tin plate and looked around. He held the plate out to one of the other men and said, "Take this to the lady."

The man took the plate and started toward Eden. He was young and darkly handsome. She recalled hearing one of the others call him Chico. He smiled broadly at her as he came up and hunkered on his heels in front of her.

"Here you go," he said as he extended the plate to her.

"Thank you," Eden said. She could at least be polite to him. She saw the interest in his eyes as he looked at her and figured it wouldn't do any harm to play up to him a little. Somewhere along the way, she might be able to turn that to her advantage. "I really appreciate it."

"It's not much," he said. "But I suppose it's better than nothing."

"I could use a cup of coffee, too."

"I'll get one—"

That was all he got out before Caleb came up behind him and demanded angrily, "What the hell are you doing?"

Tatum knew he needed to control his temper, but when he saw that damned Chico Flynn making eyes at Eden, emotion boiled up inside him. He'd already had to put up with Hannah and her jealousy, and now he had a smooth-talking greaser moving in on Eden.

He had seen it plenty of times before, seen how Chico thought he could bend any woman to his will just by smiling at her and flirting. Most of the time he was right, too.

Of course, none of those women had been prisoners, but that didn't really change things. No doubt Chico thought he had a clear field with Eden because of the way Hannah figured she had Tatum under her thumb.

They were all about to find out different, Tatum told himself. It was a vow he intended to keep.

Chico straightened and turned to face him.

"I just brought the lady her supper, Caleb. Dave asked me to. And she wants a cup of coffee, so I figured why not?"

Tatum felt his eyes narrowing involuntarily as he said, "Is that all you figured why not about, Chico?"

"What does that mean?"

"It means I know how your mind works. You're thinking that you're going to have some fun with this woman. As you put it, why not? She's our prisoner, she can't do anything about it. And all women are just panting to have you make love to them, aren't they?"

"You got this all wrong," Chico said. "She won't be any good as a hostage if we let her starve to death or die of thirst, will she?"

"You're not fooling me for a second." Tatum looked around at the others. "None of you are. You keep your hands off this woman, you hear? Nobody touches her."

"Unless it's you, eh, amigo?" Chico drawled with an insolent smile on his face.

Tatum knew it was the wrong thing to do, but he did it anyway.

He swung his fist and planted it right in the middle of that smile.

Chapter 23

Chico probably hadn't been expecting that punch. It drove him backward off his feet. That sent him crashing down on top of Eden. She let out a startled cry as the outlaw's weight landed on her.

For a second, the butt of the revolver holstered on his hip was within her reach. She knew how to use a handgun. She could have grabbed it and opened fire on the men around her.

That would be the same thing as committing suicide. To protect themselves, the outlaws would have no choice but to return her fire. Hannah, especially, would be quick to do so, Eden knew.

Such a move would save her from the inevitable degradation she would suffer at their hands. Caleb might be able to keep them from molesting her for now, but sooner or later that would change. Either he would take her for himself, eventually tire of her, and turn her over to the other men, or he would decide not to cross Hannah and abandon her to the others right away.

Either way, she could spare herself that fate.

But it would mean giving up any chance of escape or rescue. It would mean never seeing Bill again.

In the split second those thoughts flashed through Eden's mind, she knew she couldn't do that.

Then Chico rolled off of her, and the gun was out of reach. The young outlaw might have been surprised when Caleb attacked him, but he recovered quickly. He threw himself at Caleb's knees, tackling the leader of the outlaws and bringing him down.

Hannah pointed her rifle at Eden and warned, "Don't try anything!"

Eden pressed her hands to the ground and sat up. She shook her head at Hannah, indicating that she wasn't going to try to escape.

Chico scrambled on top of Caleb and swung his fists. Caleb blocked one of the blows but the other punch landed cleanly and rocked his head to the side. Chico twisted and tried to dig his knee into Caleb's groin.

With a grunt of effort, Caleb heaved himself up off the ground and threw Chico off to the side. He rolled and kicked the younger outlaw in the belly. Chico gagged and curled up around the pain in his midsection, but only for a second. Then he struggled to his feet.

Caleb was up first and met him with a wildly swinging fist. Chico went over backward again, but as Caleb closed in on him, evidently intending to stomp him into the ground, Chico got a foot up and rammed it into Caleb's belly, returning the brutal favor from a moment earlier.

Eden had witnessed enough violence so that she didn't sit there horrified as she watched the two outlaws clash. As far as she was concerned, they could beat each other to death and it would be just fine.

Hannah continued to watch her, menacing her with the rifle. The other outlaws gathered around in a circle and yelled encouragement to the two battlers. As far as Eden could tell, most of the sentiment seemed to be on Chico's side, telling her that Caleb's hold on the gang might be more tenuous than it had first appeared.

After the kick in the belly, Caleb managed to stay on his feet, but he was too shaken to continue the fight for a few seconds. That gave Chico the time to roll away, come up on hands and knees, and then surge upright. He lunged at Caleb, who recovered just in time to meet the younger man's charge.

For a long moment they stood toe-to-toe, slugging away at each other, each man obviously more concerned with the punishment he could deal out than with the blows he was taking. Caleb finally landed a punch to Chico's solar plexus with stunning force. Chico let his guard down, and Caleb hammered a looping left to his face, following with a right uppercut that put Chico on the ground again.

This time Chico didn't even try to get up. He just lay there breathing hard and whimpering. His face was swollen, bruised, and bloody. He didn't look handsome now.

Neither did Caleb, but he wore an expression of triumph as he turned away from his defeated opponent.

"Make you feel better to beat up a boy?" Hannah asked with a sneer. "A boy who didn't do anything wrong."

Caleb dragged the back of his hand across his bleeding lips.

"He got too big for his britches," he snapped. "And that's what any man'll get who does the same."

"Don't worry, Caleb," one of the outlaws said. "We know you're the boss."

Eden wasn't sure, but she thought there might have been the faintest trace of mockery in the man's voice. Several of the others glanced at Hannah, as if they were saying that they knew who the boss was, all right . . . and it wasn't Caleb.

Caleb must have seen that, too. His face darkened. But he must have figured that there had already been enough trouble for one night, because he didn't say anything else. Instead he turned away, and a couple of the men went to help a groggy Chico to his feet.

The fight hadn't cleared the air. Tension still hung heavy in it during supper, so that later in the evening, when hoof-beats thudded in the night the sound made all the men stand up and turn toward them, hands hovering over their guns.

Judging by the sound, two riders were approaching the camp at a good clip, but they weren't galloping as they would have been if the posse was hot on their heels.

The horses came to a stop while they were still outside the circle of light cast by the fire. A man called, "Hello, the camp! It's just us."

"That's Lou," Caleb said. He raised his voice to say, "You and Andy come on in, Lou."

The two men walked their horses into the light. They seemed calm, which Eden found disappointing. If they had been upset, it would have meant that the posse was closing in.

Caleb waited until the men dismounted, then asked, "Did you find them?"

"Yeah," one of the outlaws replied. "We saw the light of their fire and got closer on foot so they wouldn't hear our horses. It looked like a posse, all right."

"How many?"

"More than a dozen," the other outlaw said. "Fifteen or sixteen, I'd guess."

"We thought about trying to cut down a few of them with our rifles," the first one said. "They wouldn't have known what hit 'em."

Eden went cold all over at the thought of a bullet screaming out of the darkness to strike Bill.

"Then we figured that it might be smarter not to let them know we were there," the second outlaw said. "They might have been able to follow us back here, and we knew you wouldn't want that."

Caleb rubbed his jaw and frowned in thought.

"I was hoping we'd lose them on the rocks," he said. "They must have managed to stay on our trail, though. How far back are they?"

"Six or seven miles." The man who had spoken nodded toward Chico, who stood off to the side wearing an angry glare on his battered face. "What the hell happened to Flynn?"

"He got too friendly with our hostage," Caleb snapped. "I had to keep him in line."

The two men who had gone on the scouting mission glanced at each other and shrugged. Eden thought they looked like they were just as glad they had missed the ruckus.

"If those damned lawmen are still that far behind us, the

chances of them catching up to us before we make it to the badlands are pretty slim," Caleb went on. "We'll keep moving fast, though, just to make sure."

Eden felt her spirits sinking at Caleb's words. She wanted to remain hopeful, but it was getting more and more difficult.

"Maybe they'll give up and go back home before they ever get that far," one of the men suggested.

"Maybe. I wouldn't count on it."

Eden couldn't speak for the other men in the posse, since she didn't know who had come with Bill, but she knew in her heart that her husband would never turn around and go back to Redemption without her. He would keep coming until he found her, no matter how far he had to go or how long it took.

If he had to come alone, though, what chance would he have against this band of ruthless killers? Maybe it would be better if he *did* give up and assume that she was lost to him. He would be safer. He could go on with his life . . .

And that would never happen, she thought. Not Bill. "Quit" wasn't in his vocabulary.

Chapter 24

Virgie hadn't snuck out of the house the previous night, but Tom didn't expect her to go two nights in a row without seeing her lover.

So he wasn't surprised when he heard the faint creak of the floorboards in the hallway as he lay in the spare bedroom, pretending to sleep.

Not wanting Virgie to hear him reacting, he remained motionless. It was possible that she *wasn't* going to leave the house, that she had gotten up for some other reason. Tom didn't believe that, but it wouldn't hurt anything to be certain of what she was doing.

Things had been chilly as always between them. He had ridden out to the ranch to work some more with the gray stallion, and she had spent the day—so she said—at her parents' house. When he'd asked her how her father was doing after the bank robbery, she had said that he was all right but still angry that he hadn't been able to go along with the posse.

The idea of dried-up old Walter Shelton riding with a posse after a bunch of outlaws was laughable to Tom. He could imagine his own father doing that, but not Virgie's.

He supposed he believed her about where she was during

the day. It would be hard for her to rendezvous with Ned Bassett in broad daylight. Somebody would be too likely to see her sneaking into his house. He might have customers calling, too. He was a watchmaker and both sold and repaired watches and clocks.

After a minute Tom sat up and noiselessly swung his legs out of bed. He hadn't undressed tonight, except for taking his boots off. He stood up and moved to the window, parting slightly the curtains that hung over it.

A shadow moved outside the house.

With his heart pounding, because a part of him—still, after all this time—hoped he was wrong, he watched. The slender figure moved through the shadows in back of the house, and Tom knew he was right.

There she went, off to meet Bassett.

Tom left by the front door, hurrying but not being careless. He didn't want his wife to know that her affair had been discovered, not just yet. He would take a different route to Bassett's house. He actually knew the streets of Redemption better than Virgie did. He had lived around here longer.

He was ensconced in the thick shadows under the tree when she ghosted past and went to the house. He held his breath, but his heart seemed to be beating so hard and so loud that he was a little surprised she didn't hear it.

His heart slugged even harder when his fingertips brushed the butt of the gun tucked into the waistband of his trousers.

It would serve them both right, he thought. He could burst into the house, catch them all tangled up with each other, and empty the revolver into them. Bassett wouldn't be able to stop him. The man probably didn't even have a gun of his own in his house.

Nobody else would do a damned thing about it, either. It was the unwritten law. A man had every right to kill an unfaithful wife and her lover.

The more he thought about it, though, the less Tom wanted to kill Virgie. He might hate her, but he still loved her at the same time. He supposed he could even forgive what she'd done, if she would just go back to the way she used to be, before she decided that she hated him.

Bassett, though . . . that son of a bitch deserved to die.

Not tonight, Tom told himself. Soon, maybe, but not tonight. And once Virgie saw the light, maybe Bassett would just slink on out of town and Tom wouldn't have to kill him at all.

Tom stood there for an hour or so that seemed more like a day. Then the back door of Bassett's house opened and Virgie snuck out, the same way he had seen her do several times in the past. She and Bassett embraced and kissed, then she started toward home.

Home, thought Tom. That was laughable. The house he shared with Virgie wasn't a home and might never be. Not unless he was able to set things right.

He waited until Virgie was gone before he approached the house. Bassett couldn't get off scot-free from what he'd done. And there was no hurry about getting back. Virgie might worry if she found that he was gone, but let her worry. Let her stew in it.

Tom knocked on the back door, not loudly but insistently enough that Bassett had to hear it.

The door swung open, and Bassett said, "What's wrong, Virginia? Did you forget—"

He stopped short as Tom raised the gun, pointed it at his face, and eared back the hammer.

"Yeah, she forgot something," Tom said. "Forgot that she had a husband, you bastard."

"Gentry! My God, man, be . . . be careful with that gun."

Bassett's voice held the accent of his eastern origins. He held his hands up as he backed away. Tom stepped into the kitchen and kept the gun trained on him.

Bassett wore a shirt and trousers but was barefooted. His brown hair was in disarray, probably from rolling around in bed with Virgie. He was handsome, in a weak way, Tom supposed. Virgie probably thought so, anyway.

"My wife's been paying you visits," Tom said. "I thought it was past time I did, too."

"Whatever you're thinking, it . . . it's wrong, Gentry," Bassett protested. "There's nothing going on between Virginia and me. We're just friends. We were acquainted in Wichita—"

"I'll just bet you were," Tom cut in. "So you knew her before I did, eh? I'll bet that's not the only thing you did before me."

"Please don't be crude. There's no need for a scene—"

Tom interrupted him again.

"What there's a need for is for me to pull this trigger and splatter your brains all over the wall."

Bassett's eyes widened with terror.

"But I'm not gonna do that," Tom went on. "I don't think a sorry son of a bitch like you is worth the price of a bullet."

He tipped the gun barrel up and lowered the hammer. Relief flooded Bassett's face.

That reaction lasted only a second. Then Tom took a swift step forward and smashed the gun across Bassett's face.

Bassett cried out in pain and went down. Blood poured from his broken nose and welled from the long cut on his cheek that the gun had opened. He clapped his hands to his face and might have screamed if Tom hadn't kicked him in the belly, driving all the air from his lungs. After that all he could do was lie there gasping.

"Stop your damn sniveling," Tom said as he loomed over the fallen man. "You deserved a lot worse, messin' around with a married woman that way. I could kill you and most folks would think I did a good thing. You better remember that. And if I was you, I'd pack up and leave Redemption, first thing in the morning."

He turned away. Behind him, Bassett mewled in pain. Disgusted by the man, Tom stalked out of the house and turned toward his own place.

He seemed to be walking in a daze. He hadn't really planned what he was going to do tonight. He hadn't actually known that he was going to confront Bassett until his steps were carrying him to the man's back door.

Now, though, he knew that he couldn't wait any longer about letting Virgie know how things were going to be. The secret was out. If he waited, Bassett would tell her that he knew about their affair, and Tom wasn't going to let that happen. He wasn't going to deprive himself of seeing the look of surprise on her lovely face.

He slammed the door as he came into the house. Virgie popped instantly out of the bedroom, showing that she was still awake. She came toward him, tying the belt of her robe around her waist and saying, "Tom? Is that you?"

He struck a match and lit the lamp in the living room.

"It's me," he said as he turned toward her. "Didn't even bother to check and see if I was still in the spare bedroom, did you, Virgie?"

Her gaze dropped to the gun he still held in his hand. Maybe she saw Ned Bassett's blood on it. Her eyes widened and she cried, "Oh, my God, Tom! What have you done?"

"Something I should have done a long time ago. You won't be havin' any more truck with Bassett." A humorless laugh came from him. "Hell, the way I left him looking, you won't *want* to have anything to do with him."

"You killed him," she said in a hushed voice.

Tom shook his head.

"No, he was alive when I left. Hurting, but that's all. It's over between the two of you, Virgie. I've seen to that. I told Bassett to get out of town."

He set the gun on the table next to the lamp.

She breathed, "You can't . . . Tom, what do you think was . . . was going on?"

"I know damned well what was going on! You want me to spell it out for you? Better yet, why don't you tell me all about it? Why don't you tell me all the things that he did to you . . . and that you did to him?"

He saw the look of cold hatred that swept over her face, along with pain as his words lashed at her.

"Why don't you just go to hell?" she snapped.

Unwanted though it was, a feeling almost of contrition came over him. He shook his head and said, "I didn't want this, Virgie. I just wanted you to love me again."

She shook her head.

"That won't ever happen."

"No, I guess it won't."

He had thought when he came in that he would beat some sense into her, but that seemed futile now. As much as he didn't want to admit it, even to himself, she loved Bassett, he supposed. And the hot rage inside him had been replaced by a cold feeling of emptiness.

He started past her, saying, "I'll get my gear and move out to the ranch in the morning."

She moved behind him. He heard a noise, the scrape of metal on wood, and some instinct warned him what she was doing. He whirled around to see that she had picked up the revolver from the table and was pointing it at him. The barrel shook as she said, "Don't look so surprised. You've got it coming."

Her finger tightened on the trigger.

Chapter 25

When nothing happened, she looked shocked. So shocked that Tom had to laugh.

"You have to cock it first," he said.

He didn't give her a chance to do that. Instead he sprang forward, his left arm coming up and around in a sweeping blow that struck her right arm and sent the gun flying from her fingers. She let out a cry.

The next instant, he buried his fist in her belly.

Tom Gentry had never hit a woman in his life, not even a whore. But what was that Virgie had just said? The words echoed in his head.

Don't look so surprised. You've got it coming.

She sure as hell did.

The pounding on the door of the marshal's office roused Mordecai from his restless sleep. He had locked the door before he turned in, but the key was still in the lock. All he had to do was go out there, turn the key, and open the door.

Easier said than done, he thought as he used his good arm to lever himself up from the cot in the storage room. His

wounded arm ached, but not too bad. The injury slowed him
down, though, as he climbed to his feet and started from the
back room into the office.

"Hold your dang horses!" he yelled to whoever was out
there hammering a fist on the door. "I'm gettin' there, I'm
gettin' there."

It occurred to him that the door pounder might be looking
for trouble. Lawmen had enemies, after all. He hadn't made
any really bad ones in the time he'd been working as Marshal
Bill Harvey's deputy, at least as far as he could remember,
but there was no telling about these things.

Getting rousted out of bed like this in the middle of the
night was nearly always bad news, Mordecai told himself.
He detoured back to the desk and slipped the revolver from
the holster and coiled shell belt he had left there.

When he reached the door, he realized he was going to
have trouble holding the gun and turning the key at the same
time. Since he only had the one good hand right now, he
called through the door, "Who in blazes is out there?"

The pounding stopped. Somebody said something, but
the voice was so thick and muffled that Mordecai couldn't
make out the words. He leaned closer to the door and asked,
"Who is it? What's the trouble?"

This time he understood when a man said, "I need help . . .
I'm hurt . . ."

More likely drunk than hurt, Mordecai thought. On the
other hand, the hombre really could be injured, and he had
promised Bill he'd look after the town. It wouldn't be fittin'
for Bill to get back to Redemption and find that Mordecai
had let somebody die on the doorstep of the marshal's office.

"All right, hold on," he grumbled. He was wearing only
his long underwear, so there wasn't really any place to put
the gun. He bent over and set it on the floor, then reached for
the key.

As he swung the door open, the man outside said, "You've
got to stop him . . . I think he's going to kill her!"

The man had been leaning against the door as he knocked
on it, and when Mordecai opened it, that threw him off bal-

ance. He stumbled toward the deputy, who thrust out his
good hand and caught the man by the shoulder.

"Whoa there!" Mordecai exclaimed as he held the man
up. "Who are you, mister? What's that you said about somebody gettin' killed?"

The man held one hand to his face. Dark smears on his
features might be blood, Mordecai thought.

"Virginia . . . Gentry." The man's voice had a peculiar
bubbling sound to it that Mordecai recognized from dozens
of fracases over the years. His nose was broken, and blood
still flowed from it like a river. "Her husband . . . I'm afraid
he's going to kill her!"

Mordecai had to think about it before he knew who the
man was talking about. Virginia Gentry was the daughter of
Walter Shelton, the hombre who had tried to shoot it out with
those robbers in the bank. She was married to . . . Mordecai
drew a blank on that.

"Settle down, settle down," he said. "What happened to
you?"

The man took his hand away from his face. Most of the
businesses along the street were closed for the night and
dark, but the saloons were open and gave off enough of a
glow that Mordecai was able to make out some of the damage to his caller's face. The fella's nose was busted, all right,
and he had an ugly gash across his left cheek. He'd been
holding it together. Now the wound sagged open grotesquely.

"Tom Gentry did this," he got out. "H-he pistol-whipped
me. Then he went after his wife."

Mordecai didn't like the sound of that. When a man went
after another man like that and the first hombre's wife was
involved, usually there'd been some sort of improper fooling
around going on.

"It ain't the law's business to get mixed up in problems
'twixt a husband and wife," he said.

"But he's going to kill her!" the man insisted. "That's
murder!"

Even that was debatable in the eyes of the law, thought
Mordecai. But on the other hand, he didn't want Bill coming

back to find that there had been an unnecessary killing while he was gone.

Mordecai recognized the name Tom Gentry, too. The fella was one of the Gentrys who had a horse ranch outside of town. Mordecai had had a run-in or two with old Burk Gentry, the patriarch of the family, and considered him to be an arrogant, high-handed troublemaker. If his son Tom was anything like him . . .

"All right, damn it," he said. "Let me get my pants on. You go in and sit down. You're hurt."

"I . . . I'll be all right. I'll come with you. I can show you where they live."

That would save time, all right, since Mordecai didn't have a clue where that was. He was familiar with the big Shelton house on the edge of town, but not where Shelton's daughter and son-in-law lived.

"What's your name, mister?"

"Bassett . . . Ned Bassett."

"Fella who repairs watches and clocks? Yeah, I know who you are. Hang on."

Mordecai picked up his gun, went back to the desk, and holstered it. He opened a drawer and found a rag, then took it over to Bassett.

"Here. Mop up some o' that blood."

Bassett took the rag and held it to his face while Mordecai retreated to the storeroom where his cot was and awkwardly climbed into his trousers. He pulled on his boots and returned to the office to buckle on the gun belt. It wasn't an easy chore to perform one-handed, but he had learned to manage.

"All right, come on," he told Bassett. "Lead the way, mister."

They moved swiftly through the darkened streets. Mordecai listened tensely for a gunshot. If Tom Gentry had pistol-whipped Bassett, that meant he was armed. He might decide to shoot his wife. Obviously that was what Bassett was afraid of.

Bassett groaned as he hurried along, still holding the now-bloody rag to his face.

"Don't go lookin' for any sympathy from me because you got hurt," Mordecai snapped. "Fella who'd mess around with another man's wife is just about the lowest form of humanity there is, far as I'm concerned."

"It's not like—" Bassett began. He broke off with a shake of his head and another moan. "It doesn't matter now. I just don't want him to kill her."

"Neither do I," Mordecai said. "How much farther is it?"

Bassett stopped and pointed to a house.

"That's it right there."

As far as Mordecai could see, no lights were burning in the house. It looked quiet and peaceful, as if the folks who lived there were sleeping.

Or dead, he thought grimly. He drew his gun and told Bassett, "All right, you stay back. I don't want you gettin' in my way."

"I'll open the gate in the fence for you."

"Well, that'd be helpful, seein' as I got this bad wing."

Bassett swung the gate open. Mordecai went through, stalked up a flagstone walk, and climbed three steps to the small front porch. He glanced over his shoulder at Bassett, who stood waiting just outside the gate.

Mordecai used the barrel of his gun to rap sharply on the door and called, "Wake up in there! Open the door! This here's the law!"

There was no response from inside. Mordecai drew back a foot and kicked the door, hard.

"Open up, I say! Tom Gentry! Open this damned door!"

Nothing.

"You have to break the door down," Bassett called from the fence. "You need to get in there right away. She may already be dead!"

"Do I look like I'm in any shape to go bustin' down doors?" Mordecai demanded irritably.

"I'll do it."

Without waiting for Mordecai to tell him it was all right, Bassett came through the gate and started up the walk toward the house.

"Dadgum it—" Mordecai stopped his protest. Maybe between the two of them, they could get the door open, he thought.

When Bassett reached the porch, the deputy went on, "Try the knob, just to make sure it ain't already open."

Bassett rattled the knob, then shook his head.

"It's locked," he said.

"All right, we'll both kick it at the same time," Mordecai said. "You ready?"

Bassett nodded.

"When the door opens, you back off, quick-like," Mordecai added. "If Gentry's in there with a gun, he's liable to shoot. I don't want no innocent bystander gettin' shot . . . although I ain't so sure how innocent you are."

"Let's worry about that later," Bassett said.

"Yeah. Get ready."

The men braced themselves as each lifted a foot and poised it. Together, they rammed their legs forward. Their boot heels crashed against the door, and with a splintering of wood as the jamb broke, it flew open.

Mordecai thrust his good arm in front of Bassett and shoved the man back. He swept his gun forward again and moved fast into the darkened house, halfway expecting to see Colt flame bloom in the shadows.

Nothing happened. Mordecai stopped a few steps into the house and listened. At first he heard only the pounding of his own pulse, but then he caught a faint whimper coming from somewhere nearby.

He needed some light. To get it meant that he would have to holster his gun, but it looked like he was going to have to take that chance. He pouched the iron and reached in his trouser pocket for the tin of matches he always carried.

Again it was awkward because he had only one hand, but he managed to fumble out one of the lucifers. A flick of his thumbnail snapped it to life.

As Mordecai lifted the match, the glare from the little flame washed over the room. He squinted against the sudden light and looked around.

The first thing he saw was a man slumped, apparently

senseless, in an armchair. Then his eyes moved down to a huddled form lying on the floor. That shape trembled, and another whimper came from it. The figure was that of a woman in a blood-splattered robe, Mordecai realized. She lifted her head.

From behind the deputy, Ned Bassett whispered, "My God. My God."

Those were Mordecai's sentiments exactly.

Chapter 26

"I thought I told you to stay outside," Mordecai croaked.

Bassett ignored that.

"Look . . . look at what he did to her." He took a step toward the man in the armchair. "That bastard!"

Mordecai had already spotted a pistol lying on a small round table next to the armchair. He got between Bassett and the man in the chair and said, "Take this match, damn it!"

He wanted his own gun in his hand again. That revolver was in easy reach of Tom Gentry, if that was who the fella in the chair was, as seemed likely.

Bassett hesitated, then took the lucifer from Mordecai. Mordecai gave him the tin with the other matches in it and ordered, "Find a lamp and get it lit."

Keeping his eyes on Gentry, he drew his gun again. The young man still hadn't moved. His eyes were open, but other than that he might as well have been unconscious. He didn't seem to be aware of what was going on around him.

Yellow light welled up as Bassett lowered the glass chimney on the lamp he had just lit.

Now that Mordecai could see better, he stared at Virginia Gentry and struggled to control the impulse he felt to blast a couple of holes in the man who had done this to her. At this moment it didn't matter to him that Tom Gentry was her husband.

Nobody had a right to do this.

The woman hadn't been pistol-whipped like Ned Bassett. Mordecai could tell that much. This damage had been done with fists.

Fists slamming savagely into Virginia Gentry's face again and again until every bit of it was swollen and smashed. Her eyes were closed, her nose and mouth were crushed and bleeding. She barely looked human.

Mordecai didn't see how she got any words out of that wreck of a mouth, but she managed to croak, "H-help . . . me . . ."

Bassett took a couple of steps toward her. That movement finally got through to Tom Gentry. His eyes flicked toward Bassett, and his stunned face contorted with rage. He started up out of the chair.

"Stay away from her!" he roared at Bassett. "This is all your fault!"

Bassett changed course. Even though he was weak and shaky from his injuries, he turned and plunged straight at Gentry, tackling him around the waist and driving him backward. Both men fell onto the armchair, which tipped back from the impact and fell over, dumping them on the floor.

"Blast it!" Mordecai yelled. "Stop that, you damned fools!"

Neither man paid any attention to him. Bassett slugged ineffectively at Gentry, but there wasn't enough power behind the blows to do any damage. Gentry seemed disoriented by the attack and wasn't fighting back yet. That saved Bassett, but only for the moment.

Gentry came to his senses and grabbed Bassett around the throat. He tightened his hold and rolled over, taking Bassett with him. As soon as Bassett was on the bottom and Gentry on top, Gentry slammed his opponent's head against the floor.

"I'll kill you the way I should have before!" Gentry howled.

Mordecai reversed his grip on the Colt, stepped in closer,

and lifted the gun. He hammered the butt down on Gentry's head. The blow made Gentry fall to the side, out cold. Maybe even dead.

Right now, Mordecai didn't much care which one.

Bassett was gasping for breath now that Gentry's hands weren't trying to choke the life out of him. His nose and the gash on his cheek were still bleeding. His whole face was a gory mess. He and Virginia Gentry were a pretty good match for each other now, Mordecai thought.

He needed help. He couldn't handle this crisis on his own. He didn't want to leave Tom Gentry here with the injured woman while he went to fetch somebody, either. If Gentry regained consciousness, there was no telling what he might do.

That left Bassett to go for help.

Mordecai holstered his gun, bent down, and got hold of Bassett's arm. With a grunt of effort, he helped the man stand up.

"You got to go down to the Prairie Queen Saloon," Mordecai told Bassett. "The bartender there, Glenn Morley, has experience patchin' up wounded folks. He can help you, and Miz Gentry needs help, too. You got to go fetch him."

"What . . . what about Gentry? He might try to . . . hurt her again."

Mordecai shook his head.

"That's why I'm stayin' here, to make sure he don't. Now go on, Bassett. I know you're in bad shape and it's askin' a lot of you, but there ain't no choice in the matter. You're the only one who can do this."

Bassett nodded, causing the loose flap of flesh on his face to move.

"Yes. I'll be back. Don't let him hurt her again."

"He ain't gonna," Mordecai promised. "I'll shoot him in the knee if I have to."

Stumbling and staggering, Bassett left the house. Mordecai hoped he made it to the saloon without collapsing.

A desk sat on one side of the room. Mordecai went over and leaned on it, feeling the exhaustion in every fiber of his being. He was injured, too, and his arm ached almost intolerably even though he'd been able to avoid using it. Just moving around as much as he had tonight made it hurt.

He could hear Tom Gentry's harsh breathing, so he knew the man was still alive. So was Gentry's wife, although she had slumped to the floor again and lay there making tiny noises of pain. The fingers of one hand flexed slowly against the floor.

Mordecai had never been married, but back in his fur-trapping days he had spent some winters with the Indians and taken a squaw for a wife as long as the cold weather lasted. He'd never laid a hand in anger on any of those gals. He had known plenty of men who swore that a fella had to beat his wife every now and then just to keep her in line, but it had always seemed to Mordecai that there were better ways.

Anyway, what Gentry had done to *his* wife went beyond that. This was the act of a crazy man. He had beaten Virginia to within an inch of her life.

What was Walter Shelton going to do when he found out what had happened to his daughter?

And how was Burkhart Gentry going to react when he heard that his son Tom was in jail?

Because the one thing Mordecai knew for sure was that Tom Gentry was going to end this night behind bars, locked up like the loco animal he obviously was.

"Dear Lord," Annabelle Hudson breathed when she followed Morley into the room and saw Virginia Gentry lying on the floor. "What did he do to her?"

"It's pretty bad," Mordecai told the woman. "Where's Bassett?"

"The man you sent to the saloon to get Glenn?" Annabelle asked. Morley was already at Virginia's side, gently turning her over so that he could see the extent of her injuries. "I have some of my girls looking after him. He insisted that he would be all right and said Glenn should come down here right away to tend to the woman. Then he passed out."

"He'd lost a lot of blood, by the looks of it," Morley said

over his shoulder, "but I think he'll be all right. I can sew up that cut on his face once I get back to the saloon and try to set his nose. I'm not sure it'll ever be the same, though."

"How about Mrs. Gentry?" Mordecai asked. He kept an eye on Tom Gentry, but the man still seemed to be unconscious.

"She hasn't bled as much," Morley said as he took hold of her jaw and carefully moved her head back and forth a little. "No telling how bad she's hurt inside, though. Anybody who gets hit in the head as many times as she obviously has, as hard as she was hit, runs a real risk of something being wrong with their brain." He spread the robe open. "From the looks of the bruises he punched her quite a few times in the belly and chest, too." Morley gave a grim shake of his head. "All I can do is clean her up, then we'll wait and see."

Mordecai nodded and said, "All right, do your best." He turned to Annabelle. "Did you bring anybody else with you?"

"Some of my customers followed us down here, of course," she said. An edge came into her voice as she went on, "People are always eager to witness any sort of tragedy as long as it doesn't involve them."

"I'd be obliged if you'd go out and get a couple of men to haul this varmint down to the jail for me."

"You're going to lock him up?"

"You're dang right I am!"

Annabelle's mouth twisted as she said, "It's my understanding that this woman is his wife."

"Yeah, so?"

"Most people believe a man has the right to do whatever he wants to his wife."

"Look," Mordecai said. "The best I can figure it from what I heard, that fella Bassett and Miz Gentry were messin' around with each other. If Gentry had come in and found 'em together like that and shot 'em both, I don't reckon anybody would've done a blasted thing about it. Ain't sayin' that's right or wrong, just the way it is. And I ain't even all that concerned about what he done to Bassett, if you want the truth. But beatin' his own wife damn near to death . . . I can't stomach that."

"But yet it would have been all right if he'd shot and killed her."

Mordecai heaved a sigh. This argument was wearing him out.

"Ma'am, are you gonna help out here or not?" he asked.

"All right. I'll go get some men." She glanced at Tom Gentry's unconscious form. "But as far as I'm concerned, you could just put a bullet in his head and save us all some trouble."

"Maybe, but that ain't gonna happen."

Annabelle left and came back a minute later with two burly townsmen who took hold of Tom Gentry by the shoulders and feet and lifted him. Mordecai drew his gun, just in case Gentry came to and tried to put up a fight, and told the men, "Take him down to the jail and put him in a cell. I'll be right behind you."

He glanced at Morley, who was using a wet cloth to clean blood off Virginia Gentry's face.

"Somebody needs to stay with her once you've done all you can for her," the deputy said.

"I'll do that," Annabelle told him. "Glenn can go back to the saloon and see if he can help that young man."

"I'm obliged to both of you," Mordecai said.

He hurried out and caught up to the men carrying Gentry.

A few minutes later, Mordecai clanged the cell door closed. Gentry shifted on the bunk inside the cell and groaned. He was starting to come around.

When he woke up, let him wonder what the hell had happened, Mordecai thought as he went out into the office and closed the cell block door. He had some wondering of his own to do, he thought as he sank wearily into the chair behind the desk.

Mainly, he wondered just how much more hell was going to break loose around here before Marshal Bill Harvey got back to Redemption.

Chapter 27

True to his word, Bill kept the posse riding like hell the rest of the day after picking up the outlaws' trail again. His hope was that they might be able to see the dust raised by the horses they pursued, or even spot the bank robbers themselves.

But the northern horizon remained mockingly empty.

While they were camped that night, Bill dozed restlessly in his blankets when it wasn't his turn to stand guard. Once, far into the night, his eyes snapped open and he sat up abruptly. He would have sworn that he'd heard the distant drumming of hoofbeats somewhere on the prairie.

"Something wrong, Marshal?" Jesse Overstreet called softly. The young cowboy was standing guard, along with one of the men from Redemption, and must have noticed Bill's movement.

Bill pushed his blankets aside and stood up. Keeping his voice low so he wouldn't disturb the other men, he asked, "Did you just hear something, Jesse?"

Overstreet shook his head.

"Nope, not really. What are you talkin' about, Marshal?"

"I thought I heard horses."

Overstreet straightened from his casual pose.

"A lot of 'em?" he asked. "Like that bunch of outlaws doublin' back to jump us?"

Bill had been aware all along that was a possibility, although it seemed more likely the gang would make a straight run for its hideout.

"No, this was more like just one or two horses," he was forced to admit. "I don't think it was the whole bunch."

"Sorry, Marshal, I didn't hear anything like that," Overstreet said.

The other guard had walked over to listen to their conversation. He said, "Neither did I, Marshal. Maybe you dreamed it."

Bill felt a surge of anger. He wasn't prone to dreaming things and then believing they were real.

But giving in to that anger wouldn't help anything, so he said, "Yeah, maybe so." He listened intently for a moment and then shook his head. "I don't hear anything now, that's for sure."

It was true. The plains were as quiet and peaceful as they could be.

Bill went back to his blankets, but his slumber was even more restless the remainder of the night. He didn't know if he had really heard riders, and even if he had, there was no way of knowing if they were part of the outlaw gang. Other people might be traveling out here.

Despite knowing that, his instincts told him what he'd heard might be important, and that was a prod that kept him awake until exhaustion finally forced him to succumb.

Bill had the members of the posse up early the next morning, and after a hurried breakfast, they set off again as soon as it was light enough to see the tracks they had been following. Bill set a fast pace again today, thinking that this might be the day they would catch up to their quarry at last.

Chico Flynn was surly the next morning after his battle with Caleb, but he didn't say anything, evidently content to keep his distance and glare in Caleb's direction every now and then.

He glanced at Eden, too, but didn't approach her.

That was somewhat disappointing. She had hoped to drive a wedge between the members of the gang. She knew that if it came to a showdown between Chico and Caleb, some of the outlaws, maybe even most of them, would support Chico.

On the other hand, Caleb seemed to be devoted to keeping her alive and relatively unharmed, even if it was only because he wanted her for himself, eventually. If he wasn't around anymore, there was no telling what the rest of the gang might do.

For one thing, Hannah would probably want to go ahead and just shoot her. It was clear that the redhead hated her.

No, as bad as it seemed on the surface, the status quo was probably preferable right now, Eden decided.

That might all change when they reached those badlands they kept talking about.

Hannah brought her half a cup of coffee and a stale biscuit for breakfast. Eden had been hog-tied the night before as Hannah had threatened. Her wrists were lashed behind her back, her ankles were tied, and a length of rope ran between wrists and ankles so that her body was bent and cramped in an awkward, uncomfortable position. She was grateful when Hannah untied her and allowed her to sit up and eat.

"Will we get to the badlands today?" she asked.

"What business is that of yours?" Hannah snapped.

"I'm just curious, that's all," Eden said with a shrug. "I've never ridden this far before. I'm tired."

"I've told you before, things ain't gonna get better for you once we're there."

"Anything will be better than bouncing in a saddle all day."

That brought a laugh from Hannah.

"I'll ask you in a week or so if you still feel that way," she said.

Eden didn't say anything else, just drank the coffee and gnawed on the hard biscuit. She was growing numb in both mind and body. She didn't know how long she could survive this ordeal.

She wasn't going to give up, though, because she knew that Bill wouldn't.

At one point during that long day, she found herself wondering just why she had so much confidence in him. True, he had stood up to the dangers facing Redemption, but she had known him less than a year. Did she really know how determined he would be to follow the outlaws and rescue her? She didn't doubt his love, but would his despair overwhelm it in the end, causing him to abandon the chase?

She wouldn't allow herself to think that. She just couldn't.

Sometime during the afternoon, she realized that something lay ahead of them on the horizon. For days now she had seen nothing but the endless prairie around them and had grown so accustomed to that monotony that at first she didn't even notice anything different.

But when she did, it was shocking. The thing, whatever it was, jutted up in sharp contrast to the plains surrounding it.

"What in the world?" she muttered under her breath.

Hannah, riding beside her, must have heard the startled question.

"Castle Rock," the redhead said. "Ever see anything like it?"

Eden hadn't.

It was a huge rock formation, reared up from the surrounding plains by some geologic upheaval in ages past, and as a matter of fact, it did look a little like the sort of storybook castles Eden had seen pictures of. Four thick, towering stone spires were crowded together at their bases as they rose from the prairie. The formation gleamed a grayish white in the sun.

"There's a lot of chalk in the rock," Hannah said. "That's what gives it that color."

Castle Rock itself wasn't the only thing different, Eden realized. Beyond it lay a dark line rising from the prairie, and as the riders came closer she began to be able to make out details. The line was actually a series of jagged, rocky ridges that rose a hundred feet or more from the plains, extending to the south like gnarled fingers and forming a twisting maze of canyons.

"Those are the badlands," she said.

"Yeah," Hannah said. "The Castle Rock badlands, because

of the rock standin' there like a sentinel in front of 'em." The woman went on in smug satisfaction, "I told you, it'd take an army to get us out of there."

Looking at the badlands now, Eden saw that Hannah was right. She felt her heart sinking. Bill didn't know this country. He might not even be able to find her in that maze, let alone rescue her from the outlaws. For the first time since being carried out of Redemption as a prisoner, she felt hope slipping away from her. Out here on the plains, she might have stood a chance in a running fight between the outlaws and the posse . . .

But now it seemed there was no chance for her to escape her fate, whatever that might be.

Tatum reined to a halt in the shade of the huge rock formation and the others did likewise. He turned in his saddle to look at his men and said, "All right. Dave, Roy, you're the best rifle shots. You know what to do."

The men nodded and dismounted.

Eden asked, "What are they going to do?"

Tatum smiled at her. Her face was gray with fatigue and hopelessness, but she would come around once she realized she might as well make the best of the situation, he told himself.

"They're going to take their rifles and climb up to the top of the rock," he explained. "From up there they'll be able to see for ten miles or more. If that posse is still on our trail, Dave and Roy will see them coming."

"So they can signal you?"

"Well . . . it won't work exactly like that."

Tatum saw the young woman's eyes widen as she realized what he was talking about. She said, "Oh, my God. You wouldn't—"

"That gap there is the best approach to the badlands," Tatum went on, pointing. "But nobody can get to it without riding right past Castle Rock. And nobody can ride past Castle Rock as long as my men are up there with plenty of ammunition." Tatum shrugged. "Of course, it probably won't come to that. Dave and Roy will let them get close before opening fire. That posse won't know they're up there. It'll be like target practice for them."

"You . . . you . . ." Clearly she was struggling to find something bad enough to call him.

"Careful now," Tatum warned with a smile. "You may not realize it, but I'm just about the only friend you've got." He lifted himself in the stirrups to ease his muscles, then waved the others forward. "Come on. We can make the hideout by nightfall."

Chapter 28

Bill hauled back on the reins and brought his horse to a stop. Beside him, Josiah Hartnett did likewise. Behind them, Jesse Overstreet and the rest of the posse followed suit.

Crossing his hands on the saddle horn and leaning forward to peer into the distance, Bill asked, "What the devil is that?"

"Got to be Castle Rock," Hartnett answered with a smile. "I've never laid eyes on it myself until now, but I've heard about it. I don't know what else a thing like that could be, out here in the middle of nowhere."

Neither did Bill. He had heard that there were some pretty spectacular rock formations out in west Texas, but he had never seen them. In the part of Texas where he had grown up, there were some good-sized hills here and there, but the countryside was mostly flat and grassy, much like Kansas in the area around Redemption.

"That'd be the badlands on the other side of those rocks?" he asked Hartnett.

"Yep. It's pretty rugged country. Folks don't think of there being anything like that in Kansas."

Bill certainly wouldn't have, if he hadn't been forced to chase those outlaws up here. It made sense that they would choose the most rugged terrain they could find for their hideout.

Overstreet brought his horse up alongside Bill's mount and said, "Looks like the tracks run straight at that thing."

"Yeah," Bill agreed.

"You don't reckon they're hidin' behind it, waitin' to jump us, do you?"

Bill frowned in thought and looked over at Hartnett.

"Is it big enough for that?"

"Like I told you, I've never been here, either," the livery-man replied. "And from this distance, it's hard to tell exactly how big it really is."

"Maybe we should swing wide around it."

"We could do that," Hartnett said, "but the way it looks from here, the gap leading into the badlands is right behind it, so we'd just have to come back."

Bill studied the layout for a moment and then nodded.

"You're right," he said. "But I don't like the idea of ridin' right past it without doing some scouting first. The rest of you stay here. I'll ride on ahead and see if the way is clear."

"You mean ride right into an ambush if there is one?" Hartnett asked. "I don't think that's a good idea."

"You got a better one?"

"I do," Overstreet said. "Let me go."

"I don't know—" Bill began.

"Didn't we have this talk before, Marshal? You're in charge of this posse, and in charge of law and order for a whole town as well. I'm just a shiftless cowboy. If I get killed, the posse can still go on." Overstreet grinned. "And you'll know for sure that it's a trap, won't you?"

"I won't ask any man to do something I won't," Bill insisted.

Overstreet pulled his horse to the side, snatched his hat off his head, and said, "You ain't askin' me, I'm volunteerin'!"

With that, he slapped his horse on the rump with his hat and sent the animal lunging forward into a gallop.

Bill bit back a curse.

"Not very good about followin' orders, is he?" Hartnett said.

"Texans usually aren't," Bill said. "Come on. We'll close up behind him. Those rocks are at least a mile off. We can stay out of easy rifle range and maybe still be close enough to give him a hand if he gets in trouble."

The posse rode toward Castle Rock at a slower pace. Overstreet steadily drew out farther in front of them. Bill didn't watch the young cowboy. He knew what Overstreet was going to do.

He kept his eyes on the rock formation instead, searching for any sign of an ambush.

That alertness was why he saw something: a flash of color, a glint of late afternoon sunlight on something shiny and metallic. The spires that formed Castle Rock were a dull, chalky grayish white. The sun wouldn't be reflecting on them.

Bill threw up a hand in a signal to stop and then reached for his rifle as his horse skidded to a halt.

"What is it?" Hartnett asked.

"The spire in the center," Bill said. "There's somebody up there!"

Moving quickly, he pulled his rifle from the saddle boot, worked the lever, and lifted it to his shoulder. The posse was still half a mile, maybe a little farther from Castle Rock, but Jesse Overstreet was closer, well within rifle range. Bill raised the barrel of his Henry, angling it up in hopes of gaining more distance.

He saw a puff of smoke from the center spire.

Overstreet toppled off his horse.

Bill pulled the trigger.

With a whipcrack report, the rifle kicked back hard against his shoulder. He worked the lever again and called to Hartnett and the rest of the men, "Open fire on that rock in the center!"

The men spread out and did so, sending a rain of .44-caliber rounds toward Castle Rock. Bill figured most of the bullets fell short, but some of them might carry that far. Mainly he was just trying to distract the men who had waited in ambush up there, maybe make them duck their heads and hold their own fire for a few minutes.

He cranked off several more rounds as fast as he could jack the rifle's lever and squeeze the trigger, then rammed the Henry back in its sheath.

"Keep pourin' it on 'em!" he told Hartnett. "Advance and fire!"

"What are you going to do?" Hartnett asked over the roar of gunfire.

"See if Jesse's still alive!"

Bill kicked his horse into a run.

He leaned forward in the saddle, holding the reins with one hand while he pressed his hat to his head with the other to keep it from flying off. Overstreet had landed in some tall grass, so Bill couldn't see him anymore, but he knew about where the young cowboy had fallen. Overstreet's horse, obviously badly spooked, had galloped off in the other direction.

Bill glanced up at the rock formations as he rode. He didn't see any more gunsmoke rising from the one in the center, but that didn't mean anything. The bushwhackers could still be firing down at him. But he hadn't felt or heard any bullets, so he didn't swerve from his course.

Suddenly, as he neared the spot where Overstreet had pitched from the saddle, an arm thrust up from the grass and waved. Bill veered his mount closer. Overstreet leaped up and ran to meet him. Judging by the way he was moving, he didn't seem to be hurt too badly.

Dirt jumped in the air as bullets struck the ground just behind the running man. The bushwhackers were still alive up there.

Bill slowed his horse and reached down as Overstreet reached up. The two men clasped wrists. Bill hauled up as hard as he could, swinging Overstreet onto the horse behind him.

After that he didn't hesitate. Turning around and trying to rejoin the posse was just about the worst thing he could do. So instead he sent the horse pounding hard toward the base of the massive spires.

"That's good thinkin'!" Overstreet yelled as he hung on

for dear life. "We get close enough and they won't be able to fire down on us!"

That was the way Bill saw it, too.

It took only a couple of minutes for them to cover the rest of the distance to Castle Rock, but those were a long two minutes to Bill, never knowing from one second to the next when a bullet might smash into him, end his life, and end any chance he had of rescuing Eden. All he could do was keep going, though.

Keep going and hope.

When they reached the base of the spires, Bill reined in and dropped out of the saddle, pulling his rifle out again as he did so. Overstreet slid down from the horse and joined him. They crouched next to the chalky rock face that rose almost straight up.

"How'd they get up there?" Overstreet exclaimed. "They must've flown like damn buzzards!"

Bill figured the rock had to be rough enough in places that a man could climb it with a rifle slung on his back. He put that matter aside and asked Overstreet, "How bad are you hit?"

"I'm not hit," the cowboy replied.

"How come you fell off your horse, then?"

"I didn't fall, I jumped! Those fellas had the range and the elevation on me. I knew if I stayed on my horse they'd be able to pick me off. There's no real cover out there for a man on horseback. So I jumped off and got down in that grass where they couldn't see me anymore."

That was pretty smart, thought Bill, and he was glad that Overstreet wasn't wounded. But they had other problems now. He waved his rifle over his head to let the other members of the posse know they were all right and then motioned for them to back off and spread out.

Hartnett must have understood what Bill meant. The men peeled back, splitting up as they did so. They turned and raced away from Castle Rock, not stopping until they were out of easy rifle range again.

"If we'd just ridden up bold as brass, they would have shot

half of us out of the saddle before we knew what was happening," Bill said.

"I'm surprised they didn't wait until I was closer so they could be sure of drillin' me, anyway," Overstreet said.

"They might have if I hadn't spotted the sun reflecting off a rifle barrel or something else up there. When they saw me pull out this Henry of mine, they knew we weren't gonna waltz right into their ambush. That's when they opened fire on you."

"They came mighty close," Overstreet said with his easy grin. "I swear I heard a bullet whistle past each ear at the same time. That's why I think there are two of 'em up there."

Bill tilted his head to look up.

"As long as they're up there, the posse can't get past," he said.

"But as long as we're down here, the bushwhackers can't get away."

"That's right."

"Then it looks like we got us a Mexican standoff."

That was true, Bill thought, but it meant something else as well.

While the posse was stuck here, the rest of the outlaws were getting farther into the badlands . . . and taking Eden with them.

Chapter 29

A few more scattered shots rang out from the top of the spire, then silence fell over the prairie except for some fading echoes.

"They figured out they're just wastin' ammunition," Overstreet said.

"Yeah," Bill agreed. He was still studying the rock formation that towered above him.

Overstreet frowned and said, "You're not thinkin' about climbin' that damn thing, are you?"

"They got up there somehow."

"Yeah, but I'll bet by now one of them's coverin' their horses and the place they climbed up, just in case we decided to do it, too. We wouldn't have a chance in hell, Marshal."

"I know. I never was much of one for climbing, anyway. I'd rather wait and let them climb down."

"Why would they do that? Then *we* could pick *them* off without any trouble."

"That's right. They won't budge from up there unless they think we're gone."

"Why would they think that?"

Bill glanced at the sky and said, "Because as soon as it starts to get dark, we're lightin' a shuck out of here."

"You mean we're givin' up?" Overstreet sounded like he couldn't believe that.

"No, but that's what I want them to think." The plan continued to form in Bill's head. He put it into words because that helped him think it through. "When it's too dark for good shooting but still light enough that they can see a little, we're going to head back to the posse, riding double on my horse. They'll probably take some shots at us, but I'm countin' on the poor light to make them miss."

"That's a pretty big gamble," Overstreet said.

"I know, but it's the best I can come up with."

"So we go back to the posse—"

"No, you go back to the posse," Bill said.

"But you just said—"

"We'll leave together, but when we get a few hundred yards out, where they won't be able to see us, I'll drop off the horse. Then I'll use the grass and the darkness to cover me while I crawl back here. You'll go on, riding hard so they can hear you the whole way, and join up again with Josiah and the rest of the posse."

"You don't think they'll suspect something like that?" Overstreet asked.

"Not if they see both of us riding out and the horse never slows down."

"So you're gonna risk breakin' your neck when you jump off, too."

"That's what you did earlier, and you survived."

"Yeah, but I'm too damn dumb to get killed that way. That's why they call it dumb luck."

"Maybe I'll have some dumb luck on my side," Bill said.

Overstreet thought it over for a moment, then said, "You're the boss, Marshal, so I reckon you're callin' the shots. Say that you don't break your neck and you're able to get back here without them knowin' about it. Then what?"

"Then I wait for them to come down and ride off. Or try to, anyway."

"What if they've got enough food and water to stay up there for days and keep us pinned down?"

"Then I'm no worse off than I am right now. Besides, you're gonna tell Josiah that I said for the whole bunch of you to pull back a couple of miles and make camp. Build a good-sized fire. I want them to see you."

"You want them to think we're all pullin' out."

"That's the idea," Bill said. "The way I see it, there are two ways of lookin' at this. It could be that those fellas are supposed to stay up there and keep us pinned down for days. But it's possible they were just supposed to do as much damage as they could and slow us down, then light out for wherever the rest of the gang is holed up. That's what I'm hoping. For one thing, I don't think it's too likely they'd want to be separated from their share of the loot for that long, and I can't see them carrying it with them to the top of this damned rock."

Overstreet rubbed his chin in thought and shrugged.

"You might be right about that, Marshal. I got to admit, it makes sense. If they think we're all sittin' out there two or three miles away on the prairie, they'll have plenty of time to climb down and get away."

"And when they do, I'll be waitin' for 'em," Bill said.

"The only problem with that notion is that there's at least two of them and only one of you."

Bill nodded and said, "Yeah, but I'll have surprise on my side. I'll get the drop on them. If I do, I'll fire three shots, spaced out a little, as a signal for the rest of you to come on in."

"And if they kill you?"

"Then it'll be up to Josiah . . . and you . . . and the rest of those men to keep on after them, recover that money, and rescue my wife."

"We'll do it, Marshal," Overstreet vowed. "I know you don't have much reason to believe me, but shoot, after the hell I raised back in Redemption, not many lawmen would've even let me come along on a posse like this. I appreciate you havin' a little faith in me."

"You haven't done anything not to deserve it so far," Bill

pointed out. "Other than bein' a little reckless and foolhardy now and then."

Overstreet grinned and said, "Well, hell, that comes natural to us Texans, don't it?"

Bill sure couldn't argue with that.

The posse had drawn back well out of rifle range. From time to time Bill caught a glimpse of one of them. They were probably wondering what was going to happen next.

They would find out when the time came, he thought as he looked at the sky again. The sun had lowered close to the western horizon. A few high, wispy clouds hovered like rose-colored streamers in the pale blue sky. Another hour and true darkness would begin to settle over the landscape.

The timing of the plan was crucial. Bill wanted to catch that moment—what was the word for it? the gloaming?—when the last light of day made it too dark for accurate shooting but bright enough that the bushwhackers would be able to see that both he and Overstreet were on the horse.

Bill was glad his horse hadn't bolted when they reached Castle Rock. The plan couldn't have worked without the animal. He held on to the reins and stroked the horse's neck as they waited.

Hunkered against the base of the spire, Overstreet asked, "What made you decide to settle down in Redemption, Marshal? I can't imagine bein' tied down so I couldn't drift on whenever the notion struck me. No offense."

Bill smiled faintly.

"None taken," he said. "A year ago, I'd have said that I felt the same way, Jesse. I'd been on my own for a while, cowboyin', trailin' cattle up to the railhead, and I didn't see how anybody would want to do anything else. Sure, it's hard work, but a fella who does it is free."

"Damn right," Overstreet nodded.

"Yep, free to eat dust and burn in the sun and freeze in the rain and try to stay out of the way of proddy steers that want to trample him. Free to drink rotgut until you puke in an alley behind a saloon and then give what few coins you've left to some gal who doesn't give a damn about you and just wants you to get finished so she can move on to the next poor cowboy."

"Well, hell," Overstreet said, "when you put it like that it don't sound all that good! What about seein' new country and wakin' up every mornin' not knowin' what's gonna happen that day? What about the way the air smells and the sky looks after a prairie thunderstorm? What about the pards you make who'll never let you down, come hell or high water?"

"There's all that to consider, too," Bill allowed. "Your life, my life, they're more alike than they are different, a mix of good and bad and things you never expect. If I hadn't gotten gored in the leg and landed in Redemption, I'd have gone on cowboyin' and never known the difference." He paused. "But that *did* happen, and I have made a difference, I think. I'm not braggin', but if I hadn't been there, there's a good chance Redemption might've been wiped out, either by outlaws or Indians. There are folks alive today who probably wouldn't be if I hadn't been around to rally the townspeople into fightin' for themselves and their families. I'm not saying that I saved each and every one of those folks, not hardly, but me bein' there helped. I figured out that's worth something to me."

Overstreet had listened quietly. Now he said, "I realize I ain't known you for long, Marshal, but I think that's the most words I ever heard you speak at one time."

"Yeah, well, that was my one and only speech," Bill told him with a grin. "Don't expect to hear another one."

"What you say makes sense, I reckon, but you left out one thing."

"What's that?"

"You got to marry a mighty pretty girl, too."

Bill laughed.

"That's true. But I didn't know you'd ever seen my wife."

"Oh, I haven't," Overstreet said. "I'm just goin' by how bound and determined you are to get her back. She must be mighty special."

"She is," Bill said. "You'll get to meet her before this is over."

"It'll be my honor, Marshal."

"Jesse, one more thing . . . why don't you call me Bill? I've never been one for standin' on ceremony and worrying about titles and such."

"Why, sure, Bill," Overstreet said with a grin.

A short time later, the sun slipped below the horizon. Bill felt himself growing more tense. He hadn't heard a sound from the top of the spire for quite a while now, but he knew the outlaws were still up there. They had to be. They couldn't have climbed down and ridden off without Bill and Overstreet hearing the horses.

Now that time was short, the waiting grew even harder. The glow faded from the western sky, and in the east the heavens shaded from dark blue to purple. As Bill looked out over the prairie, the occasional clumps of brush grew indistinct with the dwindling light.

Finally, he followed his instincts and said, "Mount up, Jesse. It's time to go."

Chapter 30

Overstreet climbed into the saddle, then extended a hand for Bill to grasp. Bill swung up behind the cowboy. He looped his left arm around Overstreet's waist and held the Henry in his right hand.

"Remember, don't slow down," he said. "Keep the horse at a gallop. When I think we're far enough away, I'll drop off."

"Good luck, Marshal. I mean, Bill."

"Thanks." Bill smiled in the gathering darkness. "I reckon I'll need it."

Overstreet dug his heels into the horse's flanks and sent the animal lunging forward. Both he and Bill leaned forward to make themselves smaller targets.

As they rode straight out, away from the rock formation, one of the outlaws shouted to the other. Shots blasted from the center spire. Bill heard a bullet whine through the air fairly close to them, then another.

His gamble was paying off, though. In the poor light, the bushwhackers were trying to draw a bead on him and Overstreet, but they couldn't quite do it. Fifty yards passed under the horse's racing hooves, then a hundred. The outlaws continued firing, but none of the shots came close enough for Bill to hear the bullet's song.

The shooting stopped when they were a couple of hundred yards from Castle Rock. By then the outlaws had figured out that they were just wasting shells. Overstreet kept the horse moving at the same pace, though. The rapid drumming of its hoofbeats filled the evening air.

Bill waited until they had covered another hundred yards. Then he said in Overstreet's ear, "Don't forget to tell Josiah what I told you!"

"I—"

That was all of Overstreet's response that Bill heard. He let go and pushed himself off the horse, throwing himself to the side and twisting in the air so he would land on his shoulder and roll. That was the plan, anyway.

Bill crashed to the earth with such force that the rifle was jolted out of his hand, despite his best intention to hang on to it. His momentum carried him over and over, so many times that he couldn't have counted the rolls even if he'd tried. When he finally came to a stop he was gasping for breath because the collision with the ground had knocked all the air out of his body, too.

He lay there for a long moment, half stunned and unable to do anything except try to drag breath back into his lungs. He heard the continued swift rataplan of hoofbeats as Overstreet galloped away into the shadows. The men on the rock spire could probably still hear that, but Bill was confident they hadn't been able to see him dive off the horse. Gloom lay thick on the prairie now.

He moved his arms and legs, gratified to discover that they seemed to be working all right. He hadn't broken his neck or anything else in the fall. The only real damage he had suffered were bruises and some scratches on his hands and face from rolling through the low brush. His bad leg ached, but that was nothing new.

Now he had to find his rifle and get back to Castle Rock.

Easily ignoring the small pains, he crawled back toward the place he thought he had landed. The Henry ought to be somewhere around there, he thought. He had trouble finding it, though, and that frustrated and irritated him as he continued to search. He had to make it back to the rock before the outlaws climbed down and got away. His plan depended on it.

A minute or so later, as he ran his hands over the ground, he touched the rifle's barrel. A feeling of relief went through him as he ran his hand down the barrel to the breech and gripped it.

Now that he was fully armed again, he started toward Castle Rock. He stayed low, on his belly. That made for slow going, but at least he made steady progress. Even in the fading light he could see the towering rock formation because it was lighter in color than the landscape around it.

His hope was that the outlaws wouldn't climb down and head for the hideout right away. They would wait until they were sure the posse was withdrawing, he told himself. But the uncertainty he felt made him move a little faster. He had to suppress the impulse to get up and run toward the rocks. Movement like that would give him away faster than anything.

As he crawled, he listened for the sound of horses moving away. He had known all along that the outlaws had to have their mounts tied on the other side of the formation. Earlier in the day he had considered sneaking around there and running off the horses, trapping the two outlaws on top of the spire.

Ultimately he had decided that wouldn't do any good. He had no way of knowing how much food and water the men had up there. They might be able to stay for days, and Bill didn't have that much time to waste. It was too big a risk.

Better to try to draw them down off the fortresslike formation, he had decided. He had a use for them, but only if they were down here on the ground where he could get to them.

He didn't hear anything, which was good. He had almost reached the rocks when a glowing spark fell out of the sky and landed in front of him, startling him into catching his breath.

It was the butt of a quirley one of the outlaws had tossed off the top of the spire, he realized. That was proof they were still up there.

The question now was how long they were going to stay up there.

Bill couldn't answer that. All he could do was wait and see. He started crawling again, going around the still-glowing cigarette butt, and a few minutes later reached the base of the towering spires.

Bill rolled against the rock and lay there for several moments, resting and gathering his thoughts. He knew that where he was now, the outlaws couldn't see him, so he climbed to his feet and leaned against the chalky stone wall.

While he was waiting there, he saw a small orange glow on the prairie. As it grew larger, he knew it had to be the campfire he had told Overstreet to have Josiah Hartnett and the other men build. If Bill could see it, he knew the men on top of the spire could, too. They had a better view of it than he did and could estimate that it was several miles away.

Now to see how they would react, he thought.

A moment later he heard voices. He couldn't make out the words, but they were having quite a discussion up there. Bill figured they were talking about whether to go ahead and pull out now that the posse had retreated and the ambush had failed.

On the chance that they would, Bill knew he had to get around on the other side of Castle Rock where the horses had to be.

As silently as possible, he began working his way around the formation toward the other side. He stuck close to the rock. When he reached the last spire, he slid along its base and held the rifle ready in both hands as he followed the curve of the formation.

The last of the sunlight was gone now. The sky was black from horizon to horizon, but millions of stars dotted the blackness and cast a faint silvery illumination down on the earth. In that dim light, Bill made out two dark shapes that had to be the horses.

More important, he heard a rock clatter down the spire. Tilting his head back, he looked up and saw another shape, this one man-sized, moving against the lighter face of the rock.

"Careful," the other man said from the top of the spire.

"I know what I'm doin'."

He was moving down too quickly to be descending by way of handholds and footholds, Bill realized. Those outlaws were canny. Sometime in the past, a man had climbed to the top of the spire with a rope and attached it somehow, so they could get up and down easier. Even with a rope, the descent had to be nerve-wracking, and a man would still have to be pretty careful.

Clearly they didn't trust the rope to take the weight of more than one man at a time, because the second man didn't start down until the first one was on the ground. Bill knew there were only two outlaws because he could see two horses.

With his back pressed against the rock, just around the curve of the spire, he waited while the second man climbed down as well. The outlaw heaved an audible sigh of relief when his boots were on the ground again.

"I don't know about you," he said to his companion, "but I'd be happy if Caleb never sent me up on that damn rock again."

Caleb, Bill thought. That had to be the leader of the gang. Bill wondered if this Caleb was the man who had grabbed Eden off the street.

The other man laughed and said, "It's your own damned fault for bein' such a good shot with a rifle."

The second man let out a disgusted snort.

"You wouldn't know it by what we accomplished today. I can't believe we didn't kill a damned one of those possemen."

"Don't worry about it. I don't believe they're really turnin' tail, so you may get another chance at 'em."

"I doubt it. They'll never find the hideout."

Bill stepped around the rock, brought the rifle smoothly to his shoulder, and said, "How about if I give you another chance right now?"

Chapter 31

He didn't wait for the men to react, although in his anger he hadn't been able to keep from throwing out that challenge. His finger squeezed the trigger as soon as the last word was out of his mouth. He kept firing, aiming low and shooting fast as he worked the Henry's lever. Muzzle flashes lit up the face of the rock formation.

The hail of lead tore through the legs of the outlaws as they tried to turn and claw the guns from their holsters. Bill didn't give them a chance. He shot their legs right out from under them, his bullets ripping through flesh and smashing bones. Screaming, both men pitched to the ground.

Bill held his fire and rushed forward. One of the men tried to stand up and thrust a pistol toward Bill. Still moving fast, Bill used the Henry's barrel to knock the gun out of the man's hand and then backhanded him on the side of the head with it.

The other outlaw howled in pain, but he managed to get his gun out, too. Bill twisted away as the gun roared. He thought he felt the slug pluck at the side of his shirt, but that could have been his imagination.

He didn't have time to be fancy, so before the man could squeeze off a second shot, Bill finished swinging the Henry around and fired it one-handed. The muzzle was so close to the man's chest that sparks from the shot landed on his shirt and started it smoldering as the bullet drove him back to the ground.

Firing a rifle one-handed like that was a good way to break a wrist, or at least sprain it, but Bill hadn't had any choice. And at point-blank range like that, accuracy didn't matter a whole hell of a lot, either. The outlaw was down and out of the fight, and that was all Bill cared about at the moment.

Another worry reasserted itself a second later. He whirled toward the first man and then backed off so he could cover both of them. He had no way of knowing how badly wounded the first man was. The outlaw might bleed to death, and Bill couldn't have that. He moved around so that the first man lay between him and the body of the second one, then approached carefully. He set the rifle aside and drew his Colt as he knelt beside the outlaw.

Bill found a pulse in the man's neck and felt relief at that. In the middle of a desperate fight like that, it was usually easier to kill a man than it was to wound him and take him alive. He picked up the pistol and rifle the man had dropped and slung both of them well out of reach, then rolled the man onto his back. He was still out cold.

Both pants legs were dark with blood. Bill holstered his gun and drew his knife from its sheath. He cut strips from the man's shirt and tied them around his upper thighs, pulling them as tight as he could. That would slow down the bleeding, anyway, and maybe keep the man alive for a while.

A while might be all he needed, Bill thought.

He rolled the senseless outlaw onto his belly and cut another strip from the man's shirt, then used it to tie the man's hands behind his back. Once that was done, he cautiously checked on the second outlaw and found that the man was dead, just as Bill had thought he would be.

With those grim chores taken care of, Bill picked up his rifle again and fired three evenly spaced shots into the air. He was pretty sure Hartnett, Overstreet, and the other members of the posse had started in this direction as soon as they heard all the shooting, but that signal would tell them that he was all right and it was safe for them to come on in.

By the time the posse rode up with a flurry of hoofbeats, Bill had dragged the unconscious outlaw over to the rock and propped him up against it.

"Bill, are you all right?" Hartnett asked anxiously.

"Fine, Josiah." Bill didn't waste any time on explanations or platitudes. He said, "I need some light. Somebody gather up some brush and make a torch out of it."

One of the men came up a moment later and lit the make-shift torch with a lucifer. By the light of the flames, Bill knelt and cut away the outlaw's trousers to examine his wounds. It looked like the man's left thigh bone was broken, but his right thigh was just badly grazed. All the bullet holes were still oozing blood, but it wasn't flowing freely anymore.

"That fella looks like he's half dead," Hartnett said.

"Half is fine as long as he doesn't up and die the rest of the way," Bill said.

"I don't savvy," Overstreet said. "Why do you care if this varmint lives or dies?"

Bill glanced up and said, "Because he's got to live long enough to tell us how to find the hole where the rest of 'em are hiding."

Night had fallen by the time the outlaws reached their hide-out. Gloom had closed in almost as soon as they entered the sharp-ridged canyons with their prisoner, and as the sun set, darkness clamped down hard and fast on the rugged terrain. Eden couldn't even see where she was going, but it didn't matter because her captors seemed to know, and one of them led her horse.

They entered a narrow defile where the shadows were even thicker, so thick that moving forward was almost like pushing through black fog. Eden couldn't see the rock walls on either side of her, but she could sense them. She thought that if her hands were free, she could have reached out and touched both of them. The outlaws were riding single file now. The trail through these badlands was too narrow to do anything else.

Hannah rode right behind her. The redhead laughed and said, "You'd never find your way out of here even if you got loose now. And these rocks are sharp. They'd cut your shoes to ribbons and slice the flesh off your feet right down to the bone!"

"I'm not going anywhere," Eden said quietly.

"Damned right you're not."

After what seemed like an hour or more of riding through that slash in the earth, the path opened up abruptly. Eden could see more than a slice of starlit sky again. They had come out into a bowl shaped like an irregular circle. It was about two hundred yards across at its widest point. The rough walls surrounding it were steep enough that while a man could probably climb them, a horse couldn't.

The starlight was bright enough that Eden could also see several crude cabins with stone walls. Nearby was something that might be a brush corral; she couldn't be sure about that.

"We'll stand our usual guard shifts," Caleb said as he reined to a halt in front of the largest cabin. It figured that one would be his, Eden thought. He went on, "Hannah, bring the prisoner in."

"You're gonna keep her in there with us?" Hannah demanded, not bothering to hide her irritation.

"That's right. I want her where I can keep an eye on her."

Hannah snorted and said, "You want to keep something else on her. You're not foolin' me, Caleb Tatum."

So that was his full name. Caleb Tatum. Eden had never heard of him. Maybe she should have, she told herself. Maybe as a lawman's wife, she ought to keep up with such things as wanted bandits.

Caleb dismounted and snapped, "Just take her inside."

"And put her in your bunk?"

For a second Eden thought Tatum was going to answer in the affirmative. But then he said, "You know better than that. Make a pallet on the floor for her, and see to it that she's tied so she can't get away."

That didn't sound appealing, but right now Eden was going to be grateful for any small favor she could get, like another night without being molested. That run of good luck was probably coming to an end soon, but any respite was better than none.

Tatum's head came up sharply as the sound of distant gunshots drifted into the bowl. On their way deeper into these badlands, they had heard scattered shots several times, as well as one prolonged volley. Every shot Eden heard sent pain jabbing into her heart, because she knew the outlaws who'd been left behind at Castle Rock were engaged in battle with the posse. Bill might have been killed already . . .

She didn't believe that, though. She was confident that if he died, she would know it, even at a distance of several miles. And every instinct in her body told her that he was still alive.

Now, after the shooting had been over for a while, suddenly there was another flurry of gunfire, and Eden had no idea what that might mean. It probably wasn't anything good for her, though.

Tatum laughed and said, "That posse probably tried to slip past our boys in the dark. I reckon they found out that can't be done. There's enough starlight that they can see everything from the top of Castle Rock."

Hannah untied Eden's hands from the saddle horn and hauled her down from the horse. Eden didn't put up a fight. She still refused to believe that Bill was dead, but this new outbreak of gunshots didn't bode well.

Hannah prodded her in the back with the rifle barrel.

"Get in there," the redhead ordered. "It's been a long ride, and I'm tired, damn it. I want some shut-eye, and the sooner I got you trussed up like a pig on its way to market, the sooner I can get it!"

Chapter 32

Bill held the flask to the wounded outlaw's mouth and forced some whiskey between his lips. The man gagged and coughed, but he swallowed some of the fiery liquor, too, and it roused him from his stupor. He lifted his head and looked around, blinking bleary eyes against the glare from another torch made from dry brush.

His eyes widened as they fastened on the blade of the knife Bill held right in front of his face. Torchlight flickered red on the steel.

"That was my wife you sons of bitches carried off from Redemption," Bill said.

The outlaw pressed his head back against the rock as if trying to get it farther away from the knife, but there was nowhere for him to go. He swallowed hard, licked his lips, but didn't say anything. His gaze flicked from side to side. He seemed to be looking for some reason to hope, but if so, he didn't find it in the grim expressions of the men gathered around him.

"What's your name?" Bill asked softly. The hard planes of his face reflected the torchlight almost as much as the knife blade.

"M-my name?" the outlaw husked.

"That's right."

"It's D-Dave. Dave Belton." A moan escaped the man's lips. "You shot the hell out of me! My legs are ruined."

"Well, Dave, that won't be the only thing ruined if you don't tell me what I want to know."

Bill lowered the knife away from Belton's face. The man tried to look down and follow the blade's motion, but Bill used his other hand to grip the outlaw's chin and wrench his head back up.

"Better if you don't look," Bill told him. "That way maybe it won't hurt as much when I start carvin' on you."

"Look, mister, I . . . I," the prisoner babbled. "It wasn't my idea to grab your wife! That was all Tatum's doin'!"

"Tatum?"

"Caleb Tatum! He's the boss of our bunch, plans all the jobs."

"Why did he take my wife?"

"He said . . . he said she might come in handy." As Bill's expression hardened, the outlaw hurried on, "As a hostage, you know, in case a posse caught up to us! That's all he ever said about doin' with her, mister, I swear it!"

Overstreet said, "He's a mite more talkative than I thought he might be, Marshal. I figured you'd have to cut at least one of his balls off to get him to talk. This ain't much fun so far."

"Oh, it'll be fun," Bill said with a smile. "Tell me, Dave . . . you know how to get to the hideout the rest of the bunch was headed for, don't you?"

"I . . . I don't," the outlaw answered. "I really don't."

Still smiling, Bill said, "You're lyin' to me, Dave. I know it, you know it, and the rest of these fellas know it."

"Now this is gonna be entertainin'," Overstreet said.

"Josiah, come hold his head."

Hartnett said, "Bill, I don't know if I want—"

"I'll do it," Overstreet said. He stepped forward quickly and took hold of the outlaw's chin, forcing his head back even more than Bill had. "Go ahead, Marshal. He can't see what you're about to do now."

"All right."

Belton whimpered, but tied up like he was, there was nothing he could do.

Bill unfastened the man's trousers. A moment later, the prisoner gasped as he felt the touch of cold steel against his skin. Then he shrieked as that steel bit into flesh.

"I'll tell you!" he screamed. "I'll tell you how to get to the hideout!"

"You'll do more than that," Bill told him. "You'll take us there, and you'll show us the best way in."

"I . . . I can't! I can't ride! I'm hurt!"

He screamed again as Bill moved the knife.

Overstreet's eyes bugged out a little, too, as he watched.

"Wh-whatever you say!" the outlaw gasped. "I'll help you, I swear! Just don't do it, mister! Don't do it!"

"That's more like it," Bill told him. He wiped the blade on the prisoner's shirt and slid it back into its sheath. As he stood up, he looked at a couple of the possemen and added, "Keep an eye on him."

He turned and walked out of the circle of light at the base of Castle Rock. As soon as he was sure the other men couldn't see him, he lifted his hand. He could feel it trembling.

Hartnett followed him. He asked quietly, "Bill, are you all right?"

"Yeah, I'm fine," Bill said. He clenched that trembling hand into a fist.

Overstreet came up to them and said, "You know, Bill, for a second there I thought you were really gonna cut his balls off. You just barely nicked his belly with that knife and he sure screamed like you were doin' it, though."

"I think that's what Bill wanted him to think," Hartnett said.

"Yeah," Bill said. "That's what I wanted him to think."

He didn't know if the other two men could hear the hollow note in his voice, but he certainly could.

Earlier, Bill had bound up the wounds in Dave Belton's legs. Now he gave the man another drink of whiskey and some bacon one of the posse members had fried up before they returned to Castle Rock. Belton was more interested in the liquor.

"You reckon I'll ever walk again?" he asked.

"Damned if I know," Bill told him. "I've got a bad leg, and I get around pretty good most of the time. I wouldn't worry about it too much, considerin' that you're probably gonna hang."

The outlaw shook his head.

"No, sir," he said. "I robbed quite a few banks and held up a few stagecoaches, but I never killed anybody in my life. Maybe not for lack of tryin' now and then, but the fact of the matter is, I never did. They can put me in prison, but I hadn't ought to swing."

"That's for a judge and jury to decide. But if you help us out, like you said you would . . . well, I'd be more inclined to stand up in court and say that maybe you shouldn't hang after all."

"I'll help you, but there's something else you got to do for me."

Bill smiled and said, "You're not in very good shape to be dictating terms."

"No, I mean it. When you fight it out with the gang, you've got to kill Caleb Tatum. It don't really matter that much about any of the others, but Tatum's got to die. Otherwise, he'll know that I told you how to find the hideout, and he'll come after me. If he thought somebody double-crossed him, he'd track 'em to hell and gone to settle the score with 'em."

"Tatum's the one who grabbed my wife, you said?"

"That's right, Marshal."

Bill shook his head.

"I can't promise you I'll kill him. I'm sworn to uphold the law."

The prisoner heaved a sigh and said, "Well, it probably don't matter all that much, anyway. Tatum won't be taken alive."

Bill talked with the man for a good hour, getting him to go over the route they would take into the badlands. According to Dave Belton, the gang's hideout was in a bowl closed in by high, steep walls, and the only good way in or out was a trail through the surrounding ridges that was only wide enough for one man on horseback at a time.

"They guard that trail around the clock," Belton said. "There are always two men watchin' it. But hell, one man with a good rifle and enough ammunition could hold off an army there."

"That's not the only way in, though, is it?" Bill guessed. "You said it was the only *good* way."

Belton shrugged.

"A man could climb down the walls . . . if he could get to them. Problem is, there's a ridge that runs through there and cuts off the bowl from this side and it's too steep to climb just about everywhere."

"Just about, you said," Bill repeated.

The prisoner sighed and said, "Yeah. I reckon most of the fellas don't even know about this, but one time Tatum and Lou Price and me were explorin' around there . . . just passin' time between jobs, you know . . . and we found a place where somebody, Indians most likely, had carved handholds and footholds into that stone wall. I'd sure hate to have to climb it, though. Not Tatum. He was loco enough to do it. When he didn't come back, we circled around, went back to the hideout the usual way, and when we got there he was sittin' there grinnin'. He'd come over the ridge and down the far side into the bowl. Said it wasn't easy, but he'd proved it could be done."

"Can you find that place in the dark?" Bill asked.

"I think so. It shouldn't be too hard, and you can use torches to help find it. From inside the bowl, nobody can see what's goin' on out there."

Bill thought about it for a second and then nodded.

"All right. But if you're trying to trick us and send us into some sort of trap, you can be sure of one thing. I'll have a man watching you all the time, and at the first sign of anything wrong, his only job will be to put a bullet in your head."

"No tricks, Marshal," Belton promised. "I give you my word on that. Shot up as bad as I am, I know my only chance to live is to go back and take what's comin' to me, even if that means prison." He took another sip from the flask Bill had allowed him to keep. "I don't understand what you're plannin' to do, though. Even if you get a man inside the hide-out, he's still gonna be outnumbered."

"You let me worry about that," Bill said. He wasn't going to reveal all the details of his plan to the outlaw, just in case something happened and the man got away somehow. As badly wounded as Belton was, the chances of that were mighty slim, but Bill didn't want to run any unnecessary risks.

Not with Eden's life probably depending on what happened between now and the time the sun came up in the morning.

Chapter 33

It would have been just fine with Mordecai Flint if he had woken up to find that the events of the night before were nothing more than a grotesque nightmare.

Unfortunately, that wasn't the case, and the muttered cursing that came from the cell block as Mordecai stumbled into the office was proof of that.

Tom Gentry was awake.

For the moment, Mordecai ignored the prisoner. He went to the potbellied woodstove and got a fire burning so he could boil some coffee. He dumped the dregs from the previous day and got fresh grounds. He wanted the brew as strong as he could get it.

"Hey! Hey, out there!" Tom Gentry called from the cell block. "What the hell!"

"Yell all you want," Mordecai muttered to himself. His arm hurt, and he was disgusted.

He had a strong hunch that things were going to get worse before they got better, too.

It didn't take long for that to happen. The office door swung open, and Walter Shelton stalked into the room. The man's face was tight with cold fury, and he had a gun in his hand.

"Where is he?" Shelton demanded. "Where is that son of a bitch?"

Mordecai turned slowly from the stove and rested his hand on the butt of his own revolver, glad that he had buckled on his gun belt before he started fixing the coffee. He didn't know if he could draw fast enough to stop a man who already had a gun in his hand, but he hoped that with the power of the law behind him, it wouldn't come to that.

"Mr. Shelton," he said, "I know what you're feelin' right now, but I don't appreciate you bustin' in here wavin' a hog-leg around." He added, "You didn't even knock."

"That son of a bitch you've got locked up back there didn't ask permission before he did his best to kill my daughter, either," Shelton snapped. "I want to see him . . . now!"

Mordecai shook his head.

"I reckon we've established that Tom Gentry is a son of a bitch," he said. "But he's also my prisoner, and I wouldn't be doing my duty as a lawman if I let you go back there and shoot him, Mr. Shelton."

"I'm not going to shoot him."

"Then what's that gun for?"

Shelton looked down at the revolver in his hand as if he had forgotten that it was there. He frowned and said, "I suppose maybe when I started over here I planned on shooting Tom Gentry. But now I just want to see what sort of monster could do that to a poor innocent girl like Virginia."

Based on what he had heard the night before, Mordecai had his doubts about Virginia Gentry being totally innocent in this matter, but that wasn't really relevant. He held out his left hand and said, "If you ain't gonna shoot him, then you won't mind givin' me that gun, will you?"

Shelton stared at the gun for a moment longer, then gave it to Mordecai. The deputy felt a little better once the visitor was disarmed.

"I'll let you see the boy," he said, "but first I want to know how your daughter is doin' this morning."

Shelton was hatless, and his thinning gray hair was mussed. He tangled it up even more by running his fingers through it as he sighed.

"She's at my house, of course. That man Morley sent word to me that she was injured, and I went right to Gentry's house. When I saw the kind of shape Virginia was in, I had a wagon brought and took her back to my house. Her mother is with her now."

"She was out cold the last time I saw her. Has she come to?"

Shelton nodded.

"She was able to speak to us. Morley came by this morning to see about her and told us that was a good sign. He thinks she's going to be all right."

"I'm mighty glad to hear that," Mordecai said, and he meant it.

"She may recover physically," Shelton said, "but I'm not sure she'll ever get over what that bastard did to her."

From the cell block, Tom Gentry called, "I can hear what you're sayin' out there, old man! You just shut up! You don't know a damned thing about it!"

Shelton turned sharply toward the cell block door. Mordecai was glad he had gotten the gun away from the man. Judging the expression on Shelton's face, he might have started trying to shoot through the door at his son-in-law.

"Let me back there," Shelton said as his hands clenched into fists. "You told me I could see him."

"Don't bring that old fool back here, Deputy! I don't want to see him!"

That rubbed Mordecai the wrong way. He raised his voice and said, "What you want don't mean a damned thing to me as long as you're locked up in this jail, mister." He plucked the ring of keys from the desk and jerked his head at Shelton. "Come on."

He unlocked the cell block door and swung it open. Shelton stalked past him.

"Stay away from the cell door," Mordecai warned.

Shelton stopped out of reach of the bars, just in case Tom

Gentry tried to stick an arm through them and grab him. Mordecai stood in the doorway with his hand on the butt of his gun again.

Gentry was on his feet, standing about halfway between the bunk and the cell door. He and Shelton glared at each other for a long moment before Shelton said, "You worm. You pathetic excuse for a man."

Gentry sneered.

"That shows what you know," he said. "You're the pathetic excuse for a man. That's what it'd take to raise a daughter who's nothin' but a no-good whore."

Mordecai expected Shelton to throw himself at the bars and try to get at Gentry. Instead the man just stood there, trembling slightly with rage.

"Here now," Mordecai snapped at Gentry. "There'll be more more of that kind of talk."

"Why not?" Gentry demanded. "It's the truth, Deputy. You know that. You talked to Ned Bassett."

Shelton slowly turned his head to look at Mordecai.

"What's he talking about? What's that watchmaker got to do with this?"

Before Mordecai could answer, Gentry let out a scathing laugh.

"Don't you know, old man?" he asked. "Bassett's the man who's been bedding my wife."

"You're a damned liar," Shelton said coldly.

"I've watched her sneak out at night and go to his house a dozen times. She didn't deny it when I accused her of it, either. She knew it wouldn't do her any good to lie."

Shelton still tried to look stern and angry, but Mordecai could tell that he was shaken by what Gentry had just said.

"I don't believe you, but even if you were telling the truth, that wouldn't justify what you did."

Gentry laughed again.

"Doesn't it? What would *you* have done thirty years ago if you'd found Clarissa in bed with another man? Not that anybody but you would've ever wanted her, but you know what I mean."

"You really *are* a monster," Shelton whispered.

"You're just saying that because you know I'm right . . . about everything."

From the door of the cell block, Mordecai said, "This ain't doin' anybody any good. I reckon it's time for you to leave now, Mr. Shelton."

Shelton didn't argue. He started to turn toward the door, but he paused and pointed a finger at Gentry.

"You'll pay for what you've done, Tom," he said. "I promise you that."

Gentry just sneered.

Mordecai stepped back and motioned for Shelton to go on into the office. He closed and locked the door after them, tossing the key ring back onto the desk.

"What are you going to do with him?" Shelton asked in a dull voice.

Mordecai nodded toward the outer door, indicating that Shelton should step out onto the boardwalk in front of the office. When they were both out there, Mordecai closed that door. The office was pretty small, and he didn't want Gentry eavesdropping from the cell.

"I don't rightly know just yet what I'm gonna do with him," Mordecai said. "I'll have to talk to Judge Dunaway. I ain't never been a lawman until just a few months ago, you know."

"He should be hanged . . . or shot. At the very least horse-whipped."

"I won't argue with that last sentiment. But whatever happens to him, I reckon it'll have to be done legal-like."

"You still have my gun, you know."

Mordecai took the revolver from his waistband and handed it back to Shelton. "Until that bank robbery the other day, I didn't even know you had a gun," he commented.

"I'm sure there's a great deal you don't know about me." Shelton looked up and down the street. The hour was early, but Redemption was fairly busy already. "For example, did you know that I was here long before the town was?"

"You mean before Redemption?" Mordecai asked with a frown. "I thought you come from somewheres else."

"I lived in Wichita for a long time, but I grew up right here. Well, just outside town along the creek. That's where I camped after the Pawnee jumped my family's wagon and killed my parents and brothers and sisters thirty years ago. The only reason I survived was because I was out hunting for some fresh meat. I heard the shots, but by the time I got back it was too late. I was twenty years old."

Mordecai tried not to stare at the man. He never would have guessed that Shelton had such a tragedy in his background.

"In those days it was several hundred miles back to civilization," Shelton went on, the tone of his voice telling Mordecai that the man was momentarily lost in the past. "We were on our way to Santa Fe, but that was hundreds of miles away, too. Anyway, I didn't want to leave. I buried my family. I used to know exactly where the graves were, but now . . . now I'm not sure I could find them again. So much time has passed. So much has changed."

"It has, for a fact," Mordecai said quietly.

"And it wasn't just that I didn't want to leave my family. I thought that some of the Indians who killed them might come back. So I waited . . . and they did. Not all the members of the war party, I'm sure. Only four."

"What'd you do?"

"I killed them," Shelton said. "I had my rifle and one they had overlooked in the wagon, plus a couple of pistols. And a knife. It was enough."

Mordecai had believed what everybody else in Redemption did about Walter Shelton: that the man was just a mild-mannered, retired storekeeper. But Shelton's words had the unmistakable ring of truth to them.

The man turned to look at Mordecai and went on, "So you see, Deputy, Tom Gentry's lucky. There was a time in my life I lived for murder and revenge on whoever hurt my family. Back then I probably would have shot you for getting in my way and then gone after him."

"Well, I'm mighty glad it didn't come to that. Best thing for you to do now, Mr. Shelton, is to go home and see that Miss Virginia's well taken care of."

"Yes," Shelton said with a nod. "But I meant what I told Tom. He's going to pay for what he did. I'll see him hanged or in jail, one or the other."

"That'll be up to the judge."

Shelton shook his head. "No. You tell Kermit Dunaway what I said."

Mordecai might have argued more with the man, but at that moment he was distracted by the appearance of several riders at the western end of Main Street. They approached the marshal's office in a hurry, dust billowing into the air from their horses' hooves.

Mordecai recognized the man in the lead.

Burkhart Gentry had come to town.

Chapter 34

Jesse Overstreet tilted his head back to look up at the sheer wall of the ridge that rose above them. He shook his head and said, "Not even a mountain goat could climb that."

"The Indians did," Bill said. "I can, too."

"But it's not just straight up!" Overstreet protested. "Look at the way the wall bulges out here and there. A fella'd practically have to hang upside down to make it!"

"Then that's what I'll do."

The torch that Josiah Hartnett held over his head to light up the ridge where the outlaw Dave Belton had brought them finally burned down to his fingers. Hartnett shook out the flame and said, "I think Jesse's right, Bill. Maybe some wiry Indians were able to climb that, but I don't see how we're going to."

"Not we," Bill said. "Just me. If that fella Tatum can do it, so can I."

From where the three of them stood, the ridge rose sheerly above them and also fell off in a more gentle slope the other way. They had left the horses and the other members of the posse a couple of hundred yards away at the base of that slope. The horses probably could have climbed up here, but there was no reason for them to try. Once they reached this point, there wouldn't have been anywhere for them to go.

Belton was down below, too, tied onto the saddle on one of the horses he and his fellow owlhoot had had at Castle Rock. The dead outlaw's horse had been brought along as an extra mount. All the way here, Belton had complained bitterly about the pain of his wounded legs. Every step of his horse had brought a fresh curse to Belton's lips.

Bill didn't feel any sympathy for the outlaw, knowing that he'd been part of the gang that had kidnapped Eden, even if grabbing her had been Caleb Tatum's idea alone. And they never could have found their way through the badlands without Belton to guide them through the twists and turns of the mazelike trails.

Belton had ridden at the head of the posse with Bill, Overstreet, and Hartnett, and Overstreet had kept his revolver pointed at the outlaw most of the time.

"If I see anything that looks like you're tryin' to trick us or lead us into a trap," Bill had warned, "I'm gonna tell Jesse to blow your brains out."

"You'd never find the hideout if you did that," Belton had said. "Hell, you might not even be able to find your way back out of here."

"We'll worry about that later. Either way, you'll be dead."

With that unmistakably genuine threat hanging over his head, Belton hadn't tried anything funny. He had led them to the ridge, and the ancient handholds and footholds were there, just as he had promised.

Bill took off his hat and handed it to Hartnett.

"Stuff it in my saddlebags when you go back down to the horses," he said. "It'd just fall off if I tried to wear it."

Overstreet snatched his hat from his head and held it out to Hartnett, as well.

"You can take care of mine, too," he said.

"What're you doin' that for?" Bill asked with a frown. "I'm the only one goin' over the ridge this way."

"That fella Belton said there were two guards on the bottleneck most of the time," Overstreet reminded him.

"I know. I'm gonna take care of them, and then I'll let the rest of you know that it's all right to come on in."

"Two against one?" Overstreet shook his head. "Those aren't very good odds."

"I can handle 'em."

"Two of us would stand a lot better chance."

"He's probably right about that, Bill," Hartnett put in.

"Hell, a few days ago I knocked you out and threw you in jail!" Bill said to the young cowboy.

That brought a chuckle from Overstreet.

"Yeah, and I reckon I had it comin', too," he said. "Anyway, you ought to know that one Texan can't let another Texan go into a fight by himself. Us sons of the Lone Star State got to stick together."

Well, that was true, Bill thought. If the situation had been reversed, he probably would have felt the same way.

"I thought you said nobody could climb that wall."

"Yeah, but if anybody could—"

"It'd be somebody from Texas," Bill finished the thought for him. "You've got your mind set on it, don't you?"

"I sure do."

"All right. But I'm goin' first, and you don't start up until I'm at the top. If I fall, I don't want to knock you off, too."

"How'll I know you made it? It's mighty dark on top of that ridge."

"I'll whistle like a bobwhite," Bill said. "You hear that, you'll know it's all right for you to start climbing." He paused. "And if I don't make it, I reckon you'll hear the thud when I hit the ground, so you'll know that, too."

With that grim comment, he reached up on the stone wall and felt for the first handhold. Hartnett asked, "You want me to light another torch?"

"No, the light wouldn't reach to the top, so I've got to be able to find them on my own, anyway."

Bill dug his fingers into a small crevice in the rock. He got a boot toe in a similar niche lower down and used it to lever himself upward. He reached above his head with his other hand and searched for a second handhold.

It wasn't exactly like climbing a ladder, but for the first dozen feet or so it wasn't too bad. The ridge was about fifty feet high, so Bill figured he had covered a fourth of the distance without much trouble.

But then the wall began to slant out. The angle was so slight that it was almost imperceptible at first, but Bill soon felt it. His fingers wanted to slip out of the little cracks in the stone. He had to grip the handholds tighter to support himself. His hands began to cramp and ache.

Caleb Tatum had done this, he reminded himself. And Tatum was probably older, too, not as young and spry as Bill was.

Of course, he wasn't as young and spry as he had been, Bill thought. His bad leg started to ache worse than usual.

He clung fiercely to the ridge and continued to climb. After a few feet the angle eased. In fact, the wall was no longer perpendicular but rather leaned in slightly, which allowed him to rest some of his weight against it and take a little strain off his hands and feet.

Unfortunately, that didn't continue. The wall bulged out again. But Bill knew what to expect now, and he didn't think this part of the climb was quite as hard as it had been lower down.

It didn't help matters that the stone had enough chalk in it to make it a little slick. He tried to make absolutely sure of his grip every time before he trusted any weight to it. If one hand slipped off, he might be able to support himself with the other hand and his feet.

If both hands slipped at the same time, he was gone. He would plummet straight down to the slope that ran away from the ridge. The fall would probably kill him. At best, he would break an arm or a leg . . . or both.

Darkness had closed in so thickly around him that he was climbing strictly by feel. He wasn't even aware that he was approaching the top of the ridge until he reached up and felt its flat surface. A feeling of triumph raced through him as he pulled himself up and rolled onto the rocky crest. He had made it!

But he still had a long way to go before Eden was safe and free.

His muscles were quivering from the effort it had taken to climb the ridge. He lay there for a few moments to catch his breath and let his hammering pulse slow down a little, but he knew he didn't have time to waste. When he felt stronger, he rolled onto his belly and crawled over to the edge. He stuck his head over and whistled like a bobwhite. The bird call drifted through the night air.

An answering call came up from below, telling Bill that Overstreet had heard the signal. He lay there waiting.

Minutes dragged past. Bill couldn't see much when he peered down the face of the ridge.

Then a small, lighter-colored patch came into view. It moved, and Bill realized he was looking at the thatch of blond hair on Jesse Overstreet's head. He listened intently, and he could hear Overstreet's labored breathing, too.

"Keep coming, Jesse," he called softly. "You're almost there."

"Damn!" A second went by after the startled exclamation, then Overstreet said, "You dang near spooked me right off this rock, Bill."

"Sorry. You've only got a few more feet to go. When you get closer, I can reach down and give you a hand."

Overstreet continued laboring upward. Finally Bill was able to grasp his arm, and he hauled the young cowboy onto the top of the ridge. Overstreet flopped down limply beside him.

"Lord have mercy! I don't want to *ever* do anything like that again."

"Yeah, I feel the same way," Bill said. "But we made it."

"Now all we've got to do is jump those guards and get rid of 'em without makin' enough racket to wake up the rest of the gang."

"Yeah," Bill agreed dryly. "That's all."

After a few more minutes, they climbed to their feet. Belton hadn't been able to tell them how to get down into the bowl where the hideout was located, because he had never been this way. But he'd assured them that they ought to be able to find it.

"Climbing down in there won't be easy in the dark, but it shouldn't be near as hard as it is goin' up the other side of that ridge," Belton had said.

Bill knew the general direction they were supposed to go. When he sniffed the air, he realized they had another guide besides the stars overhead.

He smelled woodsmoke. The outlaws had small stone cabins, according to Belton, and each of those cabins had a fireplace. They must have kindled fires for cooking and boiling coffee, and now the scent lingered from the embers of those fires.

He touched Overstreet's arm and pointed. They needed to be as quiet as possible from here on out.

Following his nose and the stars, Bill led the way across the ridge. The terrain was rugged, cut by fissures and littered with boulders, but after that climb it seemed like a cakewalk.

The smell of smoke grew stronger. After a while Bill realized that something else was blending in with the woodsmoke. Tobacco, he thought. Somebody was smoking a quirley. Had to be one of the guards down in the bottleneck. That narrow passage would funnel any night breezes up into the open air.

Belton had explained that they would have to get down in the bowl itself to reach the sentries. The walls of the passage were too steep and smooth to descend. So Bill pushed on, and after half a mile or so he and Overstreet came to a drop-off. The bowl opened up in front of them.

Bill put his mouth close to Overstreet's ear and whispered, "Be mighty careful going down. If we start any rocks fallin', the racket will bring those guards on the run."

"I savvy," Overstreet whispered back.

Bill went first, feeling his way along. The slope was steep enough that he had to turn around and face it so that he could hang on to protruding rocks and clumps of hardy grass as he descended. He took his time about it, making sure that he didn't kick any loose rocks and cause them to roll down the slope.

It was impossible to move in absolute silence. Every little rattle, every creak of boot leather, even the pounding of his own heart was magnified and seemed much louder than it really was.

He reached the floor of the bowl, which was covered with short grass. A moment later Overstreet was beside him. Now all they had to do was slide along the rock wall until they reached the opening into the passage. Bill continued leading the way.

He drew his knife. He didn't want to take any chances on a gun going off, so he'd made sure that Overstreet had a knife, too. Nor did he intend to leave the sentries alive behind them, even unconscious and tied up. All it would take to ruin everything would be for one of the men to wake up and get loose somehow.

The two men in the bottleneck didn't know it, but death was slipping up behind them.

Bill and Overstreet reached the passage. Resting one hand on the wall to keep himself oriented and gripping the knife in the other, Bill plunged into utter darkness. The stars in the narrow strip of sky still visible overhead didn't throw enough light down here to do any good.

Belton had said there was a little niche in the wall halfway through the passage where the men stood guard. They had to be getting close now, Bill thought. He could still smell cigarette smoke. That wasn't very smart of the outlaws. It gave away their position. But they probably thought there wasn't anyone else within ten miles.

Bill spotted a faint orange speck up ahead. That was the glowing coal at the end of the quirley he smelled. He paused, putting out a hand to stop Overstreet. Again he found the cowboy's ear and breathed, "Ten yards ahead of us, on the left. We'll rush them together—"

They didn't get that chance. Suddenly footsteps echoed along the passage. A second later a voice called, "Hey, Andy! Russ! It's Chico and T. J. Don't get jumpy."

"Damn well about time," one of the guards replied. "You were supposed to relieve us twenty minutes ago."

Bill pressed his back against the stone wall and tried to slow his frenziedly racing heart.

The odds against him and Overstreet had just doubled.

Chapter 35

Burk Gentry had four men with him. Mordecai seemed to remember that Gentry had other sons besides Tom, but he didn't know how many. All the men with Gentry might be his offspring, or some of them might be hands who rode for him.

Either way, Mordecai didn't like the looks of this. Clearly, the newcomers were bound for the jail . . . and bound on making trouble, too.

"Mr. Shelton, you get on out of here," Mordecai said tensely.

"I'll side you on this, Deputy," Shelton replied. "We won't let Gentry take his son out of jail."

"That's my worry, not yours. Nobody's takin' a prisoner outta this jail."

Not to rescue them . . . and not to lynch them, either, Mordecai thought, which was more likely something that Shelton would have in mind. Both extremes would be equally bad in the eyes of the law.

"Deputy—"

It was too late to argue with Shelton now, Mordecai saw. Burk Gentry and the other riders brought their horses to a stop in front of the marshal's office. More dust swirled in the air. All along the street, people looked, pointed fingers, and talked excitedly.

Gentry was a big man and looked even bigger on horseback, barrel-chested and looming above the boardwalk. He fixed a hate-filled glare on Mordecai and demanded, "Are you the lawman who locked up my son for no good reason?"

"No good reason?" burst out Shelton. "Why, that bas—"

Mordecai thrust out his good arm and pushed Shelton back as he stepped to the edge of the boardwalk. Shelton was just going to make things worse, he thought bitterly.

Somebody in town who had heard what had happened the night before must have ridden out to the Gentry ranch to tell old Burk all about it. Mordecai had hoped to have a little more time before he had to deal with that.

"I'm Deputy Flint," he confirmed, "and I've got Tom Gentry locked up, all right. I reckon the judge'll have to determine whether or not it was for a good reason."

All five of the men were hard-faced and determined. They all had six-guns strapped on, too. Burk Gentry lifted a hamlike hand and pointed at the office.

"You get in there and turn him loose right now, and maybe I won't whip you up this street one way and down the other. Right now, do you hear me?"

Shelton moved behind Mordecai, who shifted again to keep himself between Shelton and Gentry. Mordecai was struggling to keep his own temper under control. In the past forty years, nobody had talked to him the way Burk Gentry just had and not been made to pay for it. In fact, Mordecai had fired shots in anger with less provocation.

But even if he hadn't been wounded, he couldn't win a gunfight with these five men, and he knew it. If he'd had more time to get ready, he would have stepped out here to confront them with a shotgun, and even that wouldn't have been good odds. If he slapped leather now, he would die and probably so would Walter Shelton.

Then Gentry and his men would go in there and turn Tom loose, and their deaths would have been for nothing.

Mordecai was damned if he was going to step aside meekly, though. He said, "Gentry, your son attacked his wife and came mighty near to beatin' her to death. He's got to answer for that."

Gentry let out a disdainful snort.

"She's his wife, ain't she? He can do whatever he wants to her. It's his legal right."

"That's not a damned dog you're talking about!" Shelton yelled. "Virginia is my daughter!"

"You stay out of it, Shelton. You squeak like a damn mouse when there's men talkin'."

Clearly, Gentry didn't know anything about Walter Shelton's history, either.

Mordecai made another attempt to head off trouble. He said, "I ain't had a chance yet this mornin' to talk to Judge Dunaway. This is all gonna be handled legal and proper—"

"Would you lock a man up for getting rough with a saloon floozy?" Gentry broke in. "From what I hear, that Virgie ain't no better."

Lord, Lord, the man was just tryin' to get somebody killed with talk like that, Mordecai thought. Gentry was about to succeed, too, because Shelton ripped out a curse and grabbed for the gun he had put back in his pocket.

Mordecai moved fast, gripping Shelton's wrist before the man could pull the weapon free. From the corner of his eye he saw Burk Gentry and the other men reaching for their own guns.

The sharp crack of a shot came from somewhere else and made everyone stop what they were doing.

Mordecai looked over and saw Judge Dunaway waddling toward them. The beefy-faced lawyer and justice of the peace held a Winchester '66. He worked the rifle's lever as he approached.

"You hold your fire, Burkhart Gentry, and tell those boys with you to do the same!" Dunaway bellowed. "I do most of my work with a gavel, but I can still handle a rifle if I have to."

"By God, Dunaway, you stay out of this!"

The judge shook his head.

"No, sir, I won't. I can't. I'm the justice of the peace in this town, and that makes me every bit as much of a peace officer as Deputy Flint there. You try to interfere with the law and you'll be in more trouble than you know what to do with."

Gentry scowled darkly at the judge.

"You reckon you and this crippled old man can outshoot all of us?"

"I'm pretty damn sure I can kill *you* before anybody can stop me," Dunaway said. "What happens after that I don't much care."

Dunaway had surprised Mordecai by stepping in like this. He wouldn't have taken the judge for such a hell-raiser. But like Walter Shelton, everybody had sides of themselves that took folks by surprise, he thought.

That was confirmed when Roy Fleming approached from the other direction and said, "If you harm anyone, Burk, I'll see to it that you answer for your crimes. I'll call in the army if I have to. We've fought hard to bring law and order to Redemption, and you're not going to bull in here and run roughshod over people like it was the old days again."

"You're takin' their side against me and my sons, Fleming?" Gentry roared.

"If I have to," Fleming replied calmly.

"The best thing you can do, Gentry," the judge said, "is to turn around and ride out of here. Let the law run its course."

"You mean I should leave my son behind bars when he didn't do anything wrong?"

Shelton started to bluster again. Mordecai silenced him with a look. He had already taken the man's gun away again.

"Everybody just settle down, damn it," Dunaway said. "I'm going to have a meeting with Mayor Fleming and Deputy Flint right now, and we'll deal with the matter."

For a moment, Mordecai thought Gentry was going to continue to argue. But then the rancher drew in a deep breath and let it out in a gusty sigh.

"All right," he said. "We'll go down to Smoot's and wait a while. But you'd better come up with the right decision in this *meetin'* of yours, or you'll have more trouble than you know what to do with. You got my word on that!"

Gentry turned his horse and rode slowly toward the saloon.

His men followed him, each of them giving Mordecai a cold, narrow-eyed look of hate as they rode past.

Once they were gone, Dunaway and Fleming came up to Mordecai. The mayor was pale and sweating, despite the coolness of the morning.

"This is bad," he said. "I knew it would be as soon as I heard what had happened."

"I'm going to be part of this meeting," Shelton declared.

Dunaway shook his head.

"Sorry, Walt, but that wouldn't be right, any more than it would be to let Burk Gentry sit in on it."

"Legal proceedings are supposed to be open to the public," Shelton insisted.

"This isn't a trial or even a formal hearing," the judge said. "It's just some fellows sitting down and trying to figure out what the hell they need to do next."

"I can tell you what you need to do. Put that animal on trial, convict him, and sentence him to twenty years in prison. Either that or hang him."

Dunaway ignored that and told Shelton, "Go home. I expect both your wife and your daughter could use you there."

Shelton glared for a moment longer, then said, "All right. But while I hate to agree with Burkhart Gentry about anything . . . you'd better make the right decision, Kermit."

"Is that a threat?"

"No," Shelton said. "A promise."

Chapter 36

If there was anything at all fortunate about this most recent development, Bill thought wildly, it was that the two men coming up the passage to take their turn on guard duty hadn't brought a lantern or a torch with them. They must know the hideout so well that they didn't need light to find their way around.

He pressed himself harder against the wall and thrust his arm across Overstreet's chest to hold him back, too. With luck, Chico and T. J. would walk right past them without knowing they were there. That luck might not be forthcoming, though, as Overstreet's fair hair would make him easier to spot. Bill's long brown hair blended in more with the rock wall.

All they could do was try, Bill told himself. He held his breath as the two outlaws came closer.

The blended smell of whiskey, tobacco, and unwashed flesh drifted through the air. The men were practically on top of them now.

"Everything quiet back at the cabins?" one of the first two outlaws asked.

"Yeah, I guess."

"No trouble between Hannah and that blond girl?"

Eden, Bill thought. The man was talking about Eden.

But who was Hannah? The outlaws must have another woman with them, he reasoned, and not a prisoner, either, from the sound of it.

Well, it wasn't unheard of for a woman to ride with outlaws, he supposed, although it sure wasn't common. Bill didn't know why this Hannah, whoever she was, would have any trouble with Eden.

He found out the next moment, as the four men continued their conversation. Their talking among themselves was a good thing, because they were paying attention to that and not as much to their surroundings. Chico and T. J. started to walk right past the spot where Bill and Overstreet were standing. Bill made himself as narrow as he could to give them more room.

"Sooner or later Hannah will raise a ruckus about that girl," one of the men said. "She ain't blind. She can see the same thing that the rest of us see. Caleb grabbed her because he wants her in his bed. He don't give a damn about usin' her as a hostage."

"No, he just wants to use her," the other newcomer said.

That brought laughter from all four of them.

"Yeah, but as long as Caleb's moonin' over her, the rest of us can't have any sport with her," one of the outlaws said. "That don't hardly seem fair."

"Only if we go along with what Caleb says."

"What do you mean by that, Chico?"

"Nothing," the owlhoot called Chico replied, but it was clear from the tone of his voice that he did mean something.

"You're just upset because the two of you had that tussle the other night. Hell, I don't blame you. Although it *did* look like you were flirtin' a mite with that gal."

"I just don't like the way Caleb thinks he can lord it over all of—damn it!" Chico let out the exclamation as he stumbled over something on the rough floor of the passage. His shoulder bumped hard against Bill's chest. "Sorry, Andy.

Didn't mean to run into you. Or was that you I ran into, Russ? Can't see a damned thing in here."

"You didn't run into me," one of the guards said.

"Or me, either," the other one added.

"Then who—"

Chico was right in front of Bill, who heard the rustle of cloth as the outlaw swung sharply toward him. Sensing that, Bill didn't wait. He thrust out hard with the knife in his hand and felt the blade sink deep into yielding flesh.

At the same time he reached out with his other hand at what he hoped would be Chico's throat. His fingers closed around it and clamped down hard, cutting off any sound. Chico struggled, but his efforts were feeble, telling Bill that his knife had done some serious damage. He grimaced in the darkness as he heaved Chico around and rushed with him at the spot where he judged the two guards to be.

"What the hell!" one of them said. "Chico, what are you—"

Bill, Chico, and the two guards all came together with a crashing impact in the darkness.

Overstreet and the fourth man were still behind him somewhere. Bill didn't have time to worry about them now. He stumbled, trying to hang on to his balance as he ripped the knife out of Chico's body and slashed through the shadows with it. The blade met resistance and ripped through it. Bill felt something hot gush over his hand and hoped it was blood.

A blow swung every bit as blindly as his own smashed into the side of his head and staggered him. It felt like a gun barrel had clipped him. If the blow hadn't been a glancing one, it might have crushed his skull. As it was, he reeled to the side, unable to control himself for a second.

"Somebody's out here! Grab 'em!"

Yelling was a mistake. Bill caught his balance and lunged at the sound of the voice, chopping desperately with the knife. A man screamed, but only for a second before a grotesque gurgle cut off the sound.

Bill's legs tangled with somebody else's legs. He couldn't

stay on his feet. As he fell, he grappled with the man and jabbed again and again with the knife. Bill's hand felt like it was covered with blood now. The knife handle was slippery with it.

He hit the ground and rolled to the side. No guns had gone off, and except for that brief scream, there hadn't been any cries loud enough to be heard back in the hideout. It was possible everyone was asleep and hadn't noticed the scream. That's what Bill was praying for.

"Marshal!" That urgent whisper came from Overstreet. "Bill! You still alive?"

Bill was, but for all he knew some of the outlaws were alive, too, and Overstreet had just told them where he was. Bill listened intently for the sounds of a new struggle.

He didn't hear anything, so after a minute or so he risked a whisper of his own.

"Jesse?"

Bill heard a sigh of relief.

"I thought one of those hombres might've got you. No need to worry about mine. I got my hands on his neck and choked the life out of him."

Bill knew he was going to have to risk a light. That was going to make him a target, so he wiped off his knife as best he could on his trousers and sheathed it. He pulled his gun and used his other hand to dig a match out of his shirt pocket. Holding the lucifer out at his side at arm's length, he raised the revolver and rested his thumb on the hammer, ready to fire. Then he snapped the match to life and squinted against the sudden glare.

The bloody corpses of three outlaws were crumpled on the rocky ground around him. It was easy to pick out which one was Chico, because that body had only a single stab wound to the chest. Another man's belly was ripped open so that his guts had spilled out over his hands as he tried to stuff them back in. That was the lucky swipe, Bill thought. And the final man's face was hacked to pieces so that he didn't hardly look human anymore, plus his shirt was sodden with blood from stab wounds.

Overstreet let out a low whistle of awe.

"You really went to town on those fellas, Bill. Looks like a damned butcher shop in here."

"Yeah, well, we're mighty damned lucky that we're not the ones who got butchered," Bill said. He holstered his gun, dropped the match, and ground it out under his foot. "You can find your way back to the other end of this bottleneck," he went on. "Josiah and the rest of the posse ought to be waiting there."

"What are you gonna do?"

"Thought I'd go do a little scouting, see what the layout is inside the bowl. I'll meet you at that end of the passage."

"Don't get yourself in trouble before I get back with the rest of the fellas," Overstreet cautioned.

"I don't intend to," Bill said.

But worry gnawed at the back of his brain. From the sound of the things those outlaws had been saying, Eden hadn't been molested by the gang so far. But she was still in the hands of Caleb Tatum, and Tatum clearly wanted her.

Now that the outlaw leader thought he was safe in his den, how long would he wait to satisfy that desire?

Chapter 37

"What the hell do you mean, you can't put him on trial?" Mordecai demanded as the men stood in the marshal's office.

He would have preferred to hold this meeting somewhere that Tom Gentry couldn't eavesdrop, like Fleming's office in the bank, but he didn't want to leave the prisoner unattended as long as Burk Gentry and the other men were in town. They might try to bust him out.

There was also the chance that Walter Shelton could return and try to shoot Tom, and Mordecai didn't want to risk that, either.

"I'm just trying to explain that I don't really have the jurisdiction for a matter like this," Judge Dunaway said. "I'm only a justice of the peace, Deputy. I enforce the town ordinances and certain misdemeanors under the state statutes, and that's all. For something as serious as attempted murder, you need the circuit court judge."

Mordecai pointed at the cell block door and asked, "Are you tellin' me that I've got to keep Tom Gentry locked up until the blasted circuit rider comes around?"

"Well, to tell you the truth . . . and I don't like what I'm about to say . . . if I was you I'd probably let him go right now. Not because I like or agree with what he's done, but because I think the chances of convicting him are pretty slim."

"I saw the girl, Judge; you didn't. What he did to her wasn't hardly human."

"And she, ah, violated her marriage vows with this man Bassett, I understand. When you take that into account along with a man's natural rights as a husband . . . let's just say you'd have a hard time finding twelve jurymen who would vote to convict him, no matter how unpleasant and distasteful they might find the whole matter to be."

Mordecai looked over at Roy Fleming.

"What do you think, Mayor?"

"Why, I would defer to my good friend Kermit's vastly greater legal knowledge," Fleming said with a rueful smile on his face.

Mordecai stared back and forth between them for a second, then said, "Well, I'll be damned if I savvy what's goin' on here. Judge, you read the riot act to Burk Gentry, and Mayor, you backed the judge's play. Now you're sayin' he was right to ride in here and demand that I let his boy go?"

"I wasn't going to stand for him taking Tom out of the jail by force," Dunaway said. "That's entirely different than Tom being released after charges have been dropped."

Mordecai sank into the chair behind the desk and ran his good hand over his mostly bald head. He sighed.

"Walt Shelton's gonna take this mighty hard," he said.

"And I feel for Walt," Dunaway said. "He and Clarissa are friends of mine. To tell you the truth, I always thought they raised the girl to be a mite spoiled and flighty, so I'm not all that surprised by what she did. I'm sorry for what happened to her anyway, and I'm sorry for the pain it's brought to her parents. But none of that changes anything."

"I feel the same way," Fleming said. "Walt will just have to . . . get over it."

Mordecai looked up at them.

"How much do you know about Shelton's background?"

"I know he was a very successful businessman," Fleming said. "He still owns those furniture stores, although he's hired other people to run them now."

The judge shrugged and said, "That's about all I know, too."

Mordecai wondered if Shelton considered him to be some sort of kindred spirit as a frontiersman, and that was why the man had told him about the massacre and killing those Indians.

He said, "I don't think Shelton's gonna take this news too well. I'd better get Tom Gentry out of town before I let him know about it."

"That sounds like a good idea to me," Dunaway said.

The two officials left. Mordecai cast a longing glance at the coffeepot. He'd never even got a chance to start it boiling before Shelton came in earlier, and he didn't really have time now, either. Instead he put on his hat, picked up the keys, and went to the cell block door.

He found Tom Gentry leaning against the bars, a smirk on his handsome face.

"You don't have to tell me, Flint," he said. "I heard. You're letting me go."

"I'm turnin' you loose against my better judgment," Mordecai snapped. "And if you know what's good for you, you'll get out of town and don't come back."

"It's a free country, ain't it?"

"Yeah." Mordecai turned the key in the lock. "Which means your father-in-law is free to try to blow a hole in your worthless hide, too."

Tom laughed.

"Let him try. I'll kill him. It'll be self-defense, Deputy."

Mordecai backed off and drew his gun.

"Come on outta there," he said. "I'm takin' you to Smoot's. That's where your pa's waitin'."

There wasn't a crowd gathered around the marshal's office when Mordecai and Tom Gentry came out, but folks all up and down the street were paying attention to see what was going to happen. Mordecai ignored them. He held his

Colt down at his side as he walked behind Tom toward the saloon.

"I live here in town, you know," Tom said over his shoulder. "I have a house. I have every right to go there."

"Maybe so, but it'd be a damned foolish thing to do. Go out to your pa's ranch and stay there until things cool off."

"What about my wife? I have a right to see her, too."

"You try and I'll arrest you for disturbin' the peace. And I'll bet a hat I can make *that* charge stick."

"Fine," Tom said, and his voice was surly now. "She's not worth fighting over, anyway. I'm done with her and her prissy ma and pa."

It was a sure thing that the young man didn't really know his father-in-law, Mordecai thought. From what he had seen in Shelton's eyes, that old badger was anything but prissy.

Word of Tom's release reached Smoot's before Mordecai and his former prisoner did. Burk Gentry swaggered out onto the boardwalk to meet them, as much as a fat man could swagger. His other sons and the men who had come with him followed.

"I see you're out," Gentry said to Tom. "I told you you were makin' a mistake by marryin' that gal. She ain't our kind and never was."

"Yeah, Pa, I'd be a lot better off if I'd just listen to you all the time, wouldn't I?"

Mordecai heard the hostility in Tom's voice and knew that while the Gentry family might close ranks whenever one of them was threatened, there was a lot of friction between father and son, too.

"Listen to me, Gentry," Mordecai said. "Take your boys— *all* of your boys—and get out of town."

"You got no call to run us out of town," Gentry shot back.

"I'm charged with keepin' the peace here, and if you and your bunch are around when Walt Shelton hears about this, the peace is liable to be mighty disturbed. So for the good of the town . . ." Mordecai took a deep breath and forced himself to phrase it as a request. "I'm askin' you to ride out and take Tom with you."

Burk Gentry stood there sneering and pretending to think about it for a long moment before he finally said, "I'm sick of the place, anyway. Come on, boys. Let's go home."

"Pa, I—" Tom began.

"You got somethin' to say to me?" his father demanded, raising his voice. "You really got somethin' to say to me right now?"

Tom shook his head and said, "No, I guess not. I need to go back to my house and get my horse—"

"No, you don't. We already fetched it. It's right there at the hitch rack, if you'd just open your damn eyes and look."

Mordecai couldn't resist saying, "Mighty confident you'd be takin' him home, weren't you?"

Gentry gave him an ugly grin.

"I sure was, Deputy. I sure was."

Mordecai waited until they had mounted up and ridden hard out of Redemption, raising another cloud of dust. Then he shook his head and turned back toward the marshal's office.

He was only halfway across the street when he saw Walter Shelton hurrying along the boardwalk on the other side. Mordecai didn't see a gun in Shelton's hand this time, but that didn't mean the man was unarmed.

They reached the porch in front of the office at the same time.

"Is it true?" Shelton demanded. His narrow face was a mottled gray, and Mordecai knew he was a man who turned pale with fury, rather than flushing. "You let Tom Gentry go?"

"The judge and the mayor and I all talked about it," Mordecai replied, unwilling to throw all the blame on Kermit Dunaway. The judge had just given his honest opinion on a bad situation. "We decided that there was no point in holdin' Tom for trial until the circuit court judge comes around. Given the, uh, facts of the case, it ain't likely that any jury would ever convict him."

"So he gets away with what he did to my daughter," Shelton said, his voice shaking a little. "With what he did to my little girl?"

"I know that's the way you feel, Mr. Shelton, and I'm not

sayin' that you're wrong to feel that way. But sometimes you got to just go on."

"Where is he now?"

Mordecai didn't see that it would do any harm to answer that question.

"He left town with his pa and brothers. I reckon they're headed back out to the Gentry ranch. And I told 'em not to come back to Redemption anytime soon."

"You don't think they'll pay any attention to that, do you?" Shelton snapped. "That bunch of high-handed bastards thinks that they rule the roost around here! Well, they're going to find out that they're wrong!"

Mordecai pushed on, saying, "If I was you, Mr. Shelton, I reckon I might take my wife and daughter and go back to Wichita for a while—"

Then Shelton's last comment soaked into him, causing him to stop short in what he was saying.

"You think I ought to run, Deputy?" Shelton asked, smiling thinly. "You think I ought to run and hide my head like the meek little man all of you believed me to be?"

"What did you mean by that, about the Gentrys findin' out that they're wrong?"

"I didn't run from the Indians, and I'm not just about to run from sorry trash like the Gentrys," Shelton went on, as if he hadn't heard Mordecai's question. "I'm going to have justice for my family, and if I can't get it from the law, I'll see to it myself!"

Without thinking about what he was doing, Mordecai reached out with his good hand and gripped Shelton's arm.

"Damn it, you can't go gunnin' for Tom Gentry! He's thirty years younger'n you, and his whole family's tough as nails."

Shelton jerked his arm out of the deputy's grasp.

"They *think* they're tough as nails. But don't worry, Flint, I'm not a fool. I know I can't take them all on by myself." He was still smiling that cold smile. "But I know men who really are tough, a lot tougher than the Gentrys. And they're all going to be sorry for what Tom did. Each and every one of them!"

Shelton turned and stalked away. Mordecai could only watch him go and think how a fella should never be a big enough fool to think that the worst was over.

Things could always get worse . . . and it looked like they were about to in Redemption.

Chapter 38

Eden hadn't liked the look in Tatum's eyes as he watched her while Hannah was cooking supper at the cabin's fireplace. Eden's hands were tied, but her feet were still loose and she was sitting in an uncomfortable chair at the rough-hewn table while Tatum sat across from her.

From time to time, Hannah glanced in their direction, and the cold, implacable hatred on the redhead's face was worrisome, too. It was like a storm was building in this little, stone-walled room, and there was no telling when it might break.

An oil lamp sitting on the table filled the single room with a smoky glow. Eden glanced around. One bunk lay against the wall. A couple of blankets were spread on the floor on the other side of the room, the pallet that Tatum had told Hannah to prepare. The table, the chairs, some crude shelves formed of old crates . . . those were the cabin's only furnishings. There were loopholes for rifles in the crumbling mortar holding the stones together in the walls, but no windows and only the one door.

Only one way out, Eden thought. And Caleb Tatum wasn't likely to let her get anywhere near it.

Hannah filled wooden bowls from the pot of stew she had simmering on the fire. She brought them over and set them on the table, being none too careful about it so that some of the broth slopped over the side of the bowl she placed in front of Eden.

"Your hands are tied in front of you," Hannah said in a surly tone. "You can pick it up and eat from the bowl."

"All right," Eden said. Arguing wasn't going to do any good.

As she picked up the bowl and saw the steam rising from the hot stew, she thought about flinging the contents into Tatum's face. That ought to blind him momentarily and give her a chance to make a dash for the door.

And it would also give Hannah an excuse to grab the rifle leaning on the wall close at hand and shoot her, she reminded herself. Even if by some miracle she made it out of the cabin, she wouldn't be able to escape from the bowl that nature had scooped out of these badlands. The guards in the passage would stop her.

So she sipped the hot broth instead. She needed to keep her strength up. Maybe that was just rationalizing, she thought, but it was all she could do right now.

Hannah got a bowl of stew for herself, kicked one of the empty crates over to the table, and sat on it as she ate. The mood around the table was tense and awkward as the three of them ate in silence.

When the meal was over, Tatum leaned back in his chair and took out the makings to roll a quirley. He smoked while Hannah cleaned up. The lamp was starting to burn low.

And the apprehension inside Eden was growing.

Finally Tatum said, "You're going to be taking the blanket roll tonight, Hannah."

She stared at him bitterly.

"I knew it!" she said. "You think I'm gonna just lay there and watch while you take this whore to your bunk and have your sport with her?"

"You don't have to watch," Tatum said as his lips curved into a cruel smile. "You can blow out the lamp and just listen if you want to."

Hannah took a step toward him and said, "You son of a bitch."

"You can call me anything you want," Tatum said coolly. "You know that doesn't bother me. But don't try anything against me, either. You know better than that."

Hannah was quivering with rage, but she was able to say, "You know I'd never hurt you, Caleb."

"I didn't think so."

"This bitch, on the other hand—"

With no more warning than that, Hannah moved fast. She covered the distance between her and Eden in one swift step and whipped the knife that had suddenly appeared in her hand against Eden's throat. In that second, Eden was convinced she was about to die with her blood spilling out from a severed throat.

The knife stopped so that its keen edge barely pressed against her skin. Tatum had bolted up from his chair, and his hand rested on the butt of his gun, although he didn't draw it from his holster just yet.

"By God, Hannah, you go too far!" he burst out. "If you kill her, I'll make you regret it."

"I already regret that I didn't kill her before now," Hannah shot back. "You're fast on the draw, but not fast enough to stop me from cuttin' her throat if I want to."

"What do you want?" Tatum asked, his lips curling in a snarl.

"You grabbed her to use as a hostage, or so you said. If you'll stick to that, I'll let her live. But if you've got any notions of her takin' my place, she's got to die."

Eden sat there with her heart hammering in her chest, too terrified to move. It wouldn't take much pressure for the keen edge of that blade to bite deep into her throat.

After a few seconds that seemed much longer, Tatum laughed and took his hand off his gun.

"Fine, if you feel that strongly about it," he said. "I'll make a trade with you. The girl goes on the pallet and you go in my bunk, as usual, and you don't say anything about this to the rest of the bunch."

"Don't want them to start thinkin' that your word ain't

law, do you?" Hannah laughed. "I got news for you. Chico's already startin' to feel that way."

Tatum nodded grimly.

"I know. That's why I'm going to have to kill him one of these days soon. What about it? Do we have a deal?"

Hannah took the knife away from Eden's throat and shrugged.

"Fine. Don't know why I care so much anyway. It ain't like you're the first handsome man who wanted me warmin' his blankets."

"All right, that's settled. Put her on the pallet, tie her hands and feet, and rope her to the table leg, too. That way she can't try to crawl off."

"Wouldn't do her any good if she did. Where would she go?"

Eden had asked herself that same question and come up with the same answer.

There was nowhere for her to go. She was trapped here.

The blankets spread on the crude puncheon floor didn't make a very good bed. Eden couldn't get comfortable. Comfort didn't really matter much right now, though. Only survival did. She turned her face toward the wall and tried to go to sleep. She heard Tatum and Hannah moving around in the cabin, then the lamp went out. Utter darkness closed down around her.

She didn't really sleep, but she drifted in and out of a half stupor. She heard low voices and knew Tatum and Hannah were passing a jug of whiskey back and forth in the dark. Then she heard other sounds she didn't want to think about or even acknowledge.

Finally it was quiet in the room.

Eden dozed off then. She didn't know how long she slept, but when she came awake, it was suddenly, instinct making her strain against her bonds as Tatum's hand clamped roughly over her mouth.

"Don't raise a ruckus," he warned her in a whisper. "Hannah guzzled enough rotgut that she passed out when I was through with her, but I don't want her to wake up." He leaned close enough that Eden could smell his warm, whiskey-laden breath. "I reckon you can still make me feel mighty good without causing too much racket."

Eden felt panic inside her raging to get out. She tried to pull away from Tatum, but his grip was too tight. She felt the rope holding her to the table suddenly go slack. He must have cut it, she thought. A moment later she felt cold steel against her flesh for the second time tonight, but in this case it was against her calves. He moved the knife down and severed the bonds around her ankles.

"You just lay back and don't make a sound," he said.

Then Hannah yelled, "You sorry son of a bitch!"

It looked like he was wrong in thinking that she was passed out drunk.

A gun roared and muzzle flashes split the darkness. Hannah had a revolver in her hands and was firing blindly toward the other side of the room, not caring in her rage whether she hit Tatum or Eden. If she drilled both of them, that would probably be fine with her.

Eden heard a bullet smack into the wall somewhere above her. Tatum let go of her and twisted toward the new threat. Eden's wrists were still tied, but she was able to club her hands together and strike out with them as she lunged up from the floor. Her fists thudded into what felt like Tatum's back and knocked him away from her.

Then she used her panic to give her speed and relied on her instincts to guide her as she surged to her feet. She knew she might run right into one of those bullets, but she had to get out of here. She couldn't stand it anymore.

She ran into the wall, bounced off, and managed not to fall even though she was half stunned. Fumbling in front of her with her bound hands, she found the door latch and yanked on it. Night air spilled into the stuffy cabin as the door swung open.

Hannah screamed. The shots had stopped.

Eden flung herself through the open door and ran away from the cabin, the lengths of rope still fastened to her ankles trailing behind her.

*   *   *

Bill had just reached the end of the bottleneck and crouched behind a boulder there when he heard the blast of gunshots. He could tell the muffled reports came from inside one of the thick-walled cabins. Fear for Eden's safety gripped him tightly, squeezing his heart like a big hand, as he jerked his Colt from its holster.

Enough starlight filtered down into the bowl for him to be able to make out the squat shapes of the cabins. Suddenly the door of the center one was flung open, and a figure raced out into the night. Bill's eyes widened as he recognized the shock of fair hair. That was Eden running toward him!

Bill raced out from behind the boulder, determined to reach her and guide her to safety. She was almost back in his grasp, almost safe. He cried, "Eden!"

A figure appeared in the door of the cabin behind her. Flame stabbed from a gun muzzle, and Eden let out a cry and pitched forward.

Chapter 39

As sometimes happened, a lull settled over the town. A couple of days passed without anything out of the ordinary happening. Mordecai wasn't convinced that that good fortune would last, but he was grateful for the respite.

For one thing, it gave his wounded arm a chance to heal more. The pain in it receded so that it wasn't too uncomfortable as long as he didn't use it much. All he had to do was make his rounds every morning and evening and sit in the marshal's office the rest of the time. The Nilssons even sent most of his meals over from the café, so he didn't have to go out for them.

And thankfully, no fights broke out in the saloons. He would have had a hard time breaking them up.

Mordecai hadn't seen hide nor hair of Walter Shelton since the man had stomped off angrily a couple of days earlier, but he was able to keep up with how Shelton's daughter was doing by talking to Glenn Morley, who was still taking care of Virginia as the closest thing the settlement had to a doctor.

"She's doing as well as can be expected," the bartender reported. "No signs of brain damage or internal injuries so far, which is good. The bruises will heal. They're starting to look better already."

"What about her pa?" Mordecai asked as he stood in front of the bar in the Prairie Queen.

"What about him? I haven't seen him, only the girl and her mother."

"Just wondered what he was up to, that's all," Mordecai replied. He had an uneasy feeling about the whole situation.

At least the Gentrys were having the good sense to steer clear of town. Mordecai hadn't seen any of them in Redemption since he'd let Tom out of jail. He dared to let himself hope that the trouble would blow over, although he was still doubtful that it would.

Late in the afternoon of the second day after all the trouble, Mayor Roy Fleming appeared in the marshal's office with a worried look on his face.

"Have you heard anything from Marshal Harvey?" the mayor asked.

"Now how in blazes would I have heard anything from him?" Mordecai asked before he could remind himself that he was speaking to the mayor and suppress the impulse. "You ain't seen him and the posse ridin' into town, have you?"

"No, no, of course not." Fleming shook his head. "I'm sorry, Deputy Flint. I'm just concerned. About Mrs. Harvey, of course, and all the members of the posse."

"And the money those varmints took from your bank," Mordecai guessed.

"I'll admit it. If that money isn't recovered, it's going to be a major blow to the bank. The establishment may not be able to survive."

"I reckon Bill will do everything he can to get that money back."

"I know. But his wife's safety has to be his main concern, and I understand that." Fleming paused. "There's something else I wanted to ask you about, Deputy. That gypsy still has his wagon parked down at the end of Main Street."

Mordecai frowned and said, "That don't sound like a question."

"Well, when are you going to make him move on? The

town's been quite tolerant of him so far, but it seems like it's time he was leaving."

"I don't have any reason to run him out of town. Far as I can tell, Gregor ain't done anything wrong."

As a matter of fact, Mordecai had stopped by the wagon a few times to check up on Gregor Smolenski, and he found himself liking the man and his dog. Gregor had been a lot of different places, and Mordecai enjoyed swapping stories with him about the things they had seen and done.

"Are you saying that you haven't had any complaints about him?" Fleming demanded.

Mordecai frowned. He scratched at his beard and said, "Miz Maude Cartmill stopped by yesterday and reported that somebody swiped a buttermilk pie she had coolin' on a windowsill. She didn't see who it was."

"Mrs. Cartmill lives less than a block from the spot where that gypsy wagon is parked," Fleming said as if that proved his point. "Has there been anything else?"

"Clothes swiped off a clothesline at the Seabolt house," Mordecai admitted.

"Which is just two houses down from the Cartmill place," Fleming said with excitement in his voice now. "You see, Deputy? You have to do something about this!"

"A missin' pie and some underwear don't hardly rank up there with bank robbery," Mordecai said. "And I got no proof that Gregor Smo-len-ski"—he pronounced the name carefully—"had anything to do with either of those things."

"Make him leave town, and those thefts will stop. Mark my word on that, Deputy."

Mordecai could see that the mayor wasn't going to let loose of this. He said, "I'll take a *pasear* down there later and see if he's given any thought to movin' on. Maybe he's already plannin' to leave."

"Whether he is or not, I want him gone."

That was about as direct an order as a fella could get, Mordecai thought. And as the mayor, Roy Fleming was his boss, especially with Bill out of town. Mordecai sighed and nodded.

The door of the marshal's office was still open. Benjy

Cobb appeared there, clutching his battered, shapeless old hat to his chest.

"Dep'ty," Cobb said, "Mr. Monroe sent me down here to let you know there's somethin' you need to see."

Since returning to Redemption on the day of the bank robbery, when his efforts to pursue the outlaws had failed, Perry Monroe had stayed close to his store. Mordecai knew that Monroe must be worried sick about Eden and figured he was trying to distract himself with work.

"What is it, Benjy?" Mordecai asked as he got to his feet. "Trouble at the store?"

Cobb shook his head.

"Nope. Some fellas just rode into town, and Mr. Monroe said that he didn't like the looks of 'em."

Mordecai suppressed the urge to utter a curse. The last thing they needed right now was more troublemakers riding into Redemption. Things were just starting to settle down a mite.

Grabbing his hat, Mordecai headed for the door. Cobb stepped aside, and Fleming followed him. The three men went out onto the boardwalk in front of the marshal's office. Cobb pointed and said, "Down yonder at the Prairie Queen."

"What am I lookin' at?" Mordecai asked. "I don't see nothin' except some horses tied up at the hitch rack."

"The fellas that rode those horses into town went on inside the saloon. Hard-lookin' men they were, Dep'ty, and strangers, every one of 'em."

"No law against strangers ridin' into town," Mordecai said, although a feeling of unease had begun to stir inside him. Was the settlement about to be raided again by another outlaw gang?

Or were these men after something—or someone—else?

Only one way to find out, Mordecai told himself. Hitching up his gun belt, he told Fleming and Cobb, "I'll go up there and check it out."

"Do . . . do you want us to come with you?" Cobb asked.

"Nah, this is my job, not yours."

Both men looked relieved at Mordecai's answer.

He left them there, walked up the street, and crossed over to Redemption's new saloon.

When he went in, he found that an odd hush hung over the place, no doubt due to the great interest with which the customers were regarding the six men who stood at the bar drinking beers that Glenn Morley had just drawn for them. The bartender looked worried, too. Mordecai didn't see Annabelle Hudson. She was probably upstairs, he thought.

As he approached the strangers, one of them turned to face him. The man was tall and lean, well dressed in a black frock coat and black hat. His face was narrow and clean-shaven, although a blue black shadow of a beard lingered on his cheeks, jaw, and chin. His gaze touched the star pinned to Mordecai's shirt, and one corner of his mouth quirked in a faint smile.

"Marshal," he said. "Just the man I was looking for."

"Deputy," Mordecai corrected him. "Name's Flint. Marshal Harvey's out of town right now, but he'll be back any time."

Mordecai wished that was the case. In truth, he didn't know when Bill would be back . . . if ever.

"Well, you'll do just fine, Deputy Flint," the man said. "I just need to ask a question, and I figure someone in authority will probably know."

"What sort of question is that?"

"Where would I find Walter Shelton?"

That was exactly what Mordecai didn't want to hear. This man, and those with him, bore the stamp of professional gunmen. Either Shelton had sent for them, hiring them to go after the Gentrys, or the Gentrys were responsible for the hard cases being here and planned to use them to strike first at Shelton.

Mordecai figured the first possibility was the most likely. Burk Gentry and his sons were the sort of men to do their own gunfighting. From what Mordecai had seen, Shelton was, too, but he was badly outnumbered by the Gentrys and could use some men to back him up.

Either way, these strangers were trouble, and nothing but.

"You know the name, Deputy?" the spokesman prodded. "Walter Shelton?"

"I know who he is," Mordecai snapped, unable to hold in the irritation he felt. "What do you want him for?"

"That's not the law's business."

"Reckon the law's business is what I decide it is."

Mordecai saw several of the men glance at each other and smile. One of them even chuckled. He felt his face growing warm with anger. They weren't worried about him. They thought he was just a broke-down old cripple with a bad wing. Maybe they were right about that, but he was still wearing a star.

The leader must have decided that it would be easier to cooperate rather than argue. He said, "Shelton sent for us to do a job. We have mutual friends in Wichita."

"You mind tellin' me your name, mister?"

"Not at all. It's Jack Roland."

Mordecai had heard of Jack Roland, but he tried not to let that knowledge show on his face. Roland was a gunman, all right, with a reputation that said he would hire out for any sort of dirty job as long as the money was right. Mordecai had no doubt that the other men ranged along the bar were the same sort.

"If you don't know where to find Shelton, Deputy, I'm sure I can find somebody who does."

"You passed his house already," Mordecai said harshly. "You rode by it on your way into town. Big house that looks more like it ought to be back East instead of in Kansas."

Roland nodded and said, "I saw it and wondered if that was where he lived. But I wanted to be sure." He smiled. "Anyway, we were thirsty. It's been a long, fast ride from Wichita, and the boys and I needed to cut the dust." He turned to his companions. "Drink up, and then we'll go see Mr. Shelton."

Mordecai stood there. After a moment Jack Roland looked over at him again.

"Is there anything else, Deputy?"

Mordecai shook his head and said, "No, I reckon not."

"I didn't think so."

The smug tone in the man's voice almost pushed Mordecai over the brink. But he knew he was no match for six hardened killers, even on his best day, and if he tried to throw down on them, the resulting gunplay might injure or kill innocent folks. Even though turning away from the bar and heading for the door of the saloon cost him a considerable effort, it was the right thing to do. He had to let this lie until he figured out what to do about it.

Well, there was one good thing about this development, he told himself with a touch of grim amusement as he pushed throught the batwings.

With everything that was liable to be happening pretty soon, the mayor wouldn't have time to worry about Gregor Smolenski anymore.

Chapter 40

Bill howled, "Noooo!" as he saw Eden tumble off her feet. He opened up with his Colt. The revolver roared and bucked in his hand as he fired toward the cabin. The range was a little too far for a handgun, but the shots carried close enough to force the figure back inside.

With his heart slugging painfully, Bill stopped shooting and sprinted toward the spot where Eden had fallen. It wasn't possible he could have followed her and her captors this far, stayed on their trail for so long, and come this close, only to have her snatched away from him now by an outlaw's bullet.

Then, amazingly, she was on her feet again and racing toward him. Bill didn't know how that was possible—he supposed the wound she had suffered was only a minor one—but he wasn't going to turn his back on a miracle. He hurried to meet her, and she came into his embrace. He had never felt anything better in his life than closing his arms around her and hanging on tightly.

"You're . . . you're not hurt?" he managed to ask.

"I tripped and fell."

They couldn't say anything else because their mouths were pressed together in an urgent kiss.

That kiss lasted only a couple of heartbeats because they were still in a lot of trouble, even though they'd been reunited. More outlaws were spilling out of the other cabins, drawn by the gunshots, and Bill heard somebody yell, "There they are! Get 'em!"

He had emptied his gun at the man who was trying to shoot Eden, and there wasn't likely to be enough time to reload. That left him with only one option.

He took hold of Eden's hand and told her, "Run!"

They headed toward the mouth of the narrow passage that led through the ridge. Behind them, more shots rang out. Bullets whined through the air around them.

At first Bill thought the pounding he heard was his own pulse inside his head. Just as he realized it was really hoofbeats, a rider burst from the passage and galloped toward them. The rider let out a rebel yell.

Still holding tightly to Eden's hand, Bill veered sharply to the side to get out of the way as Jesse Overstreet raced past them. The six-gun in the cowboy's hand exploded again and again as he fired at the outlaws. Right behind Overstreet came Josiah Hartnett, and then one by one the other members of the posse emerged from the bottleneck and spread out. Rifles flared and cracked, horses lunged here and there, and men yelled curses.

Bill reached the boulder where he had taken cover a few minutes earlier. He steered Eden behind it. She slumped wearily against the big rock. For the first time, he noticed that her wrists were tied together in front of her.

He wanted to get her loose, but there wasn't really time. The battle between the posse and the outlaws was still going on, and he needed to be in the thick of it.

"Stay here," he told her as he thumbed fresh cartridges into the Colt's cylinder.

She caught at his sleeve with both hands.

"You don't have to go back out there," she said.

"You know I do," he told her as he snapped the revolver closed again.

Eden didn't argue. Instead she said, "Yes, I suppose you do. Leave me your knife so I can cut these ropes?"

"Yeah, sure." He passed the blade to her. "Be careful."

"You, too."

There were so many things he wanted to say to her, but for now, that laconic conversation would have to do. Gripping the Colt, he hurried back toward the cabins.

Some of the outlaws had managed to retreat into the stone dwellings and take cover, judging by the shots that came from them. Several of them had been caught out in the open by the unexpected arrival of the posse, though, and they had been cut down as they tried to flee.

Unfortunately, now that the surprise was over, the pendulum was starting to swing back the other way. The remaining outlaws were behind thick stone walls, with loopholes to fire through, and the men from the posse were out in the open. They had to scatter as gunfire raked them. A horse screamed and went down.

Bill was on foot, so he wasn't as visible a target. He crouched and ran wide of the cabins. His limp was more pronounced now, as it always was when he had to exert himself.

He reached the brush corral, where the gang's horses were milling around in confusion because of all the shooting. None of the outlaws could see him at all now. He continued to circle until he could approach the nearest of the cabins from the rear.

Loopholes were cut into the back wall, too, so defenders could fire in that direction if they needed to, but the men in the cabin didn't seem to be aware that anyone was behind them. From the sound of the shots, Bill figured there were three men inside this cabin, all directing their fire out the front toward the posse.

He felt around on the wall until he found one of the little openings. What he was about to do was a little like murder, he thought, but the outlaws had brought it on themselves. He slid the Colt's barrel through the loophole and started to fire, triggering off all six rounds as fast as he could cock the hammer and pull the trigger. He knew it would be pure luck if any of his shots struck the men inside on a straight line, but with those stone walls, the slugs would ricochet wickedly.

When his gun was empty, he pulled it out and dropped

to a knee. His ears rang from the thunderous roar of the volley.

As that ringing faded, though, he became aware that no more shots were coming from inside the cabin. A man groaned as if badly wounded.

Bill didn't trust that, but it could be checked on later. For now, he needed to reload. He did so, working with practiced efficiency even in the dark, and then stole toward the center cabin, the one from which Eden had fled a short time earlier.

No shots came from in there. The other defenders seemed to be in the third cabin. As Bill approached it, a figure suddenly appeared at the far corner. He almost took a shot at the shadowy shape before he recognized Jesse Overstreet.

"Jesse!" Bill called to the young cowboy.

Overstreet paused and whispered, "Bill? Is that you?"

"Yeah. What're you doin' back here?"

"Same thing as you, I reckon." Overstreet's teeth gleamed for a second in the starlight as he flashed a reckless grin. "Came to smoke out some rats."

He held up his flask of whiskey. He had stuffed a rag through the open neck.

"Thought I'd set this on fire and drop it down the chimney," he went on.

"Good idea," Bill said. "How're you gonna get up there?"

"Hell, after climbin' that ridge, I reckon I can clamber up on top of a little cabin like this."

Overstreet proved that by feeling for fingerholds in the gaps between the blocks of stone. Bill holstered his gun and laced his hands together to form a step. That helped Overstreet get farther up the wall. A moment later the cowboy rolled onto the thatched roof.

Bill drew his Colt again and slipped around the side of the cabin. He stopped at the front corner and tilted his head back to look up. When Overstreet struck a match and lit the crude fuse, Bill saw the brief flare. A couple of seconds went by . . .

Then the inside of the cabin lit up brightly. The flash of fiery illumination was visible through the loopholes. A man screamed. The walls wouldn't burn, but the floor and the furnishings would. Bill began to smell smoke almost instantly and wondered if Overstreet had blocked the chimney somehow.

It didn't take long for the flames and smoke to drive the outlaws from the cabin. One of them threw the door back and charged out, the revolver in his hand spitting death.

Bill fired from the corner of the building. His bullet ripped through the man and spun him off his feet.

Two more men burst out. Overstreet downed one of them with a shot from the roof. The posse members, who had taken cover anywhere they could, riddled the other man with lead.

An eerie silence settled over the bowl as the echoes of the shots faded away across the badlands.

Overstreet dropped from the roof and landed at Bill's side.

"You reckon we got 'em all?" he asked.

"I don't know. We're gonna have to check, and that could prove to be a dangerous chore."

"Did I see that you had your missus with you a few minutes ago?"

"Yeah." Bill could hardly believe it. Relief was setting in and making his knees a little weak. "I think she's all right."

"Well, you go check on her and leave those owlhoots to Josiah and the other fellas and me," Overstreet suggested. "After all this, you don't want to get yourself killed now."

"I'm still in charge of this posse," Bill said stubbornly. "I'll do my job."

Hartnett and the others were coming forward slowly now, rifles held at the ready. Bill called to them to cover him and Overstreet as they checked on the bodies of the three men who had fallen in front of this cabin. The outlaws were dead, just as Bill expected.

He started toward the far cabin to check the men in there, but he was still in front of the middle cabin when someone lunged through the door, rifle in hand. A scream of hate blended with the crack of the Winchester. The .44-40 round whipped past Bill's ear.

He reacted instinctively, thrusting the gun in his hand toward the rifle-wielder and pulling the trigger. The muzzle flash revealed the long red hair and the face of a woman as the slug drove into her chest between her breasts and flung her backward. She landed half in the cabin and half out and didn't move after that.

Bill felt hollow inside. He had just killed a woman, and even though she had done her damnedest to kill him, that fact sent a shock all the way to his core.

"You didn't have a choice, Bill," Overstreet said as if reading his fellow Texan's mind. "It'd bother me, too, but you did the only thing you could."

"Yeah, I guess so," Bill said. His voice sounded strange to his ears.

"Reckon I'd better check this cabin, too."

Overstreet stepped over the woman's body and struck a match so he could look around. He emerged a moment later to report that the middle cabin was empty.

By that time, Hartnett and a couple of posse members were investigating the third cabin. When Hartnett came out, he walked over to Bill and Overstreet and said, "There are two dead men in there and a third who's not going to last five minutes. It looks like we cleaned them all out, Marshal."

"Good," Bill said with a nod. "Did we lose any men?"

"A few wounded, but nobody's hurt too bad, as far as I know. I think we'll all make it back to Redemption."

Bill was extremely glad to hear that. The woman's death still bothered him, but he told himself to put it behind him. He had other responsibilities now.

"Bill!"

He turned at that cry and saw Eden hurrying toward him. Her hands were free now, so they were able to hold each other as they came together.

"Thought I told you to stay behind that boulder," he murmured as he felt the soft touch of her hair against his cheek.

"I had to make sure you were all right," she said.

"I am now," he whispered, and he knew he would be for as long as he could hang on to her.

He intended for that to be quite a while.

The posse rode away not long after dawn over the badlands, taking the extra horses and the bank money they had recovered from the center cabin. They had dug a grave for the woman and heaped the bodies of the other outlaws against one of the bowl's walls. Overstreet climbed up the slope and started some rocks rolling. That turned into a small avalanche that slid down and covered the corpses.

Bill made sure to keep Eden well away from that grisly sight. He hadn't let her get a good look at any of the dead men.

If he had, she would have been able to tell him that Caleb Tatum was not among them.

Chapter 41

Roy Fleming and Benjy Cobb were still standing in front of the marshal's office. Mordecai knew that the mayor wanted to find out what was going on, but that could wait.

Instead he turned the other direction and headed for the Shelton house. Roland and the other gun throwers were still in the saloon. Mordecai ought to have a few minutes before they rode back up the street to report in to Walter Shelton.

He wanted to find out exactly what Shelton had planned. The man might refuse to tell him, but as far as Mordecai could see, Shelton had always been a law-abiding man. If a deputy marshal demanded answers from him, he might . . . just *might* . . . give them.

Clarissa Shelton answered Mordecai's urgent knocking on the front door of the big house. She gave him a weak smile and said, "Why, hello, Deputy Flint. What can I do for you?"

"Is your husband here, ma'am?" Mordecai asked. "I need to talk to him."

"Yes, of course. Please come in." She ushered him into the foyer, then went on, "Walter is in his study. I'll let him know you're here."

"Ma'am . . . ?" Mordecai said as she started to turn away.

"Yes, Deputy?"

"Uh, how's Miss Virginia doing?"

Mrs. Shelton smiled again and said, "Why, she's fine, just fine," and Mordecai understood that was the only thing the woman was going to allow herself to believe.

He waited, awkwardly holding his hat in his good hand, while Mrs. Shelton went and got her husband. When they came back, Shelton had a frown on his narrow face. He asked, "What's this about, Deputy?"

Mordecai hesitated, glanced at Mrs. Shelton, and said, "Well, uh . . ."

Shelton took the hint. He turned to his wife and said, "Why don't you go upstairs and see if Virginia needs anything, dear?"

"Yes," she said with the false, bright smile. "I'll do that."

When she was gone, Shelton turned back to Mordecai and said harshly, "Well?"

"You gonna have some visitors in a few minutes," Mordecai said. "Jack Roland and some of his pards just rode into town. I talked to 'em in the Prairie Queen."

Shelton didn't smile, but a look of grim satisfaction came over his face.

"So they're here, are they? That was fast. But with what I'm paying, I expect fast service."

Mordecai struggled to control his temper.

"You admit that you hired those . . . those gunfighters to come here? They're nothin' but hired killers, Mr. Shelton. Are you gonna send 'em after Tom Gentry and the rest of his family?"

"You have that backward, Deputy," Shelton replied. "I hired Roland and his friends as bodyguards. They're here to protect Virginia."

Mordecai frowned in confusion and asked, "Protect her from what?"

"Tom Gentry sent a note to her asking to see her. He's contrite now and wants to try to talk her into giving him another chance. But if he can't, he intends to take her with him anyway, back out to that ranch. He says that's his right, since she's his wife."

Mordecai stared at the man.

"How do you know all this?"

"Because I read the note when one of the Gentrys' ranch hands delivered it, of course. I didn't let Virginia see it. That boy has caused her enough trouble."

"But you didn't think to come tell me about it? You took it on yourself to hire some gunslingers instead?"

"Bodyguards," Shelton said again, this time with a thin, cold smile.

"You said the other day you were gonna get even with Tom Gentry. You said you knew folks in Wichita—"

Shelton waved a hand.

"You can't put much stock in something said in the heat of the moment, Deputy. I'm not interested in vengeance, only in the safety of my wife and daughter."

The man was lying, and Mordecai knew it. Shelton had to have sent for those gun wolves *before* Tom Gentry sent that note to town, and the only reason to send for Jack Roland and men of his ilk was because you wanted somebody dead.

Roland and the other gunnies were already here in Redemption, so it was too late to do anything about that. Mordecai asked, "Did that note say when Tom Gentry was gonna come to town and try to talk to Miss Virginia?"

"Tomorrow," Shelton said. "Tomorrow at noon."

That didn't give Mordecai very long to ward off the trouble, but he had to try. He said, "I'm askin' you, as a favor to the law, to tell Roland and those other fellas to turn around and ride back to Wichita, Mr. Shelton."

"I can't do that, Deputy. I can't take a chance on my daughter being harmed any more than she already has been."

The answer didn't surprise Mordecai. He nodded and turned to leave.

Shelton said, "There's no need for anyone else to get hurt, Deputy. Tomorrow you should stick close to the marshal's office."

"Sorry, Mr. Shelton, but I can't do that."

Shelton shrugged and said, "I suppose we all have things we can't do . . . and things that we have to do."

* * *

It was dusk by the time Mordecai reached the Gentry ranch. After leaving Walter Shelton, he had gone straight to the livery stable where Josiah Hartnett's hostler had saddled his horse. Then he'd fogged it out here, knowing that this errand probably wasn't going to bear any more fruit than the last one had.

A couple of men on horseback rode out to meet him as he approached the ranch house. He recognized one of them as one of Tom Gentry's brothers, but he didn't know which of the young men was which. The other man was one of Burk Gentry's hands.

"Hold up, Deputy," the Gentry boy said. "What brings you out here?"

"I got to talk to your brother," Mordecai snapped.

"You mean Thurmond?" the youngster asked with a cocky smile. "What's he gone and done now?"

"Dadgum it," Mordecai said. "You know which brother I mean."

The boy shrugged and inclined his head toward the house, which was still a hundred yards away.

"Come on, then."

By the time Mordecai pulled rein in front of the house, Tom Gentry and his father had come out onto the porch. Tom stood with his hands tucked in his back pockets, his stance casual. He didn't look like the sort of hombre who would do what he'd done to his wife, but Mordecai was old enough to understand that you couldn't tell what someone was capable of just by looking at them.

"What are you doin' here, Deputy?" Burk Gentry asked. He glared at Mordecai with undisguised hostility.

"I understand that Tom here plans to ride into Redemption tomorrow."

"Not just Tom," Gentry said. "We're all goin'. Ever' one of us. We're gonna see to it that gal listens to reason. If she don't . . . well, she's comin' back here anyway. A wife's place is with her husband."

"Even when he's done what your boy did to her?"

"I'm sorry about that," Tom said, speaking for the first time. "You don't know how sorry I am, Deputy. But Virgie isn't innocent in all this. You know that."

"Blast it, you're movin' too quick!" Mordecai burst out. "Maybe you can convince her that you really are sorry, but you got to give her some time."

Tom shook his head.

"I've waited long enough. I want to put this behind us."

"What you want don't matter to Walt Shelton. He's brought in Jack Roland and a handful of other men just like him."

"Roland!" Burk Gentry said. "I've heard of him. You'll have to do something about him, Deputy. Can't have men like that causin' trouble in your town."

Mordecai felt frustration building inside him. He said, "If you and your boys will just steer clear of Redemption, Gentry, there won't be no trouble."

"We can't do that," Tom said. "I'm going to have my wife back, no matter what it takes. And you don't have any right to interfere with that, Deputy."

Gentry gave Mordecai a sly smile and said, "Fact of the matter is, it's your job to see to it that nobody interferes with us goin' about our lawful business. Ain't no law that says a fella can't go see his wife, is there?"

Mordecai bit back a curse. He was trapped as neatly as you please. The Gentrys were certainly within their legal rights to ride into town, and if Tom went to the Shelton house to see Virginia, there was nothing unlawful about that, either, as Burk Gentry had just said.

But if that happened, Jack Roland would be waiting there to kill Tom, and the other gunslingers would take care of the rest of the Gentry bunch when they tried to come to Tom's defense. It was liable to be a bloodbath, with men dying on both sides.

"I can't talk you out of this?" Mordecai asked, expecting the same sort of response he had gotten from Walter Shelton.

"My mind's made up," Tom said. "I'm going to save my marriage, whatever it takes."

What he was going to do was get himself killed, Mordecai thought.

"You want to stay for supper, Deputy?" Gentry asked. "You'd be welcome."

"Thanks, but I got to be gettin' back to town," Mordecai said.

He had to figure out how he was going to keep the streets of Redemption from running red with blood, and he didn't have much time to do it, either.

Chapter 42

"Will we make it back to Redemption today?" Eden asked as she rode alongside Bill.

"We ought to," he replied with a nod. "Ought to make it by midday. It was sort of hard to stop last night and make camp instead of pushin' on, but there was still too far to go. I didn't want to take a chance on us gettin' lost in the dark, either."

Eden sighed.

"I'm just anxious to get home, take a bath, and sleep in a real bed for a change," she said.

All that sounded good to Bill, too, especially the bed part. Out on the trail, surrounded by the members of a posse, was no place for a proper reunion between husband and wife. They had been able to talk in private enough for him to know that none of the outlaws had molested her, and he was thankful for that. He would have continued to love her anyway, no matter what, but now he wouldn't have to convince her of that. More important, she hadn't had to suffer through that ordeal.

All the men were anxious to get back home, so it hadn't been a problem maintaining a good pace. They had been able to round up most of the horses at the hideout, so they were able to keep fresh mounts underneath them most of the time.

Now, as they rode through a beautiful autumn morning, Jesse Overstreet said, "When we get back, I'd best get outfitted and head for Texas before winter sets in. I wouldn't want to get stuck and not be able to get home."

"You're goin' back to Texas?" Bill said. "I was thinking you might want to stay around Redemption for a while."

"And do what? I'm a cowboy, not a store clerk."

Hartnett said, "There are several ranches in the area that might be able to use a good man."

"At this time of year?" Overstreet shook his head. "Not likely. Maybe if it was spring."

"Well, maybe you could do something else until then. I might be able to talk the town council into hiring another deputy for the marshal."

Overstreet stared at Hartnett for a second, then said, "Me? A lawman?"

"You've been a good member of this posse. Isn't that right, Bill?"

"Don't reckon we could've rescued Eden and cleaned out that nest of robbers without your help, Jesse," Bill said. "I'm not sure there's enough law business in Redemption for a second deputy, though. It's a peaceful place most of the time."

"Anyway, I'm hankerin' to get back to Texas," Overstreet said. "But I appreciate the thought, Josiah."

They rode on south, keeping the horses moving at a brisk pace. Bill felt his anticipation growing. It wouldn't be long now before they were home.

And that made him think that less than a year earlier, he had regarded Texas as home, just like Jesse Overstreet, and he had never even given any thought to living anywhere else. But things changed, he thought as he glanced over at Eden.

Sometimes they even changed for the better.

The damn fools never even checked their back trail, Caleb Tatum thought as he rode about a mile behind the posse. Of course, one rider probably didn't kick up enough dust to be noticed, but it was the principle of the thing. They thought they had wiped out all their enemies, and that there was no one left behind them to threaten them.

They were wrong about that, and as soon as Tatum got the chance, he was going to show them how wrong.

Back in the badlands, he had rushed out of the cabin to pursue Eden and the man who had come to rescue her, probably the marshal. Then he had traded shots with the rest of the posse as they invaded the hideout.

But as the other outlaws who hadn't fallen in the first exchange of bullets had retreated into the cabins, Tatum had veered off to the side of the bowl, using the cover of darkness to make his escape. He didn't view his actions as cowardly. His plan had been to circle around behind the posse and catch them in a crossfire.

He hadn't had a chance to do that. Things had gone against the gang too quickly. And then he had seen Hannah die.

Her death affected him more than he ever thought it would. True, he had grown tired of her, especially her jealousy and her anger, and he had been ready to throw her aside for Eden.

But when he saw her fall with that bastard's bullet in her, he had realized that he still loved her, and ever since, the need to avenge her death had burned brightly within him. Those fires of hatred had kept him going as he followed the posse south.

The first night on the trail, he had considered charging into their camp on horseback and taking them by surprise. He knew he could kill several of them before they shot him out of the saddle.

That would deliver only a small measure of satisfaction, and he would wind up dead. He had no doubt about that.

So he had decided to hang back and follow them all the way to Redemption. Once they got there, they would be more convinced than ever that they were safe. He didn't really care about the other members of the posse. He wanted to kill the marshal, and he intended to kill Eden, too . . . but not until he was finished with her.

Chapter 43

Mordecai looked around at the men gathered in the marshal's office. Roy Fleming, Perry Monroe, Charley Hobbs, Leo Kellogg, the newspaper owner Phillip Ramsey, and walrus-mustached Gunnar Nilsson from the café were all good men, and they were willing to stand up and fight when it was necessary.

But none of them would be any match for Jack Roland and his band of gun wolves, and they couldn't even stand up to that tough bunch of Gentrys.

"I appreciate all of you comin' here this mornin' and offerin' to help," Mordecai said, "but there ain't really anything you can do."

"We can turn Burk Gentry and his men away at the edge of town," Monroe said. "If they don't ride in, they can't start a shoot-out with those gunmen."

That was a halfway decent idea, Mordecai thought, but he knew it would end up with some of the townsmen getting hurt or even killed . . . and in the end it wouldn't stop the Gentrys from forcing a showdown with Shelton's hired guns.

"This is my job," Mordecai insisted. "What I want you fellas to do is make sure that everybody's off the street come the noon hour. I'll deal with the Gentrys. They got to under-stand that they can't go against the law."

The words sounded hollow to Mordecai even as he spoke them. Burk Gentry didn't care about the law, and neither did his sons. And Walter Shelton sure as hell didn't.

"This is our town, too," Monroe insisted. "We've learned how to fight for it."

"The Gentrys don't have anything against Redemption," Mordecai said. "Neither do Roland and his bunch. This is a private matter, not like a raid by owlhoots or Indians. Like I told you, keep people off the street until the trouble's come and gone, and with any luck no innocent folks will be hurt."

"What about you?" Fleming asked. "If you get between those two bunches, you're liable to get killed."

"It's my job to get between 'em." Mordecai was able to summon up a chuckle. "Anyway, I ain't all that innocent."

The citizens continued to argue, but Mordecai was ada-mant and they finally gave up. With a sigh, Fleming said, "We'll spread the word that everyone needs to stay off the street for a while around noon. How will they know when it's safe to come out again?"

"I reckon they'll know when the trouble's all over," Mor-decai said. "Just wait until there's no more shootin'."

The men left. Mordecai leaned back in the chair behind the desk. He slid his left arm from the sling and moved it gingerly. Glenn Morley said that it was healing nicely, and some of the strength had returned to it. Mordecai glanced up at the gun rack on the wall. He was going to need both hands to use a shotgun, so he took the sling from around his neck and set it aside.

Anyway, there was a good chance he wouldn't have to worry about his arm after today, he thought.

From time to time he glanced at the clock on the wall of the marshal's office. When the hour stood at half past eleven, he stood up, took one of the scatterguns from the rack, and broke it open. There were shells in the desk drawer. Morde-cai slid one into each barrel and closed the shotgun. He put a handful of extra shells in his shirt pocket.

Taking the shotgun with him, he stepped out onto the

boardwalk. He looked both directions along the street, and the only thing he saw moving was a dog trotting into an alley. Redemption might as well have been a ghost town.

The Gentrys would probably enter the town from the west. Stopping them before they ever reached the Shelton house was a good idea. That was what Mordecai intended on trying to do. If he could persuade them somehow to turn around and go back to the ranch, maybe Jack Roland and his men would leave Redemption, too. Shelton wanted a showdown, and the Gentrys were playing right into his hands with Tom's demand to see Virginia. If he could head that off, Mordecai thought, then maybe Shelton wouldn't send his hired guns after his son-in-law's family. That would be little better than murder, after all, and Shelton still had to live here.

He wouldn't know how any of it was going to play out until the cards were dealt, Mordecai told himself. He walked slowly toward the western end of the street.

When he got there he paused next to Gregor Smolenski's wagon.

"You in there, Gregor?" he called. Feeling the way he did about the gypsy, Mayor Fleming might not have passed along the warning.

The door at the back of the wagon opened. Smolenski stepped out and asked, "How are you today, my friend?"

"Oh, I reckon I've been better, but I'm still here," Mordecai said.

"Where is everyone? The town looks deserted." Smolenski sat down on the folding steps that led up to the door. Tip came out of the wagon and sat down beside him. Smolenski rubbed the dog's ears.

"Trouble's on its way to town. If you and Tip stay inside the wagon, though, you ought to be all right. This is a private fight that's shapin' up."

"Ah, always trouble. People cannot get along, and often the source of the conflict doesn't really amount to all that much."

Mordecai thought about how Virginia Gentry had looked after that beating, and he said, "Well, in this case, what set it off is pretty bad, all right, but it's nothin' to do with you or most of the other folks in town. Just stay out of the way, and I'd take it kindly."

"Whatever you say, Mordecai. If there's anything I can do to help you, though . . ."

Something occurred to him. He said, "There is one thing."

"Tell me."

"Did you swipe Miz Cartmill's buttermilk pie off her windowsill and take some clothes from the line behind the Seabolt house?"

Smolenski frowned.

"You ask these things because I'm a gypsy?"

"I just want to know," Mordecai said.

"I wouldn't steal clothes. I have my own clothes and no need for anyone else's."

"What about the pie?"

"Well . . ." And suddenly Smolenski smiled. "I must admit I have a hard time resisting a fresh-baked pie. It was good, wasn't it, Tip?" He scratched the dog's ears again, then asked, "Are you going to arrest me now?"

"Over a damn pie? Not hardly. Just don't do it again. The mayor wants me to run you out of town and I keep puttin' him off about it. Don't make it harder on both of us."

"Of course. My apologies." Smolenski pointed. "Is this your trouble on its way?"

Mordecai turned and looked, saw the dust cloud rising. There had to be more than a dozen riders in that group, he thought.

But something was odd, he realized a moment later. Those riders were angling toward the town from the northwest. The Gentrys would be approaching Redemption from the southwest, unless they had gone an awfully long way around.

Mordecai walked out farther and peered toward the dark shapes at the base of that dust cloud. They soon turned into individual riders, and something about the two in the lead was mighty familiar. Mordecai saw sunlight reflect off blond hair, and he suddenly knew what he was seeing.

The posse had returned to Redemption, and Eden was with them.

Chapter 44

Bill was mighty happy to see Mordecai, but he knew right away that something was wrong. The town looked deserted, and Mordecai was waiting at the end of Main Street with a shotgun like trouble was on the way.

He swung down from his horse, gripped his deputy's outthrust hand, glanced at the colorfully clad tinker who was a newcomer to Redemption since he'd been gone, and said, "What's goin' on here, Mordecai?"

"It's a long, ugly story, Bill," Mordecai said. "But the short version is, we got a bunch of hired killers in town and some damn fools about to charge head-on into their guns."

Bill's eyes widened. He said, "I think you better tell me the long version, at least as much of it as you've got time to."

Mordecai did so as the other members of the posse dismounted and gathered around. He didn't gloss over Virginia Gentry's affair with Ned Bassett, even though talking about it made him feel a mite like a gossip. Eden let out a gasp when she heard about what Tom Gentry had done to his wife.

"That poor girl!" she said. "I always thought she was a little stuck-up and snooty, but that's terrible."

Josiah Hartnett said, "I have a hard time believing Tom

Gentry would do such a thing, but I suppose with anybody raised by old Burk, anything is possible. He's always been a fire-eater who ran roughshod over anybody who got in his way."

"Where's Bassett now?" Bill asked.

"Holed up in his house, I reckon," Mordecai said. "He's probably too ashamed to show his face around town."

"How about this fella Roland and the rest of those gunnies?"

Mordecai jerked his head toward the far end of town.

"Down at the Shelton place. Benjy Cobb did some scoutin' for me. He says their horses are tied up behind the Shelton house."

"All right," Bill said with a nod. "You've got the right idea, Mordecai. We need to stop the Gentrys from ever getting there. We'll turn them back, then go tell Roland and the others to head back to Wichita."

"They won't go," Mordecai predicted gloomily. "Shelton won't let 'em. If he can't get his showdown one way, he'll get it another."

"We'll deal with that after we've sent the Gentrys packin'."

Overstreet said, "Looks like you'll get your chance to do that mighty quick-like, Bill. Riders comin' fast from the southwest."

Bill swung to look and then gave a grim nod. He turned to Eden.

"Go to your father's store," he told her. "Stay inside with him."

"We just got back," she said. "Surely you don't have to risk your life again so soon!"

"Trouble comes on its own schedule." Bill looked around at the other men. "The rest of you head home. You've done your duty. The posse you signed up for is dissolved."

"The hell with that," Overstreet said. "Beggin' your pardon for the language, ma'am. But we stood with you against those outlaws, Bill, and we ain't gonna run out on you now."

"Jesse's right," Hartnett said. "Even Burk Gentry will think twice about trying to ride over this many men."

Hartnett had a point. And the Gentrys, while plenty tough, weren't professional gunmen, either.

Bill nodded as he came to a decision. He said, "All right, get on your horses and spread out across the street. Stay behind Mordecai and me. We'll meet the Gentrys."

Eden gave him a quick hug and then hurried toward her father's store. He was glad that she hadn't insisted on staying. If it came down to a fight, he didn't want to have to be worrying about her safety.

"Good luck, Marshal," the tinker said as he put his dog back in the wagon. "We haven't been introduced yet, but Mordecai speaks highly of you."

"Thanks," Bill said. "Better stay low. That wagon looks pretty sturdy, but if bullets start to fly, it might not stop all of them."

"Perhaps not, but the pots and pans hanging all over the walls will help, no?"

Bill pulled his rifle from its saddle sheath and walked into the middle of the street with Mordecai as the other men moved into position on horseback, arranging themselves in a single formidable line. The dust cloud slowed as it neared Redemption. The riders must have spotted the men blocking the street. They rode in slowly, the bulky figure of Burkhart Gentry in the lead. His three sons were right behind him, followed by four of the men who worked on the Gentry ranch.

"That's far enough," Bill called when the riders were about forty feet away.

"Marshal," Burk Gentry said. "Didn't know you were back in town."

"We just got back, and I don't appreciate having to deal with this trouble right away, Mr. Gentry."

"No trouble. My son's just on his way to talk to his wife. He's got a right to do that, don't he?"

"Maybe . . . but Walter Shelton's got half a dozen hired gunmen waiting down there to kill you."

"Uh, Bill . . ." Overstreet said from behind him. "I don't think that's exactly right."

Annoyed at the interruption, Bill turned, but then he saw

that Overstreet was hipped around in the saddle looking toward the east end of town. Bill looked past the posse members and saw six more men on horseback riding slowly in their direction.

"Well, hell," he said softly.

Walter Shelton wasn't waiting for the Gentrys to come to him. He had sent his hired guns out to meet them.

And Bill and his friends were right in between.

This showed signs of working out perfectly, Tatum thought as he stood just back from the mouth of an alley and watched the confrontation brewing. He had no idea what was going on here, but the feeling of impending violence was thick in the air. When the shooting started, as it seemed destined to do, he could gun down the marshal without anybody knowing. They would all think that the lawman had struck by a stray bullet.

But even as that thought crossed Tatum's mind, he realized how unsatisfying it would be. That son of a bitch had killed Hannah, and Tatum wanted to look in the man's eyes as he died. He wanted the marshal to know who had killed him, and why.

Still, if all hell broke loose, as it appeared was likely, that would provide a mighty nice distraction while Tatum took his revenge.

He settled down to wait.

Bill muttered a curse under his breath and told Mordecai, "Stay here and keep an eye on the Gentrys." He walked between two of the horses and moved to confront the gunmen.

He didn't have to tell them to stop. They reined in on their own and sat there watching him, coldly alert.

The dark, well-dressed man who seemed to be their leader edged his horse ahead a step. He said, "That badge on your shirt tells me you're the marshal. I heard you were out of town."

"Just got back," Bill said again.

"That wasn't very good timing on your part, was it? You and your friends step aside now, Marshal. We have business with those men who just got here. Private business."

"There's nothin' private about a shoot-out in the middle of the street," Bill snapped. "Innocent people get hurt that way."

The gunman smiled.

"I don't think you'll find much innocence on either side of this clash, Marshal," he said. "For that matter, it's been my experience that there's not much true innocence anywhere in the world."

"You're wrong about that. But even if you weren't, I'm not gonna let you shoot up my town. If we throw in with the Gentrys, you'll be outnumbered three to one."

The thought of siding with Tom Gentry, after what the man had done, sickened Bill. But right now, his only concern was to try to stop this battle. If increasing the odds against the hired guns would do that, he was willing to take that step.

The tactic didn't show any signs of paying off. The leader of the gunmen just smiled again and said, "Numbers don't mean much when you're talking about men like us, Marshal. You don't have any real professionals on your side."

"I wouldn't be so sure about that, mister," Jesse Overstreet called.

The gunman's eyes narrowed as he looked past Bill and asked, "Who the hell are you?"

"You ever hear of the Palo Pinto Kid?" Overstreet drawled.

For the first time, Bill saw a flicker of uncertainty in the gunman's eyes. The man said, "I've heard of him. He never operates outside of Texas, though."

"Not until now," Overstreet said with a grin.

"Don't listen to that punk, Jack," one of the other gunnies said. "Even if he is the Palo Pinto Kid, there's only one of him."

Roland hesitated. Bill began to hope that he'd gotten through to the man.

A new voice suddenly cried, "What are you doing? Why

are you just sitting there talking? I paid you to avenge what happened to my daughter!"

Bill looked over and saw Walter Shelton on the boardwalk. The businessman had come up without anybody noticing, and now he was urging his hired guns to attack.

"Ride over them!" Shelton went on in a voice edged with hate and hysteria. "Kill Tom Gentry and anyone who tries to defend him!"

"Damn you, Shelton!" Burk Gentry yelled. "Those are fightin' words!"

Bill held out a hand toward either side and shouted, "Shut up! Both of you, shut up! You're tryin' to take a bad situation and make it worse, all because of stubborn pride from both of you!"

"Pride!" Shelton said. "Don't I have a right to see justice done, Marshal? If I don't avenge my daughter, who will?"

Bill couldn't answer that, but he didn't have to. A man called, "I will!" and Bill looked over to see Ned Bassett striding toward them. Bassett still had a plaster stuck over the cut on his forehead he had gotten when Tom Gentry pistol-whipped him.

Tom pointed a finger at Bassett now and yelled, "I'll settle with you later, mister, after I've got my wife back!"

"You'll never get her back," Bassett said. "She's finished with you. But I'm not."

He started rolling up his sleeves.

Tom stared at the watchmaker in disbelief.

"You're offerin' to fight me for her? You?"

"I'm not proud of what I've done," Bassett said. "I knew it was wrong. But Virginia and I love each other, and yes, if I have to, I'll fight for her. I've thought of nothing else the past few days."

Burk Gentry said, "Damn it, Tom, let's do what we came here for. Don't let this little pipsqueak put a burr under your saddle."

"No, he's right, Pa," Tom said as he swung down from the saddle. "I never did finish handing him his needin's the other night, and when I'm done with him, Virgie won't want him anymore."

"Blast it, boy—" Burk Gentry said.

"Ned, stay out of this—" Walter Shelton began.

Neither Tom nor Bassett paid any attention to them. They rushed toward each other, forcing members of the posse to pull their horses aside. They came together in the middle of the street, fists flailing.

Chapter 45

As marshal, Bill had broken up plenty of fights, but he wasn't going to break up this one. Not when it looked like nobody was going to start shooting as long as Tom and Bassett were slugging away at each other.

Tom had a lot more experience at rough-and-tumble fighting. That much was obvious right away. He hammered a right and left to Bassett's body and then tried to kick him in the groin. Bassett twisted out of the way of the kick and snapped a hard punch to Tom's nose that made Tom take a step back.

Catching his balance, Tom launched forward again. He tackled Bassett around the waist. Both men went down in a welter of dust.

Tom landed on top and smashed Bassett in the face. The plaster on Bassett's forehead began to turn red. The wound under it was bleeding again. Bassett got his arms up and blocked one of Tom's punches. He heaved his body up, trying to throw Tom off to the side. Tom clung to him stubbornly.

Bassett managed to raise his leg enough to hook his calf in front of Tom's neck. When he straightened it, that drove Tom back and off of Bassett, who rolled to the side and pushed himself to his hands and knees. He struggled back to his feet just in time to meet another charge from Tom, who pounded him with a flurry of blows and drove him backward.

Bill wasn't sure how Bassett was able to stay on his feet in the face of that onslaught, let alone fight back. The watchmaker did, though, and he even landed a punch or two of his own. Tom was confident, though, and kept boring in.

Suddenly Bassett twisted out of the way again, and the momentum of Tom's missed blow sent him stumbling forward. Bassett grabbed him, hauled him around before Tom could catch his breath, and caught him from behind, locking an arm across Tom's throat and grasping the wrist of that hand as he drove a heel into the back of Tom's right knee. That leg buckled, and Bassett was able to ride his opponent to the ground. He dug a knee into the small of Tom's back, pinning him there.

Tom's face began to turn red from lack of air. Burk Gentry yelled, "Damn it, Marshal, he's gonna kill my boy! Stop him!"

Bill was as surprised as anybody by the sudden turn the fight had taken. Tom Gentry was bigger, stronger, and more experienced than Ned Bassett, but Bassett had him down and was choking the life out of him. No matter what Tom had done, Bill wasn't going to let Bassett kill him like that. He stepped toward the combatants, ready to grab Bassett and pull him off.

He didn't need to. Bassett abruptly let go of Tom, allowing him to slump flat on the ground and gasp for breath. Bassett pushed himself to his feet and stepped back. A crimson thread of blood wormed its way from under the plaster.

"Being beaten by the local watchmaker isn't . . . isn't punishment enough for what you did to Virginia, Tom," Bassett said. He dragged the back of his hand across his mouth. "But I'm not a murderer, and like I said, I'm not blameless in this, either." He turned to Shelton. "Tell your daughter good-bye for me, sir, if you would. I'll be leaving Redemption."

Shelton ignored Bassett. He pointed at Tom Gentry and said to his hired gunmen, "There he is! Kill him! Shoot him down like the dog he is!"

Jack Roland looked at his companions. Bill watched the men closely, but he couldn't read a thing from their expressions.

Then Roland said, "A gunfight's one thing, Shelton, but we're not bushwhackers, and that's what this would amount to. You'll get your money back, less something for our time."

He turned his horse away, and the others followed suit.

Shelton gaped at them. He said, "You . . . you can't . . . There's a debt to be paid . . ."

"Looks to me like Bassett and Tom Gentry settled that between them," Bill said. "Go home, Mr. Shelton. Take care of your family. And that doesn't mean have somebody killed."

"I . . . I . . ." Shelton's shoulders slumped in defeat. He turned away.

"What about us?" Burk Gentry bellowed. "We come to get that girl back."

"No!" Tom croaked through his bruised throat as he struggled to his feet. "I don't want her anymore. This has gone far enough, Pa. It's time to forget about it."

"Forget, hell! Ain't you got no pride, boy? Ain't you got an ounce of gumption in you? I tell you, we'll ride down there and get her, and anybody who tries to stop us will be sorry. We'll kill anybody who gets in our way!"

One of his other sons said, "Didn't you hear Tom, Pa? He said to forget about it. Hasn't this whole thing been ugly enough already?"

"But . . . but . . ." Gentry appeared to be flabbergasted that anyone would stand up to him, let alone his own offspring. "We can't let somebody else *win*!"

"That's just it, Pa," Tom said hoarsely as he trudged to his horse. "I don't think anybody's gonna win in this."

Tom was wrong about that, Bill thought as he watched the hired guns depart Redemption in one direction and the Gentrys ride out the other way, an apoplectic Burk Gentry the last one to leave. The town had won, because nobody had gotten killed.

"Lord, I think I want to sleep for a week," he said wearily as he slid his rifle back in the saddle boot.

"Well, go ahead," Mordecai told him. "I don't mind keepin' an eye on things for a spell longer."

Bill smiled as he thought about Eden and said, "Maybe I won't go to sleep right away." Leading his horse, he started toward Monroe Mercantile as the former members of the posse scattered to return to their homes and lives.

"I'll be in the office," Mordecai called after him. Bill waved a hand to acknowledge the deputy's statement.

Hartnett came up beside him and reached for the reins.

"I'll take care of your horse, Bill," the liveryman offered.

"Much obliged, Josiah. Where'd Jesse go?"

"He headed straight for the Prairie Queen," Hartnett replied with a smile. "Said something about cutting the trail dust. After everything we've gone through together, I hope you don't have to arrest him again."

"Me, too," Bill said.

He went up the steps to the high porch in front of the mercantile and started toward the door, but he hadn't gotten there when it opened and Eden stepped out. She wasn't alone. There was a man right behind her, and he had the barrel of a gun pressed into her side.

"You killed my woman, Marshal," he said, "and now you're gonna watch while I kill yours, before I cut you down."

Eden was pale with fear, but in that moment when time seemed to stop, Bill saw something else on her face. Anger burned in her eyes, and he knew she was going to do something. He opened his mouth to tell her to wait, but the words never came out. She twisted in the man's grip and the gun went off. She cried out in pain, but that didn't stop her elbow from digging into his throat and knocking him back a step. Bill's Colt came out of its holster in a smooth, instinctive draw. The barrel tipped up, and as Eden fell to the side, the gun roared, then roared again. The man staggered as both slugs drove into his chest. He tried to raise his gun but couldn't seem to manage it. As he fell to his knees, the revolver slipped from his fingers. He pitched forward on his face and lay still.

Bill rushed forward, pausing only long enough to kick the fallen gun into the street before he grabbed Eden and pulled her up into his arms.

"I'm all right, I'm all right," she babbled. "I'm not hit, Bill."

He looked down at her side, saw the scorched mark on her dress from the muzzle flash. She had come that close.

But there was no blood, thank God. He held her tightly against him, vaguely aware that people were shouting and running toward them, but none of that was important now.

He was holding on to the only thing that mattered.

"So that was Caleb Tatum, the boss of those owlhoots," Jesse Overstreet said as he strolled along the darkened street beside Bill. Overstreet had come out of the Prairie Queen while Bill was making his evening rounds and offered to join him, and Bill hadn't turned him down. "We must've missed him while we were roundin' up those varmints."

"Yeah, and then he followed us back here to settle the score for that redheaded woman, Hannah. He told Eden that much after he slipped in the back of the store and knocked out her pa."

"Is Mr. Monroe gonna be all right?"

Bill grinned and said, "Oh, yeah, he's got a hard head. He's been through a lot, though, so I hope life takes it a mite easier on him for a while."

"How about you?" Overstreet asked.

"You mean, do I have a hard head?"

"No, I'm sayin' is it time for life to take it a mite easier on you?"

"Well, that'd be all right, I suppose. I'm not gonna hold my breath waitin' for it, though. It seems like there's always some sort of hell poppin' in Redemption." They walked on in silence for a moment, and then Bill asked, "Are you really the Palo Pinto Kid?"

"I never said that I was. I just asked that hombre if he'd *heard* of the Palo Pinto Kid."

"But . . . you're not sayin' that you're not him."

"I'm just sayin' it's a beautiful night," Overstreet replied with a grin, "and you'd better enjoy it before that hell you were talkin' about starts to pop again."

Loveland Public Library
300 N. Adams Ave.
Loveland, CO 80537

Don't miss the best
Westerns from Berkley

....

LYLE BRANDT
PETER BRANDVOLD
JACK BALLAS
J. LEE BUTTS
JORY SHERMAN
DUSTY RICHARDS

....

penguin.com

M10G0610